Property Ladder

Buying for PROFIT

Remodeling Investments That Pay!

Property Ladder Buying for Profit
Editor: Vicki Christian
Contributing Project Editors/Writers: Amber Dawn Barz, Jan Soults Walker
Assistant Art Director: Todd Emerson Hanson
Copy Chief: Terri Fredrickson
Publishing Operations Manager: Karen Schirm
Senior Editor, Asset & Information Management: Phillip Morgan
Edit and Design Production Coordinator: Mary Lee Gavin
Editorial Assistant: Kaye Chabot
Book Production Managers: Pam Kvitne, Marjorie J. Schenkelberg,
   Rick von Holdt, Mark Weaver
Contributing Copy Editor: Barbara Roth
Contributing Proofreaders: Julie Collins, Teresa Krug, Lida Stinchfield
Contributing Photographer: Michael Garland
Contributing Indexer: Stephanie Reymann
Contributing Illustrator: Larry Schlephorst

Meredith® Books
Executive Director, Editorial: Gregory H. Kayko
Executive Director, Design: Matt Strelecki
Managing Editor: Amy Tincher-Durik
Senior Editor/Group Manager: Vicki L. Ingham
Senior Associate Design Director: Ken Carlson
Marketing Product Manager: Brent Wiersma

Publisher and Editor in Chief: James D. Blume
Editorial Director: Linda Raglan Cunningham
Executive Director, Marketing: Steve Malone
Executive Director, New Business Development: Todd M. Davis
Executive Director, Sales: Ken Zagor
Director, Operations: George A. Susral
Director, Production: Douglas M. Johnston
Director, Marketing: Amy Nichols
Business Director: Jim Leonard

Vice President and General Manager: Douglas J. Guendel

Meredith Publishing Group
President: Jack Griffin
Executive Vice President: Bob Mate

Meredith Corporation
Chairman and Chief Executive Officer: William T. Kerr
President and Chief Operating Officer: Stephen M. Lacy

In Memoriam: E.T. Meredith III (1933-2003)

Property Ladder

ABOUT THE SHOW

Buy a house, fix it up fast, and sell it for a huge profit; that's the premise behind The Learning Channel's (TLC) series, Property Ladder. The show takes you through the process known as flipping, where novice real estate developers attempt to renovate properties considered "diamonds in the rough" and resell them for a profit. Testing the adage, "you have to spend money to make money," each episode follows one do-it-yourself real estate developer from beginning to end as he or she purchases a property, rehabilitates it, and sells it. The moment of truth comes when the show reveals whether the flipper's sweat equity pays off—or not. For more information about Property Ladder, visit www.TLC.com.

DCI team:
General Manager, TLC: David Abraham
Executive Producer, TLC: Julie Rose
VP, Licensing: Carol LeBlanc
VP, Creative Services: Elizabeth Bakacs,
Publishing Manager: Elsa Abraham
Publishing Associate: Erica Rose
Marketing Associate: Caitlin Erb

Contents

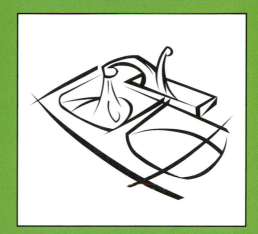

Chapter 3—Makeover magic **146**

Discover how to complete home improvement projects successfully with this handy do-it-yourself guide.

Chapter 4—Project price guide **218**

This dollars and sense section provides you with the approximate costs for a variety of redos and the best places to buy quality materials. Architectural templates enabling you to lay out every room in your home are also provided.

Property Ladder

BUYING FOR profit

Make renovations that pay off

I t's the hottest trend in the real estate market—buy a house, fix it up fast, and sell it for a significant profit. The Learning Channel's Property Ladder show offers an inside look as novice real estate developers renovate properties in an attempt to make a significant profit when they sell them a few months down the road.

Real-life advice

If you are considering the same challenge or have already purchased a property in need of a little tender loving care (whether or not you plan to sell it), you've come to the right place for help. With advice from TLC's real estate experts and real-life case studies gleaned from the Property Ladder show, this book guides you through the steps of making your property more valuable and salable by helping you decide what to replace, what to salvage, when to call in the experts, and when to consider tackling the work yourself.

   For your reading ease, the book is divided into four chapters that break down the flipping process into easy-to-follow steps.

Chapter 1: Case studies

Filled with color photos from the most popular episodes of Property Ladder, this chapter follows the process of do-it-yourself renovators as they purchase a property, rehab it, then sell it for—they hope—a handsome profit. Within each case

■ Real estate agent, designer, and *Property Ladder* host Kirsten Kemp has more than 10 years of experience flipping property for profit.

study you'll find before and after photographs of exteriors and interiors. The episode's summary includes the challenges and successes—and the profit percentage the developer actually made. Insightful Property Ladder Lessons cover everything you need to know about home inspections, neighborhood analysis, property comparisons, time and money management, and much more.

Chapter 2: All around the house

Before you begin tackling individual room renovations, you'll want to consider the easy-to-follow suggestions outlined in this chapter. Affordable surface changes, such as repainting and recarpeting, can make many rooms look new. In some instances you'll need to replace windows and doors, tear down walls, and replace cabinets and fixtures.

This chapter will help you make the right call for each room in your property, such as determining what to salvage and what to scrap. You'll discover today's remodeling hot buttons that are worth the additional expense because they appeal to so many potential buyers. Plus you'll find advice on revamping room layouts affordably, choosing the hottest-selling materials and surfaces for your redo, and furnishing the room to make the best impression.

Chapter 3: Makeover magic

You can save yourself thousands of dollars in repair and remodeling costs by doing some of the renovation work yourself. This chapter outlines easy jobs you can do, when and how to hire a professional, and step-by-step advice on painting

Push your personal tastes aside and look at flipping property as a business.

■ **First impressions are lasting. Make the front entrance as inviting and welcoming as possible.**

everything from cabinetry to woodwork. You'll also learn about tiling and how to replace flooring and countertop materials.

Chapter 4: Project workbook

This insightful chapter provides cost guides that identify how much you can expect to pay for the individual line items your project requires and where to shop for these materials. Templates for laying out the individual components of each room and a purchasing checklist are also provided. With this book in hand, you're ready to make smart renovation choices. Here's wishing that every flip you undertake is fun and profitable!

Property Ladder

CASE studies

Tune in to these tantalizing episodes for firsthand lessons that can help you transform your property into a stylish showcase you can flip fast.

Put on a fresh face

A real estate agent by trade, first-time property flipper Nicole Posca knows a home bargain when she sees it. And when she saw this condo on sale for far less than the other condos in the area, she snapped it up and decided it would be the perfect property to flip.

Here's why the condo was a bargain:
• The kitchen and bath cabinets, fixtures, and appliances had not been updated since the condo was built more than 40 years ago.
• The carpeting and wall color gave the house a cold and uninviting feeling.
• A separate kitchen and living area made both rooms seem small.
• The only room that had a ceiling light fixture was the dining room.

■ **ABOVE** Beautifying the exterior was as simple as replacing overgrown bushes with smaller ones.
■ **OPPOSITE** A coffee table with thin tapered legs keeps the look airy in the living room.

• There was very little architectural detail—not even window or door trim.
• The kitchen lacked a dishwasher.
• There were no hookups for a washer or dryer.

BEFORE

Property stats

Original purchase price:	**$235,000**
Additional investment:	**$30,000**
Number of weeks required for remodeling:	**9**
New listing price:	**$339,000**
Amount of weeks on market:	**less than 1 week**
Amount property sold for:	**$339,000**
Profit:	**$74,000**

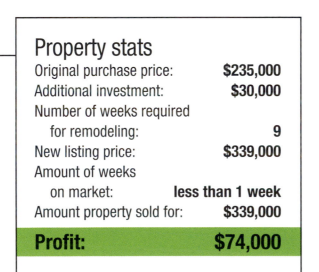

During the nine-week renovation, Nicole lived with her parents, another cost-saving measure.

The makeover

With Property Ladder host Kirsten Kemp's advice, here's what Nicole did to transform the condo:

All around the house

Nicole ripped up all the old carpeting and vinyl flooring throughout the house. For more continuity, she hired a mason to lay natural travertine stone on the floor in every room.

At the same time, she replaced all the laminate countertops with mahogany-color granite.

To give all the gathering areas more architectural interest, Nicole had crown molding installed.

The base molding throughout the home was also replaced. The doors and windows were given new interior trim.

Ready-made drapery panels and sheers purchased from discount department stores adorn every window. The remaining furnishings, accessories, and bedding were brought from Nicole's home, allowing her to affordably and attractively stage the entire home for showings.

Kitchen and bath

Nicole hired a contractor to remove all the existing cabinetry, appliances, and fixtures, including the kitchen sink, bath sink, bathtub, and toilet. She then hired a carpenter to make custom cabinets for the kitchen, bath, and dining room buffet. New appliances purchased from a local department store make the kitchen appear fresh. A new dishwasher fills the space once allocated to a base cabinet.

To open the kitchen to the living room and make both spaces appear larger, Nicole had the contractor cut a large pass-through above the cabinetry on one wall of the kitchen, which instantly united both rooms.

■ **A day bed makes the area in front of the living room's picture window the perfect place to retreat with a good book or the morning newspapers.**

■ Topping the new cutout between the kitchen and living rooms with stone creates a breakfast bar—another selling point.

Laundry

A hall closet (not shown) was reworked to make room for a washer and dryer. Although Nicole did not include the appliances, she did add the necessary plumbing and electrical hookups.

Bedroom

Only one window was replaced: The bedroom window was cracked, so she installed a new one.

■ **ABOVE An extra-deep kitchen sink serves as an affordably priced luxury.** ■ **LEFT Laying the flooring on the diagonal lends interest and makes the room appear wider.**

Find the right property to flip

Real estate agent Nicole Posca was able to find an affordably priced property to flip by weekly browsing the multiple listings—available only to licensed real estate brokers. You can achieve the same result by surfing the Internet. Most major real estate brokers now have websites that show photos of the properties they are marketing. To find the listings in your area, use your web browser and type in the name of a local real estate company and the name of your town or city. If you are uncertain of the names of the real estate companies in your area, check the business listings in your phone directory.

Property Ladder Lessons

"My biggest mistake was to have the custom cabinets built before I purchased the appliances. I had to return and buy the kitchen appliances three times before I found ones that would actually fit," Nicole says. Even then, the cabinetmaker had to build a frame around the dishwasher because it was still too small. "I'll know better next time," Nicole says. And yes, she says there will be a next time: "I plan to invest the money I made into my next flip."

Property Ladder host Kirsten Kemp says appliance installation is often a headache for anyone remodeling a property to live in or flip. "Before you buy an appliance, you'll need to ensure it will fit through the exterior doorway. Make sure it can also pass through any hallways or interior openings that it must go through on its way to the kitchen," she says.

■ ABOVE Once an empty box, the dining room becomes an architectural asset when fitted with a new buffet and a stunning low-cost mirror that complements Nicole's existing dining table.

■ **RIGHT** A tub made from a combination of polished travertine and slate makes the 5×10-foot bath feel like a private retreat.

Innovative thinking solves problems

Whether you're a seasoned remodeler or a rookie, remodeling dilemmas are a near certainty. For example, the stone counter in the bath blocked the door swing by a few millimeters. To solve the problem, the countertop fabricator trimmed the edge to make it fit.

■ **ABOVE LEFT** and **ABOVE** One bathroom sink and the open knee space beneath the counter reduced plumbing and cabinetry costs.

■ **LEFT** The nightstands, bed, and lamps are from Nicole's apartment, thus saving staging money. The bedding came from a local linen store.

Compare prices

Most properties are marketed on real estate broker websites. In only a few minutes, you can see the asking price and the number and type of rooms. You'll also discover a list of the home's most memorable selling features.

Most properties featured on the Internet also display a photo of the home's exterior and the asking price. If you're lucky, the site will offer a pictorial tour of the home,

showing photos of most rooms in the house. If some property information is not listed on the page, you can call the listing broker (his or her name and phone number will be on the listing) and ask for additional information.

You can also see what other homes in the area have sold for by accessing your county assessor's website. The assessor's website will show when a home sold, for

what price, who it was sold to, as well as the number and type of rooms. The assessor's website also describes other basic amenities for homes in your county. The information is public record, so you can access it free. To find the assessor's address, type into your web browser the name of your county followed by the word "county," then your state's name followed by the word "assessor."

Make a clean start

As a mortgage consultant, Steve Bernal is quick to spot a good real estate deal. So when he received a call about a property with minor water damage and anxious sellers, he and his wife Sherry Martyn decided this was the house to buy, fix up, and resell for a profit.

Here's why the 1,615-square-foot ranch-style house was priced low for the neighborhood:

• Built in 1965, the 3-bedroom, 2-bath house had never been updated.

• The ceiling sported "cottage cheese" texture and many walls were dressed in wood paneling.

• Poor backyard drainage had resulted in water spilling through the back door, soaking carpeting in the dining and living rooms and breeding mold.

Property stats

Original purchase price:	**$435,000**
Additional investment:	**$59,000**
Number of weeks required for remodeling:	**10**
New listing price:	**$599,000**
Amount weeks on market:	**21**

Anticipated Profit: $105,000

■ **Taupe paint unifies the stucco and wood panel siding on the exterior. Darker taupe on the trim lends interest.**

The makeover

A few clever changes made Steve and Sherry's new purchase into a stylish and desirable property.

All around the house

Top priority for the property was to resolve the backyard drainage issue. Steve and Sherry hired a landscaping professional to install a drainage system and add an irrigation system.

In the meantime the couple focused on ridding the property of the abandoned junk inside and outside. They decided to hire people to help remove all the trash. Ultimately they filled four remodeling-size waste-dumping bins.

BEFORE

BEFORE

■ **ABOVE** A larger dining room sliding door—measuring 10 feet wide—had to be custom ordered.
■ **LEFT** Refurbishing the fireplace was as simple as painting the brick white and adding a new mantel.

EPISODE 203

Inside, the cottage cheese texture was removed from the ceilings. The wood paneling and old carpets were also removed. "We basically gutted the house and scrubbed remaining surfaces with bleach," Sherry says, pointing out that they paid particular attention to eliminating mold. (See "Remove mold," on page 27.)

Along with solving the drainage issues, they replaced several windows and a sliding door and added a patio door. The house featured a slate roof and eaves in good condition. Fresh paint for the

■ **Pewter-tone hardware dresses up the stock white-painted cabinetry, complementing the appliances.**

Analyzing a neighborhood

Prior to purchasing the property, Steve and Sherry sized up the neighborhood. "The area is in transition," Sherry says. "There are a lot of people coming in and renovating, but there are also several houses that are not fixed up. But the trend is definitely on the upswing." How do they know? Properties in the neighborhood adjacent to theirs are priced in the $1.2 million range, and an upscale open-air mall is located just a few miles from the property. Here's a rundown of what you'll likely find in a viable, growing neighborhood:

• Most homes are neat, well kept, and well landscaped. New residents landscape, remodel, and add on to their homes.

• Neighborhood public services include well-maintained streets, parks, and—depending on the location—safe, convenient public transportation. The area is well served by city or county services, such as garbage and trash pickup and snow removal.

• New homes are being built in or adjacent to your property's neighborhood if land is still available. The new homes are as large as or larger than existing homes. Subdivided lots are a sign of a neighborhood in demand.

• Time on the market for selling a house is comparable to or less than on-the-market times in other neighborhoods in the area.

• Neighborhood shopping areas hum with business, including retail stores, specialty shops, and services. Retail businesses are appropriate to the neighborhood. Zoning ordinances, however, protect residential areas from commercial intrusions.

BEFORE

■ ABOVE and RIGHT Oversize 18-inch-square tiles laid on the diagonal make the refreshed kitchen and family room area appear larger.

■ **ABOVE** In the master bedroom new patio doors replace a window creating a more spacious appearance. ■ **RIGHT** Green houseplants placed throughout the interior help enliven spaces for showing.

"Be **very careful** when measuring and don't go by memory—write it down."

Sherry Martyn

stucco and wood siding, trim, and double front doors gave the exterior broad appeal.

After removing a large tree that was lifting the home's foundation, the couple put in flowerbeds, a small tree, and sod in the front yard. More flowerbeds and a stone patio perk up the backyard.

Sherry and Steve hired an interior designer by the hour to help them make good choices about colors, components, and surfaces. "The bill was $800 and it was completely worth it," Sherry says.

Kitchen

For the kitchen new white painted cabinets from a home improvement store cost $1,800, plus $500 for installation. "Wood cabinets in our price range looked cheesy," Sherry says."

Sherry found appliances at a warehouse for a great price—$1,500 total for a stainless-steel range, refrigerator, microwave oven, and dishwasher.

To save money on countertops without giving up the rich look of granite, the couple chose $4-a-foot

■ Once the soffit was removed from the old shower, the showerhead was raised to a more functional height. Tumbled tile gives the shower interior a high-end look.

granite tiles instead of a more costly slab. An outlet warehouse yielded tumbled travertine tiles.

Living areas

In the family room, adjacent to the kitchen, a half-wall that had been filled in is restored to half-size, opening the space to the kitchen.

In a section of the living room, and in the dining room, entryway, and hallway, bamboo floors lend elegance and continuity.

Bedrooms

To make the small master bedroom special, they added crown molding and traded a small window

BEFORE

■ **Furnishing this bedroom as a nursery helps potential buyers envision the property as a functional family home.**

for a large French door that opens onto a garden and stone patio.

An accordion wall located between two other bedrooms became a solid wall, transforming the house from a 3-bedroom to a 4-bedroom property.

Bathrooms

The old master and hall bathrooms were gutted. To make the tiny master bathroom seem more spacious, a soffit above the shower was removed and tumbled

stone tiles were used to line the entire stall.

Finding a sink cabinet to fit into the shallow 14-inch space was a challenge. After nixing a pedestal sink for lack of storage, they finally found an espresso-stained wood cabinet to fit.

For the hall bath, Sherry took a tiling class at a home improvement store and then added clean white tiles around the bathtub. Neutral paint, tile flooring, and a prefabricated countertop and vanity give this guest bath a clean finish.

"Definitely comparison shop! It is surprising how much better of a deal in materials and in labor costs you can find if you shop around." *Sherry Martyn*

BEFORE

■ Soft neutral color on the bedroom walls promotes tranquillity and lets the white furnishings and woodwork stand out.

Remove mold

Before buying the property, Sherry and Steve researched how to rid a house of surface mold. Here are the steps they took:

1. Opened doors and windows to provide optimum ventilation when working with bleach and to allow the interiors to dry thoroughly.
2. Scrubbed all moldy surfaces with a solution of trisodium phosphate (TSP) and water.
3. Scrubbed a second time with undiluted bleach.
4. Knocked holes into the walls to inspect for mold growing beneath drywall. They left the openings in the walls until all surfaces were completely dry. "The mold went away and it didn't come back," Sherry says with satisfaction. Once they finished extracting the mold, Sherry and Steve hired a California firm that specializes in checking for mold to inspect the property, and the house was given a clean bill of health.

Update the outdated

Actor Jacque Arnold and his wife Melissa decided to purchase a property in need of an update, fix it up, and sell it for a profit when Melissa became pregnant with their first child. "We looked at flipping as a way to boost our income and still pursue our career and parenting goals," Jacque explains, "so we decided to give it a try."

To determine what price range of home they could afford to flip, the couple went to a mortgage lender and prequalified for a mortgage loan. "Prequalifying lets you know in advance how much you can borrow, which provided us with our ballpark purchase price, less the several thousand dollars we knew we'd need for improvements," Jacque explains.

The ranch-style home the couple eventually purchased was located in a well-kept neighborhood, but the home's decor and floor

■ **Fresh paint, a few new plantings, and trimmed bushes give the ranch curb appeal.**

plan were outdated, which made the property more affordable to purchase and a prime candidate for a quick flip:

• Although the house was built in 1949, the roof, windows, and siding were in good shape.

• The floor plan needed a little help: The kitchen was closed off from the living area and the fourth bedroom could be entered only by crossing through the third bedroom.

• The kitchen and the two existing bathrooms had never been updated.

• Many interior walls had dated paneling.

The makeover

Here's what Jacque and Melissa did to make their purchase into a highly sought-after property:

The exterior

A fresh coat of paint on the trim and on the siding gives the home more curb appeal. Trimming the bushes around the house also updates the appearance of the exterior, as does planting a few new bushes and adding fresh sod to areas of the lawn that look thin and shabby.

Property stats

Original purchase price:	**$675,000**
Additional investment:	**$62,000**
Number of weeks required for remodeling:	**9**
New listing price:	**$850,000**
Amount of weeks on market:	**less than 1 day**
Amount property sold for:	**$830,000**
Profit:	**$93,000**

■ Refurbishing the fireplace was as simple as painting the fireplace surround white. Leaving the windows bare was a conscious decision. "The windows allow in more light and views, so we decided against covering them," Jacque explains.

Living area

To make the living room feel more connected to the kitchen, the couple cut a new opening between the two rooms, making the floor plan feel more up-to-date and family friendly. The same crown and base moldings used in the kitchen and dining area were extended to this room. The oak floors were already in place; the couple simply buffed them to make them look new. The fireplace surround was freshened with a coat of white paint.

BEFORE

■ INSET and ABOVE Granite countertops, stainless steel appliances, and maple cabinetry bring the kitchen into the 21st century. Opening the kitchen to the living room makes the area a favorite gathering space.

BEFORE

Kitchen and dining area

The appliances, fixtures, cabinetry, and flooring looked worn and dated, so the couple opted to remove everything and start over. They tore up the worn linoleum and replaced it with a warm, neutral-color Italian ceramic tile. New 4-inch-wide baseboards add more interest, as does new crown molding. The ceiling—originally decorated with "fake" beams—was drywalled over and given a fresh coat of paint. New maple cabinets replaced worn painted ones.

Conduct home inspections

"Always have a property inspected before you buy it. That way you will be aware of any potential red flags," Kirsten Kemp says. In most states, a home inspection is part of the purchasing process.

After making an offer, potential buyers typically have from 7 to 14 days to have a certified inspector look over the property and make a report. Based on the report, the buyers may request the seller to fix certain items or rescind their offer. The inspector observes the items listed below and notes anything that isn't in proper working order or may be a safety hazard:

Plumbing lines, to ensure there are no leaks.

Plumbing fixtures, including sinks, faucets, tubs, and toilets, to ensure they are in working order.

Electrical wiring, to ensure it meets code.

Light fixtures, switches, and fuse box, to ensure they meet code.

Appliances, to ensure they are in proper working order.

Furnace and air-conditioning (including approximate age, degree of efficiency, and time estimate of when these items might need replacing).

Water heater (including approximate age and time estimate of when it might need replacing).

Gas lines and gas appliances, to ensure there are no leaks.

Windows and doors, to ensure they open, close, and lock properly.

Walls, to check for cracks or bowing.

Attic, to ensure it is properly insulated, ventilated, and sealed.

Basement, to ensure there are no leaks or bowing walls and that the sump pump (if there is one) is in working order.

Roof, to determine if there are leaks and when it might need replacing.

Gutters, to ensure they are in proper working order.

Garage door and openers, to ensure they are in proper working order and meet current safety codes.

The inspector's report typically lists items that do not meet current safety codes first, followed by items that may need to be replaced within the next year, followed by any other items that raise any kind of concern.

BEFORE

■ **ABOVE Furnishing this bedroom as a child's space helps potential buyers envision this space as a family home.**

■ **ABOVE A neutral color scheme creates a serene master suite.**

Bedrooms

Wall paint, new carpeting, and wide base moldings give the bedrooms a fresh look. Because the fourth bedroom was not very useful—it was accessible only from the third bedroom—the space was reworked into a new master bath, which now connects directly to the existing master bedroom. This made the residence into a three-bedroom, three-bath home, a change that Kirsten suggested would make the home more valuable.

Install smoke detectors

Install and maintain smoke detectors according to the manufacturer's instructions and to comply with your local building code. At minimum your home should have one detector on every floor and by each bedroom door.

■ **THIS PAGE** The master bedroom features multiple windows and French doors. The French doors connect the suite to a covered patio.

BEFORE

■ Staging the outdoor gathering area with inviting furnishings and accessories enables potential buyers to see the space's possibilities.

> "To finish your project in a timely fashion, come up with a **plan of attack.** List exactly what needs to be done and **how and when** you plan to complete it." *Kirsten Kemp*

Bathrooms

The new master suite features a spacious walk-in closet, an attractive ceramic tile floor, a whirlpool tub, a double-sink vanity, and a separate shower. The light, airy decor makes the room feel tranquil and inviting. The other two baths were also fitted with new fixtures and cabinetry and their old tile floors were replaced with new, more contemporary slip-resistant ceramics. "You can't tell they are the same rooms," Jacque says.

BEFORE

■ **ABOVE** White cabinets combine with sand-color tiles to make the bath look crisp.

Rehab a hacienda

Husband and wife Darren and Tristen Moffett along with Darren's brother, Tyler Moffett, and Tristen's cousin, Philip Daro, individually had some remodeling experience. So they decided to pool their talents and resources to form a company, The Moffett Group, and together purchase a property with potential that they could fix up and flip for a profit. Darren functions as the money man and Tristen, Tyler, and Philip would head up renovations. Their first project was this 1920s Spanish bungalow located in a family-oriented community with an award-winning school district. Although many homes in the area sell for more than a million dollars, the

group snapped up this property for $590,000. Here's why the team was able to negotiate a rock-bottom price:

• The 1920s house had two bedrooms, but only one bath. Prior to buying the property, the team made certain there was a good location in the house where they could fit in a second bathroom.

• No updates had been made to the property since the 1970s. The kitchen and bathroom required a complete remodel and all the doors and windows needed replacing. Wood paneling on a number of walls in the house had to be removed. The team also determined that they would update interior moldings throughout.

• In addition to the property lacking grass and landscaping, the stucco exterior of the home was painted pink and the terra-cotta tile roof had been painted white.

Property stats

Original purchase price:	**$590,000**
Additional investment:	**$53,800**
Number of weeks required for remodeling:	**9**
First listing price:	**$775,000**
New listing price:	**$738,500**
Amount weeks on market:	**15**
Anticipated Profit:	**$97,400**

The makeover

Here's what the team did to make their purchase into a prime property:

■ **OPPOSITE and ABOVE: Creamy white paint, new landscaping and sod, and a tiled walkway enhance the Spanish charm of this 1920s bungalow.**

The exterior

Rather than spend thousands of dollars on a new tile roof, Philip painted the tiles a more natural terra-cotta color. The team worked together to replace all the windows themselves and paint the stucco exterior a creamy white. Tristen undertook the landscaping, including building planter boxes and doing all the planting herself. She worked with Tyler and Philip to lay new sod around the property and then Tristen hired a subcontractor to lay saltillo tiles on the patio, walkway, and stair treads. As a finishing touch, she highlighted the risers with colorful, handpainted Spanish tiles.

Living room

Tristen considered the living room fireplace—with a petrified log embedded in the brick facade—the property's biggest eyesore. To give the fireplace a fresh, Spanish flavor, the offending brick was smoothed over with plaster. Rounding the plaster edges and finishing the fireplace with a distressed knotty alder mantel gives the fireplace "a very Old Mexico look," Tristen says,

pointing out that they installed a new front door made of the same wood. She found large, thick stones in the garden department of a home improvement store and used them to surface the hearth. Refinishing the wood floor, painting the walls, and adding new recessed lighting completes the living room transformation.

■ **ABOVE RIGHT** To make the new knotty alder mantel look old, Tyler and Philip beat it with chains and hammers. The same wood was used for the new front door to create an "Old Mexico" flavor that enhances the architecture of the house.

■ **ABOVE** Tristen sewed all the curtains, including these panels in the living room, to make the interior more homey.

Kitchen

The only good thing about the kitchen's existing metal cabinets was that there were very few of them to pull out. The team started fresh with new maple stock cabinets customized with crown molding and new hardware. "It's not a huge room, so we were trying to keep it light," Tristen says.

As a contrast to the light cabinetry, black granite serves as the countertops. New stainless steel appliances add shine while new recessed lights brighten the room. A new arch-shape above the formally square opening between the kitchen and the living room adds architectural interest.

BEFORE

■ **ABOVE** Tristen opted for plain black granite countertops devoid of speckles and other markings. "I wanted to keep the look very simple," she says.
■ **LEFT** The group saved money by purchasing stock cabinets and giving them a custom look with crown molding and new wrought-iron knobs and pulls.

EPISODE 211

■ **BELOW and RIGHT** Downscaled furnishings make rooms appear larger. Decorative accessories give the rooms a chic, yet homey look.

■ **LEFT** and **ABOVE** French doors give one bedroom access to this new tiled patio.

Respect architectural styles

Tristen and her colleagues appreciated the Spanish character of their bungalow property and played up its best attributes.

It's worth understanding the architectural heritage of your house so you can respect and enhance the features. There's no mystery to house styles and types. Just as fashions and automobile styles change through the years, so do houses—though less rapidly. When, where, and by whom your property was built largely determines its style. As for so much of 20th-century social and cultural history, World War II marks the great divide in house styles. That doesn't mean that houses built before or after the war are more or less desirable. Houses of all periods and styles offer advantages and disadvantages. Housing vastly expanded after World War II with great building booms and decades of prosperity. Current updating focuses largely on properties less than 50 years old.

If you own an older home built in the 19th century or prewar 20th century, you'll likely have a definite style as a starting point. The key, of course, is to be sensitive to style, which may include reversing poorly conceptualized remodelings.

Research the house style at the library and on the Internet and familiarize yourself with the characteristics of the style. It's also smart to walk through your property's neighborhood to observe what other homeowners are doing to achieve successful, style-compatible results. You may want to consider a consultation with an architect, who may be willing to offer style insights and design advice on an hourly basis.

Bedrooms

The team decided that the front bedroom would best serve as the master bedroom of the house, because a bathroom could replace a former closet (see "Bathrooms," page 43). The team sealed up one large, oddly placed window in the new bedroom and updated the space with new carpeting and fresh paint.

BEFORE

For the home's second bedroom, they refinished the wood floor, pulled down the wood paneling, and painted over the pink ceiling with a neutral color. The highlight of this space is the new French doors, which lead out onto the saltillo-tile patio that Tristen designed.

Bathrooms

The existing hallway bathroom had a conglomeration of blue tile, a tub with no shower, and a pink toilet. The group gutted the space and started anew, discovering that the walls weren't drywall but were instead plaster and lath. "This type of construction is a little harder to work with, because you can't really attach anything to plaster and lathe," Tristen says, admitting that they hadn't thought about inspecting the walls before purchasing the property. Installing a new shower meant replacing all the plaster with moistureproof drywall materials. They completed this bath with a corner shower unit, a pedestal sink with a brushed nickel faucet, and a new toilet. Creamy neutral tile finishes the floor.

To create a second bathroom, which would serve the master bedroom, the team reframed a space once occupied by a large closet. It was only after tearing out the old closet walls that they discovered the extensive evidence of a former termite infestation. Progress was delayed for about a week as many insect-riddled 2×4s had to be replaced. Once this was done, the bathroom was fitted with new components, including a tub and shower combination.

■ **ABOVE A former closet was reframed to create this bathroom for the master bedroom.** ■ **OPPOSITE Large windows make the master bedroom a sunny retreat.**

ALL AROUND the house

From kitchens and baths to bedrooms and bonus spaces, here's the advice you need on where to spend and where to save.

Make the kitchen a top priority

An attractive, hardworking kitchen is a necessity for most home buyers. Whether your investment requires a decorative facelift or a major overhaul, these tips can help you dole out your dollars wisely.

How does it look?

When it comes to resale, a kitchen's first impression is its most important one. If the room is attractive and inviting, potential buyers will linger a little longer and perhaps think about what it would be like to cook and entertain in your kitchen.

If the kitchen appears a bit worn but functions well enough to meet the needs of most cooks, you may be able to update its look in less time and for less expense than you might think.

KITCHEN MUSTS:
- Sturdy, stylish cabinetry
- Up-to-date fixtures
- Quality appliances
- Pristine countertops and floors
- Social seating
- Lots of lighting
- Ample storage

Salvage or scrap?

Cabinetry

Salvage the kitchen cabinets if they are sturdy and of a quality that matches those found in comparable homes in the neighborhood. If you don't know, attend open houses of nearby neighborhoods to see what the other homes offer. Take note of the quality of materials used in the homes that sell the quickest, and choose comparable materials for your property flip.

For more information on identifying cabinet quality, see "Quality cabinets" on page 47. If you must replace the cabinets, plan on adding several thousand dollars to your remodeling budget—on average, cabinets consume 40 percent of the cost of a kitchen remodeling. For cabinetry pricing information, see the "Kitchen Product Price Guide" on pages 221–222.

Creating display space in a **kitchen** can be as easy as

Quality cabinets

Manufactured cabinets, often referred to as stock or semicustom cabinets, have greatly improved in quality over the last decade. Today many of these cabinets have an impressive list of standard features and an upscale style formerly available only to custom buyers.

Storage options such as recycling bins, plate racks, file drawers, and lazy Susans—available for reasonable prices—increase the salability of your home.

Fine furniture details, such as crown molding, decorative glass door inserts, and footed base cabinets, make manufactured cabinets look impressive. These function especially well when the kitchen is open and on display to living and dining areas.

The materials from which any cabinet is made (stock or custom) and how the cabinet pieces are joined together provide an easy way to determine a cabinet's quality. Solid wood is rarely used for the cabinet box; instead, one of these three materials form the guts of most cabinets:

Particleboard. This engineered material forms the base of most laminate and some wood-veneered cabinets. Better quality cabinet boxes made of this material feature 45-pound commercial-grade particleboard; poorer grades won't hold screws well.

Medium-density fiberboard (MDF). This engineered substrate material is higher in quality than particleboard, offering a smooth surface and edges that can be shaped and painted.

Plywood. This wood product is the strongest of the cabinet box materials and offers the best structural support.

Joints give cabinets their strength and stability; the better the joint, the better the cabinet.

Butt joints. These joints are formed when cabinet pieces are glued or stapled together. Butt joints are the least sturdy and may come apart over time.

Dado joints. These sturdy joints are formed when the cabinet sides slide into grooves cut into the cabinet back and face frame and are reinforced with screws or glue.

Gussets. These triangular braces are glued into the upper corners of a cabinet to provide even more strength.

When it comes to cabinet drawers, look for ones that have dovetail joints that lock together like entwined fingers. Make sure the drawer glides smoothly when opened and does not wobble when fully extended.

installing a ready-made plate rack on an empty wall.

If the cabinets are high quality, paint or refinish them to cover any signs of wear and create a more up-to-date look. For advice on painting and restyling kitchen cabinets, see "Give cabinet doors a makeover" on pages 195–199.

For a simpler alternative, replace dated hardware with new knobs or pulls. To avoid drilling new holes and filling old ones, choose new hardware that fits the existing drill holes. If you plan to replace the door hinges, save the old ones to help you find a comparable substitute. Switching hinges may be tricky, but it can be worth the hassle to achieve a pulled-together look.

You may choose to replace a few solid cabinet doors with glass-front ones. Remove the center recessed panel of the door using a router, and have a piece of glass cut to fit the opening. Use glass clips to hold the insert in place.

Alternatively, you can take the door to a home center, which can switch the panel for you and cut a piece of replacement glass to fit. (A glass shop can also cut and insert a glass pane for you.)

If your kitchen cabinet doors are too damaged or even missing, you may want to order new cabinet doors. Unfinished and finished doors in stock and custom sizes are available at most home centers. You may also find good deals through online retailers; type "cabinet" in your web brower's search window.

Cut your granite costs

Although granite prices often run from $60 to $100 per square foot, installed (with standard edge), it's possible to find good deals. Here are some fast facts and ideas that could help you work granite into your budget:

Before shopping, know what color and type of granite you like and how much you'll need. It's sold by the square foot, so a counter that is 24 inches deep and 9 feet long will require 18 square feet, plus the amount needed for edging and/or a backsplash. The slabs, normally sold in 40- and 45-square-foot sizes, are generally ¾ inch thick, sometimes as much as 1½ inches thick.

To get the best price on granite, bypass kitchen shops and big-box retailers and go straight to the granite yard to select slabs.

Don't be shy about bargaining with the granite-yard salesperson. Find the granite you like best, inspect the slabs for cracks or fissures, and ask, "What's the best deal you can give me?"

You'll pay far more for the installation than for the granite itself, because the very qualities we love in granite—hardness and density—make it difficult to cut and transport. It's not uncommon to pay up to four times the cost of the granite for installation. You'll be glad, however,

Countertops

Salvage the kitchen countertops only if they are stain- and wear-free and a neutral color. If most of the homes in the neighborhood have laminate tops, you can get by with keeping them too. If they are a neutral pattern, such as a simple stone look-alike or a neutral color such as black, white, gray, taupe, or beige, consider keeping them.

If neighboring houses have upgraded countertops (such as stone, tile, wood, or ceramic tile), you'll want to match their quality. For more information on these surfacing options, as well as a few more, see "Crash Course on Countertops" right. For pricing information on various countertop materials, see page 222.

To reduce countertop replacement costs, consider replacing only the island top or using a combination of less costly materials such as stainless steel and ceramic field tiles along with a granite slab on an island or a peninsula. Visit stone distributors and countertop fabricators to look for partial slabs or ready-made countertops that meet your size requirements—they're less costly than custom-cut tops. You can also save money on granite by following the tips in "Cut your granite costs," below.

Crash course on countertops

Before you head to your favorite surfacing retailer, learn which material offers the right style and function for your kitchen.

that you spent the extra dollars on good installers—especially if you've ever seen a poor granite installation. Your potential buyers won't consider granite a plus if it looks bad.

Buying granite from a combined granite yard/fabricator can sometimes yield a better price than buying the granite first and finding the fabricator later.

Edge details also heavily affect granite prices. Finished counters look twice their thickness thanks to "bullnosing," where an edge is sheared off, glued underneath to create a thicker lip, then rounded. Dozens of other fancy edge details and bevels are available for a fancy price (add about $15 to $35 per linear foot). Save even more money if you do without the edge detail and have a carpenter or cabinetmaker add a wood edging after the countertop is installed.

As a less expensive alternative to granite slabs, consider granite tiles. Like granite slabs, granite tiles come in a variety of colors and are available in sizes similar to ceramic tiles.

Prices start as low as $2 per square foot, uninstalled, and run all the way up to $25 per square foot, uninstalled.

Durable and affordable, laminate is a popular surfacing material in moderately priced homes.

LAMINATE

Colorful and budget priced, laminate is still the most popular countertop material. Laminate is simply a $\frac{1}{16}$-inch thick polymer bonded to $\frac{3}{4}$-inch plywood or particleboard.

Available in a variety of colors, textures, and patterns, laminate countertops can be given a rolled or square edge. Edges can also be trimmed with beveled wood or metal inlays to create a custom look.

Laminate resists grease and stains and cleans up with soap and water, but it won't stand up to sharp knives or hot pans. Prolonged exposure to water may dissolve glue lines and cause warping of the subsurface. Once damaged, laminate is difficult to repair. For resale purposes, choose this material only if it is predominantly used in other kitchens in the neighborhood.

TILE

This sturdy surfacing material is available in as many colors, patterns, and sizes as you can imagine. You can customize your countertops—and control costs—by using a combination of solid-color and/or patterned tiles.

Because tile withstands hot pots and pans without scorching, it's an excellent choice for countertops that are adjacent to a range, grill, or cooktop. Tile is also moisture resistant so it works well around sinks.

Tiles with a high gloss finish tend to show wear more quickly. Tile cleans up easily with a damp sponge; for tougher dirt, use a glass cleaner.

Grout joints are susceptible to stains, so make sure the grout is a darker color than the tile itself. In many cases, grout stains can be removed with scouring powder and bleach.

STAINLESS STEEL

More affordable than stone, this sleek countertop material looks right at home in contemporary and higher-end hardworking kitchens. Impervious to hot pots and water, stainless steel doesn't require much maintenance. Scratches, scuffs, and fingerprints show up continually, however, so they can be frustrating to maintain in households with lots of kids and cooks.

STONE

Granite is the most popular stone for countertops because it resists most stains, cleans easily, and can handle water, hot pots, and sharp knives. A remodeling "hot button," stone countertops are a great asset to point out in ads and on fact sheets.

Marble's smooth, cool surface is ideal for rolling out dough, but it is not as strong or as stain-resistant as granite. If you find a bargain-priced slab, use it only in a baking center or on a bath vanity.

Like the look of a fancy edge on stone countertops? Think twice. Fancy edge treatments can double or triple a stone countertop's total cost.

SOLID-SURFACING

A stonelike synthetic material, solid-surfacing is more resistant to scratches than laminate and more resistant to stains than marble. It is lighter weight than natural stone and can be fabricated using regular woodworking tools. To clean, simply wipe it with a damp sponge.

Unlike stone and tile, solid-surfacing can be damaged by sharp knives and hot pots. However, because this faux stone is solid—the color runs throughout—shallow scratches and burns can be repaired by scouring, sanding or buffing. Color and style choices range from stone patterns to solid colors.

The material can be molded to fit any countertop configuration. Create special effects by using inlays of contrasting colors.

WOOD TOPS

Butcherblock countertops add natural warmth and elegance to a kitchen, but they do require special care. Butcherblock counters are made from hardwood strips—generally white oak, hard-rock maple, or beech—glued together.

These counters come in thicknesses ranging from 1 to 1½ inches and can be cut in any shape. Wood counters should not be used in wet areas because warping can occur.

Newly installed butcherblock countertops require oiling with mineral oil every four to six weeks. Once broken in, they need regular oiling every three months or whenever the countertop shows signs of dryness (faded spots) or splintering. Because of maintenance, limit butcherblock installations to an island or a section of the perimeter countertop.

CONCRETE

Sophisticated, industrial-chic concrete offers the same durability on countertops as it does on sidewalks. The material can also be colored to match most any decorating scheme.

Liquid sealers are recommended to prevent stains and ease cleaning. Hot pans can singe the top sealer but not the material itself. As with sidewalk installations, hairline cracks are commonplace and, according to dealers, part of the charm, but they may not be as charming to potential homebuyers who are not familiar with the material.

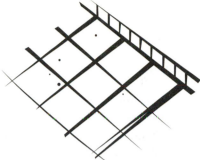

Flooring

Like countertops, kitchen flooring needs to be stain- and wear-free and neutral in color. Comfort underfoot is always a selling point as is ease of upkeep, so choose replacement materials with these features in mind. The best flooring choices link adjoining rooms together and add visual warmth to a room.

As with countertops, you'll want to choose a flooring material that is in keeping with the neighborhood. To reduce replacement costs, you may be able to lay new flooring directly over the old.

Have a professional take a look at what you're proposing to ensure that layering surfaces will not cause problems in the future.

You'll also want to ensure that the added thickness of underlayment and new flooring won't interfere with opening doors. For information on the most popular flooring options, see "Floor show" on pages 52–53.

WOOD

This classic flooring material shows its versatility as the perfect complement to any style of room. It's also a great choice for achieving a seamless appearance throughout the house.

Though a splash or two of water won't hurt, wood works best under dry conditions. Heavy traffic can leave its mark, eventually leading to refinishing. To help disguise footprints, choose a honed (or better yet, a distressed) finish.

One option is bamboo which looks like hardwood but is even softer underfoot. It is priced similar to wood. Direct sunshine can cause fading, and professional installation is recommended.

Dollars and sense

Before you solidify your kitchen makeover plans, take accurate measurements of your kitchen, then visit model displays to determine the features and components you'll need to create a salable design. As you shop various retailers, ask for price quotes.

Be certain that the dollar amount each retailer supplies is for the same size and quality of appliances, fixtures, and cabinets. Clarify delivery and installation charges, warranties, and service options. For more information on kitchen component costs, see pages 221–222.

CERAMIC

Available in colors and styles to match any decor, ceramic tile is a standout performer for hardworking kitchens. It can feel cold when working in bare feet and is unforgiving should you drop a favorite goblet or china dish.

Choose a tile with a honed finish that disguises dirt; shiny tiles look fine when just washed, but they show every dust particle, footprint, and pet hair that crosses their path. You'll also want to choose a dark grout; light grout on flooring tends to collect grime.

VINYL

This affordable, dependable choice cushions feet and stands up to moisture, and it comes in an array of colors and styles. Sheet vinyl offers a seamless appearance; vinyl tiles are easy to install.

Vinyl does scratch and dent, and dropping a sharp knife can cause permanent damage; lower quality varieties are most susceptible.

LAMINATE

Considered a rising star in midprice projects, laminate does an impressive job of replicating the look of real wood but at a lower price point and with an easier installation. Like wood, laminate is vulnerable to water damage, has a tendency to show wear sooner than real wood, and is somewhat noisier.

Appliances

Salvage appliances only if they are stylish, clean, and working well. If you must replace appliances, shop for floor models and closeouts; you'll get all the quality for about half the price. You'll have bargaining power when you need to purchase several new appliances, such as a range, refrigerator, dishwasher, and microwave oven. Check with several dealers to see who will give you the best price for a package deal. For appliance pricing information, see pages 221–222.

For finish color, choose white, off-white (especially if your kitchen is filled with creamy tones), or stainless steel.

Depending on the price range of the home you are flipping, you may be able to get by with leaving space for the fridge, but you'll want to have a dishwasher and a range (or cooktop and wall oven) installed. If your kitchen does possess a decent freestanding refrigerator, it's worth the investment to wrap the sides and top with matching cabinetry. If you replace the refrigerator, make sure that the new model you purchase will fit through exterior doors and hallways and into the allotted alcove in the kitchen.

Top-of-the-line kitchens are expected to have a cooking surface with gas burners accompanied by a pair of electric ovens. Moderate kitchens can be fitted with a smooth-top electric or a gas cooktop or range.

Stainless steel appliances add a crisp note to a kitchen filled with warm wood tones.

Because the cooking center is the focal point of this room, put your remodeling dollars into this appliance and let the other appliances fade into the background by covering them with matching cabinetry panels and/or recessing them into existing cabinetry runs. (Every cooking surface should be accompanied by a vent hood, as discussed on page 54.)

Selling points for dishwashers are ultraquiet washes, dishwashing drawers (you'll need to install two to provide enough capacity should you choose to go this route), and stain-resistant interiors. Selling points for refrigerators include ice and water in the door, door-mounted icemakers that free up storage space in the freezer, and interiors that offer lots of storage flexibility such as movable shelves, sealed edges that contain spills, and climate-controlled storage.

Vent hoods

There are two types of ventilation systems—updraft and downdraft. Either way, you'll need a ventilation system that will clear odors and smoke generated by your cooktop or range top and is as quiet as you can find within your price range.

Updraft systems have a hood that pulls air through a filter and along ductwork to the outside. Downdraft systems fit flush on a cooktop or rise above the countertop.

Both systems draw air outdoors through ductwork under the floor. Vent fan capacity is rated by how many cubic feet of air per minute (cfm) a fan moves. A conventional electric range that is used once or twice a day requires a fan rated at 200 cfm.

For similar use with a gas range, choose a hood with 200 to 300 cfm. If you plan to install a professional or semiprofessional-style gas range, you'll need up to 1,500 cfm.

Sinks and faucets

As with other kitchen components, salvage sinks and faucets if they look new, are not dated, and work well. If the sink is stained to the point of no return, or is dented, chipped, or scratched, you'll need to replace it. If you purchase a new sink, replace the faucet at the same time. Replacing sinks and faucets is relatively easy. For how-to advice, see pages 184–189. For pricing, see page 222.

SINK MATERIALS

Stainless steel is the most popular choice for the kitchen sink; it's durable, lightweight, and easy to install. Thickness and finish contribute to quality—a thick 19-gauge sink won't dent easily, a nickel and stainless composition wards off water spots, and a brushed finish conceals scratches. More good news—stainless-steel sinks are among the least expensive sink options.

Porcelain-enameled cast-iron sinks are the second most popular choice for kitchens. Available in white, cream, black, and a rainbow of other colors, these sinks are extremely durable, but because of weight they can be more difficult to install.

Vitreous china sinks have a lustrous surface, are not as heavy as porcelain-enameled cast-iron sinks, and are the most resistant to discoloration and corrosion. These sinks, however, can be chipped or cracked when struck by a heavy object.

Solid-surface sinks are also popular because—when combined with a solid-surface countertop—they appear seamless.

A pristine kitchen is a selling point. Invest in elbow grease and soap and water, and scrub down all the cabinets and fixtures.

SINK TYPES

The type of sink you choose largely depends on your countertop material. Self-rimming sinks, the most commonly used variety, are the easiest to install. With a rim that overlays the countertop, these sinks easily retrofit into existing countertops (as long as the opening is the same size).

Self-rimming sinks protect laminate countertops from moisture damage. Although debris can collect around the rim bump, it's easy to clean.

Undermount sinks mount to the bottom of a stone or solid-surface countertop, emphasizing the countertop material and making cleanup easy, because there is no rim bump.

Integrated-bowl sinks and countertops are made of one seamless material for easy cleanup. Material options are limited to higher-price stainless and solid-surface products.

Choose whether you want one-, two-, or three bowls. (Two is the top seller.) Extra-deep bowls—some as deep as 14 inches— are popular because they are useful for washing and filling tall pots.

FAUCETS

Although the sink category can be broken down into a few materials and types, the same can't be done for faucets. Brushed and polished chrome are the staples, although faucets made of brass, pewter, powder-coated epoxy, and even gold plate have joined them. A wide variety of reproduction and vintage-look styles is available, as is a range of contemporary designs.

Light fixtures

Lighting provides an easy way to make your kitchen appear livable and inviting. Installing new light fixtures is both easy and affordable. For advice on choosing and installing a variety of fixtures, see pages 200–203.

When assessing your current lighting scheme, think about natural and artificial light. Maximize sunlight by minimizing window treatments, replacing solid doors with glass ones, and if necessary, installing another window or two, even if it means sacrificing a wall-hung cabinet.

Supplement natural light with at least two electrical illumination strategies: ambient and task lighting. Also consider accent lighting.

Ambient, or general lighting, creates a uniform, overall glow in the kitchen and comes from one or more, usually overhead, sources. Backing up this general lighting plan is task lighting. These fixtures, available at home centers, are positioned to eliminate shadows in the areas where you perform specific tasks, such as cooking, eating, and cleaning up.

Accent lighting occurs when you aim light on a display space or focal point simply to show it off. You can add accent lighting for little cost by installing rope lights above wall-hung cabinets, inside glass-front cabinets, above open shelves, or beneath the cabinetry toe-kicks.

How does it function?

If a kitchen doesn't function properly, no surface changes will make it sell. To make the room functional, you may need to rework the layout. The illustrated floor plans on the following pages are the most common and all offer a high degree of function.

Floor plans

GALLEY

This setup typically is found when a kitchen doubles as a corridor between two rooms. With a walkway measuring at least 4 feet wide, parallel walls allow the cook to move easily from one workstation to another. The wide walkway also keeps traffic out of the cook's way. Housing the sink and refrigerator on one wall, with the cooktop centered on the other wall, maximizes efficiency.

Galley layouts are fine for modest-price starter homes, but you'll need to rework this layout into one of the other shapes if you're marketing the home in a more upscale neighborhood.

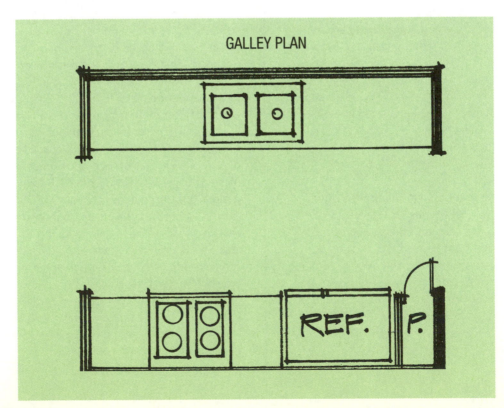

GALLEY PLAN

When possible, modify a U-shape plan so that it serves more than one cook.

U-SHAPE

This configuration, which includes one workstation on each of three walls, functions well for one cook, but it may seem cramped when two or more cooks use the space at the same time. An area of at least 8x8 feet is needed for a U-shape kitchen to provide at least 4 feet of workspace in the center of the room. You can modify this arrangement and increase its salability by making one of the sidewalls into an islandlike peninsula. This provides room for guests and helpers (especially when you add barstools to the far side of the peninsula) and creates a great-room or dining area connection.

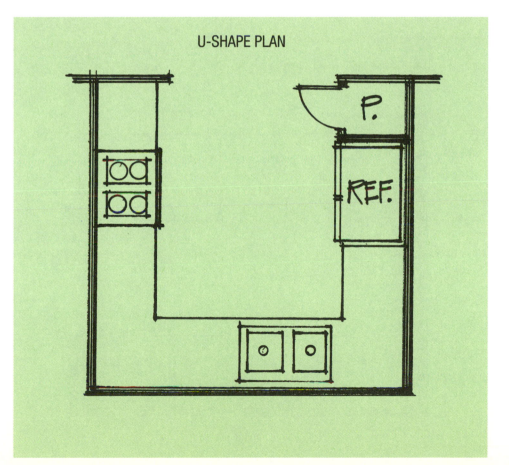

U-SHAPE PLAN

L-SHAPE

The most island-friendly configuration, the L-shape kitchen requires the least amount of space and offers the most flexibility. In this setup two workstations are situated on one wall and the third is placed on an adjacent wall. Location of the workstations is paramount: Work should flow from the refrigerator to the sink, then to the cooktop and serving area.

If there is room, add an island to this plan (see "Kitchen hot buttons" on page 61). To accommodate traffic, you'll need a minimum of 36 inches of aisle space on each side of the island, plus enough room to move appliances in and out of the room as they wear out and need replacing. Consider moving the sink or the cooktop to the island top to make the work flow even more efficient.

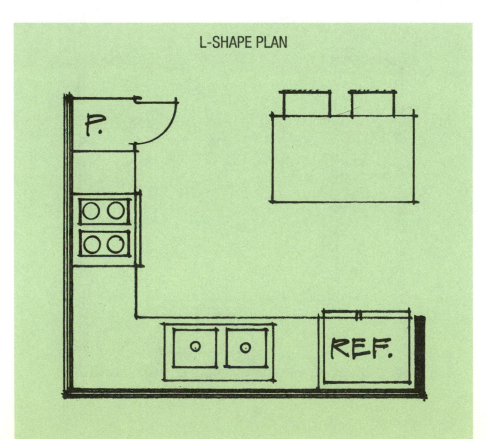

L-SHAPE PLAN

Kitchens that offer dual workstations accommodate multiple cooks and entertaining.

DUAL WORKSTATION

If you are flipping a home in an upscale neighborhood, would-be buyers will expect a kitchen plan that can accommodate a crowd. This dual workstation arrangement works well for multiple cooks and lots of visitor traffic. An island with a second sink creates a companion area to the traditional work triangle of refrigerator, cooktop, and main sink. A second work zone can become a snack center for a family on the go. Accessorize the counter with stools and a microwave so would-be buyers will immediately recognize the functionality of the layout.

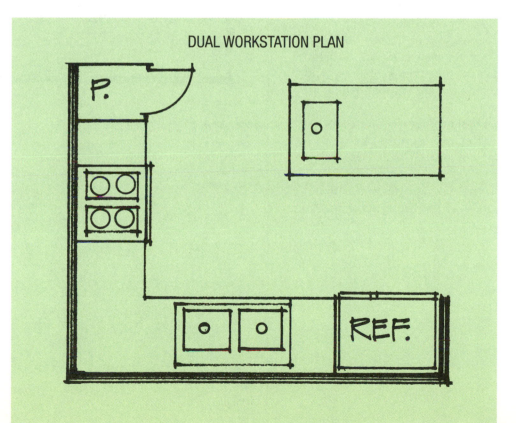

DUAL WORKSTATION PLAN

The work triangle

Each of the illustrated floor plans has a functional work triangle. This term refers to the path between the refrigerator, sink, and cooktop.

The goal is to keep the path uninterrupted by traffic or cabinetry to minimize steps between these components. Classic design principles suggest the perimeter of this work triangle should be between 12 and 22 feet, with each leg ranging from 4 to 8 feet.

The work triangle provides a good gauge of your kitchen's efficiency, but it is no longer as heavily depended on by kitchen designers as it once was. Depending on the size of your kitchen, you may want to position the refrigerator slightly outside the core work area, so other family members and guests can access its contents without getting in the way of the cook.

If the kitchen is designed for multiple cooks, you may want to create a second work triangle with the addition of a second sink. Drawing an imaginary line from a second sink to the microwave, then to the refrigerator, may also create a secondary work triangle to accommodate fast meals and snacks .

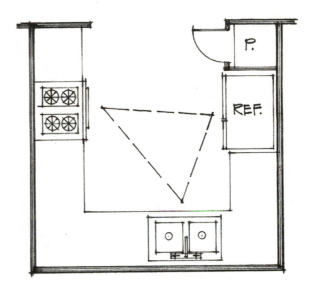

WORK TRIANGLE

Placing the refrigerator close to the **pantry** with counterspace between **simplifies** the chore of putting away **groceries**.

Push kitchen hot buttons

If you want to flip your property as quickly as possible, choose properties that have (or can be remodeled to have) the following highly sought-after features:

Open plan. Kitchen walls are coming down, sometimes to expand the rooms into adjacent spaces and sometimes to make transitions between rooms more fluid. Visual dividers—such as a taller section of island that hides the sink, or a change in ceiling height— give the kitchen an identity of its own without completely closing it off from the adjoining gathering spaces.

Social seating. The breakfast nook is disappearing, not because it isn't useful but because it is too remote. Seating in today's kitchens is about being in the thick of things—gathering where the food is prepared. Barstools or chairs around the island will help sell the kitchen as will an upholstered chair tucked in corner near (but not interfering with) the cooking action.

Display spaces. Glass inserts, open shelves, and plate racks are all affordable must-have commodities in top-selling kitchens.

Center island. Most people want one, but if your kitchen is too small to accommodate one, don't squeeze one in anyway. Instead add a narrow console table on wheels or a small butcherblock-topped table that can be moved out of the way as necessary.

Upgraded countertops. Even if you can't afford to put granite everywhere, put it somewhere, such as on the top of an island or as a 3- or 4-foot-long inset in a perimeter counter.

Storage pantry. We all want extra room to stash our stuff. Walk-ins are great, but if you don't have room, install at least one 6-foot-tall cabinet with pullout drawers that can serve as pantry central.

Activity center design

Think about the activities that commonly occur in the kitchen and you'll understand the principle behind a kitchen designed with activity or work centers. These centers are planned around specific chores, such as baking, paperwork, snacking, or buffet service. When planning a home with resale in mind, you'll want the activity centers in your kitchen to accommodate the most common kitchen activities; that way they will meet the needs of most prospective buyers.

Making space

If your kitchen is small and isolated (as most kitchens built before 1985 were), you can make it feel like a whole new space by opening it up to an adjoining dining room or family room. To do this affordably, you'll want to make sure the wall you would like to remove is non load-bearing (see page 154 for help on identifying load-bearing walls). If the wall is load-bearing, you'll need to hire a professional to determine what additional supports will be needed to make your design work.

Solving common kitchen design mistakes

Here's how to fix 10 common design ailments:

1. Avoid situating your appliances or cabinets too close to a corner because close corners restrict movement. To make appliance doors fully functional, plan for swing direction and door or drawer clearances. You also should avoid doors that bang into each other, such as a garage entry or dining room door.

2. Make the fridge accessible to passersby as well as convenient to the cooking center and cleanup area.

3. Don't underestimate the importance of a properly positioned microwave. The correct height and location for a microwave varies depending on the chef or kid-friendly requirements. As a general guide, plan for 15 inches above countertop level. For elementary-age kids, below-countertop setups are best.

4. Avoid narrow passageways by making the kitchen pathways at least 36 inches wide. Paths within the cooking zone should be at least 42 inches wide for one cook and 48 inches wide for a two-cook configuration.

5. Avoid routing traffic by the stove. In kid-friendly kitchens, keep the cooktop out of traffic areas so children don't catch pot handles and cause spills or burns when running through.

6. Break up rows of matching cabinet doors with glass-front varieties, open shelving, plate racks, wine racks, and windows.

7. Determine your island's function before determining its form. If you want to cook and eat on this kitchen oasis, plan to isolate each zone so the cooktop is safely separated from the eating area.

8. Allow 15 inches of countertop on each side of a cooktop or side-by-side refrigerator and 15 inches on at least the latch side of a standard refrigerator.

9. Avoid busy patterns or wildly bold colors. Pattern preferences vary greatly from one individual to another, so it's best to tone it down.

10. Vary the possibilities. For resale purposes consider varying the countertop height in at least one section of the kitchen. Lower counters (28 to 32 inches) are ideal for writing, kid-friendly spots, and for baking centers. Standard-height counters (36 to 38 inches) are comfortable for most other kitchen tasks (unless the cooks are very tall or very short).

Use universal design

Universal design principles make a kitchen more livable and functional for people of all ages and abilities. Where possible, follow these standards in your kitchen:

Comfortable reach. Locate door handles, appliances, electrical outlets, and switches 15 to 48 inches above the floor so that anyone can reach them comfortably.

Aisle and approach room. Aisles that are 4 feet wide comfortably accommodate wheelchairs and are recommended for multicook kitchens. Plan 5 feet of clear space for wheelchair turnarounds. Ideally there should be two turnarounds in the kitchen: one near the refrigerator and one near the cooktop or sink.

Cooking appliances. Wall ovens and separate cooktops are the safest way to go. Select front-mounted controls for easy access.

Knee clearances and toe-kicks. Wheelchair users require knee clearances that are 27 inches high, 30 inches wide, and 19 inches deep. Similarly, extra-wide 9x6-inch toe-kicks allow chair users to pull up close to counters. Some cabinet manufacturers offer these wide toe-kicks as an option; most other cabinets can be modified.

Faucets and hot water. Hands-free faucets (which turn on with a sensor) reduce the necessity to reach. Single-handle lever faucets are easier to turn on and off than two-handle varieties. To prevent scalding, turn the hot water down to 120 degrees.

Doors and handles. Plan for a door opening of 36 inches. Equip entrance doors, cabinet doors, and drawers with lever or cup handles, which are easier to operate than knobs.

Countertops. Bullnose fronts and rounded corners reduce risk of injury and help those who use a wheelchair to "shove off" from a counter using an elbow or a forearm.

Windows. Casement windows are the easiest to operate from a sitting position. Install windows 24 to 30 inches above the floor so that wheelchair users can open, close, and easily see out of them.

Color schemes

When it comes to choosing cabinetry with an eye for resale, classic white or medium wood tones are your best bets. To prevent the kitchen from looking too clinical, choose an island in a stain color that is darker or lighter than the perimeter cabinets. A wood-tone island also looks good in an otherwise white kitchen. For appliances, classic white and stainless steel are the most popular choices.

For wall color, choose a light color that provides a touch of contrast against the cabinets. Soft taupes, grays, and buttery yellow tones are good choices; they blend with most any decor. If you want your kitchen to convey more personality than a tract house down the road, avoid painting the walls basic builder white.

For a customized look, mix surfacing materials. Contrast light cabinets with a darker countertop. Select an island countertop from of a different material than the perimeter counters. For flooring, choose a neutral wood plank, a wood-look laminate, or a neutral tile or vinyl, again allowing the amenities found in surrounding homes to serve as your quality guide. Light fixtures and faucet finishes should blend with those found in adjacent rooms.

Avoid dark colors in a diminutive kitchen; dark color schemes shrink an already small space and make it feel less inviting. Use soft shades and natural light to visually expand a tiny room.

Offer dining comfort and style

The consensus varies on the percentage of prospective home buyers who consider a formal dining room a must-have feature. Yet most every buyer prefers a home with a comfortable place to eat—even if it's only a snack bar in the kitchen.

How does it look?

The top two priorities for any eating area—formal or informal—are that every surface appears clean and that the space is roomy enough to comfortably accommodate an eating surface and seating. Use these guidelines to inspect and shape up all your property's eating spaces.

Refresh the ceiling and walls

Look up and all around the dining room and assess the level of renovation these surfaces require:

DINING ROOM & EATING AREA MUSTS:
- Ample space for a table and chairs; a formal dining room should seat a minimum of 6 to 8; a kitchen eating area should seat 4 to 6
- Clean, nicely finished ceiling, walls, and floor
- Beautiful, adjustable lighting
- Inviting ambience

CEILING MAKEOVER
If you're lucky, the dining room of your property has some pleasing architectural features, such as a tray or coffered ceiling. If not, consider adding crown molding following the steps on page 172. Or beef up moldings with trim. Rather than scrubbing down a dingy ceiling, freshen it with paint. If the ceiling is stained, make sure there are no holes in the roof, then prime the ceiling with a stain-blocking primer, and repaint.

WALL UPDATE
If your dining room or eating area walls are ready for a fresh coat of paint, follow the instructions on page 156 to achieve professional results. You can also add character to plain dining room walls with moldings, such as a chair rail, or consider installing beaded-board wainscoting. For step-by-step instructions on how to install wainscoting panels, turn to page 178.

You can paint the wall area above the wainscoting or finish it with a wallcovering. If your dining room already features an attractive

Say it with trim

If your dining room features narrow molding near the ceiling, at the floor, and around doors and windows, but you wish this woodwork offered a more substantial look, try this simple trick: Secure half-round molding to the wall 2 to 3 inches below the bottom edge of the crown molding or on the wall a few inches above the top edge of a baseboard. Paint the old and new molding pieces, as well as the gap between them, the same color to create the illusion of beefy, more elaborate trimwork. Make the trim stand out by painting the wall a different color from your new, improved trim.

wallcovering, freshen the surface observing the guidelines below. Or if the wallcovering is unattractive, use the information on page 157 for removing wallcoverings, then paint or apply new wallcoverings.

WALLCOVERING CARE

Most wallpaper is made of vinyl or are vinyl-coated for durability and easy care. However, some imported, reproduction, embossed, flocked, custom-made, or older wallpapers are made of untreated or lightly treated paper. Some wallcovering companies also produce other paper-backed fabrics, most often silk. If you are in doubt about a paper or covering, treat it as plain paper.

For general dusting and to remove cobwebs, tie a dust cloth or T-shirt sprayed with a dusting agent over a broom and wipe down the walls. Work from the top down. This isn't recommended for flocked, grass cloth, or natural fiber papers, which need to be cleaned with a soft brush.

Vinyl wallpapers can be dusted or damp-wiped. Use a vacuum or wipe with a soft rag. For deep cleaning, dip a sponge in warm water and all-purpose cleaner, then wring the sponge until it's almost dry. Lightly scrub the wall in 3-foot sections, then rinse with clear water, and pat dry with soft dry cloths. Do not allow the paper to remain wet and do not let water seep through the seams. For heavily soiled areas around light switches and other often-touched places, use a detergent solution and a soft brush. Don't use abrasive cleansers, scrubbing pads, or solvent-based cleaners.

Lighting

Flexibility in lighting scenarios is key to an attractive formal dining room or eat-in area of the kitchen. Lighting connected to a dimmer switch allows you to change the mood from romantic to bright and cheerful.

You'll want an attractive fixture above the table, usually a chandelier or pendant, depending on whether the space is formal or casual. For information on installing a new lighting fixture, turn to page 202. Before hanging a chandelier, determine the most likely location for the dining table. Use a less obvious fixture if you suspect that the table will be moved frequently. The standard distance between the bottom of a chandelier and the tabletop is 30 to 36 inches. The chandelier should be 2 feet narrower than the table.

DINING ROOMS & EATING AREAS

Cleaning a chandelier

Put your eating area fixture in the best light when you follow these tips for cleaning:

CRYSTAL CHANDELIERS

Use a feather duster to freshen a dusty chandelier. For deep cleaning, turn off the power at the breaker box. Remove and wipe the bulbs. Move the dining table or other furniture from beneath the chandelier and protect the floor with heavy-duty plastic drop cloths. Mix a solution of 1 part rubbing alcohol to 3 parts water OR 1 part nonsudsing ammonia to 3 parts water. Use distilled water if your tap water is hard. Thoroughly dust the entire fixture with a clean cloth or duster. Do not use commercial dusting agents because they may leave a residue. Inspect for problems such as loose wiring. Gently wipe the fixture with a barely damp soft cloth or sponge. Cover sockets with plastic sandwich bags held in place with rubber bands. Hang a lightweight oversize umbrella, such as a golf umbrella, upside down under the fixture to catch drips. Spray one crystal with the solution of your choice, avoiding wires, hangers, and electrical components. Allow to drip-dry. Rinse crystal with a spray of distilled water, avoiding wires. If you are satisfied, spray the remaining crystals. Allow the fixture to air-dry overnight. Remove the bags from the sockets. Wipe with a soft dry cloth to ensure that there is no seeping moisture before turning on the power.

BRASS, NICKEL, OR CHROME

Turn off the power at the breaker box and remove the bulbs; dust the bulbs. Dust the chandelier with a soft cloth and polish with a cleaner formulated for the metal. Replace the bulbs and restore the power.

SCONCES

Wall sconces lend a romantic glow to a dining room. They can be mounted to flank a sideboard or an armoire or simply spaced attractively on a pair of adjacent walls.

The two types of electric sconces are direct-wire and plug-in. Direct-wire sconces have no exposed cords and are permanently wired into an outlet in the wall. An electrician is needed to install direct-wire sconces. Some direct-wire sconces operate from light switches in the room and turn on and off with the ceiling lights or from a separate switch. Others have a switch attached to the sconce and are turned on independently. Determine your needs before purchasing a direct-wire sconce. For a dining room, select sconces that turn on at the switch. (A sconce operated independently works well as a reading light in a bedroom.)

Plug-in sconces hook to the wall with brackets and are plugged into an existing outlet. Although these are easier and less expensive to install than direct-wire sconces, the exposed cord from the fixture to the outlet can be unsightly. Cord strips that are available at home improvement and lighting centers attach to the wall to encase the wire. They often match the metal in the lamp (brass, silver) or can be painted to match the painted wall color. Plug-in sconces are operated by a switch on the lamp. To turn the sconce on and off at the wall, plug the cord into an outlet controlled by a wall switch.

Most sconces fit close to the wall and direct light up and down. Uplighting enhances the room; downlighting brightens specific areas.

You can **remove crayon marks** from painted walls, wood, and washable wallcoverings: **Spray the mark** with WD-40 and wipe with a soft cloth.

Wood flooring fix-ups

Wood flooring is one of the most popular surfaces for a dining space. Beautiful and visually warming, wood flooring lends value to the property and is much easier to clean than carpeting when someone spills the spaghetti sauce. For prospective buyers who prefer the softness and color of carpeting, a rug can be rolled out over wood flooring. Wood is definitely a win-win material, so if you're fortunate enough to find a property with wood floors, pat yourself on the back.

To ensure that the wood floors are an asset when it is time to show the house, make them smooth and gleaming by following these cleaning and repair tips:

CLEAN START

Dirt, oil, and grime build up over time and aren't entirely removed by dust-mopping. Instead use a wood-cleaning product diluted according to label instructions. Saturate a sponge or rag mop in the water, then wring it almost dry so it feels only slightly damp to the touch. Damp-mop, being careful not to allow water to stand on the floor. Rinse with a clean mop dampened in clear water only if the product requires it. Wipe up excess liquid; standing water can damage wood surfaces. If the weather is humid, operate a ceiling fan or the air-conditioner to help the floor dry.

REMOVING MARKS

If the wood floor has scratches or marks, consider the floor finish before attempting to remove the mark. If the scratch or stain is on the surface, your floor probably has a hard finish. (Widely used urethane-type finishes create a hard sealant on wood floors.) If the scratch or stain has penetrated the finish to the wood, the floor likely has a soft, oiled finish—common in older residences in which the floors have not been refinished and sealed.

HARD FINISHES. Repair scratches with commercial touch-up kits from a wood flooring supplier. Never use sandpaper, steel wool, or harsh chemicals because they can permanently damage the finish.

SOFT FINISHES. Use the following techniques to restore damaged spots in the wood floor. End each treatment by staining the wood (if necessary) and waxing and buffing the spot to match the rest of the floor. Choose the appropriate remedy for the mark or stain.

• Dark spots and pet stains: Rub the spot with steel wool and floor wax. If the area is still dark, apply bleach or white vinegar and allow it to soak into the wood for about an hour. Wipe with a damp cloth.

• Heel marks: Use fine steel wool to rub in floor wax and lift the mark.

• Oil-base stains: Rub the area with a soft cloth and dishwashing detergent to break down the grease, then rinse with clear water. If one application doesn't work, repeat the procedure.

DINING ROOMS & EATING AREAS

Let the spot dry, then smooth the raised grain with fine sandpaper.

• Scratches: Repair deep scratches with a wood color stick or with a stain that matches the floor. Cover light scratches with floor wax. Let the wax dry, then buff with a cotton cloth.

• Water marks or white stains: Rub the spot with steel wool and floor wax. If the stain is deeper than the surface, lightly sand the floor, then clean with fine steel wool and mineral spirits.

REPLACING DAMAGED BOARDS

Is a wood board damaged beyond repair and in need of replacing? New tongue-and-groove flooring is expensive, and it may not match the old flooring in appearance. Also new flooring strips have to be sanded and stained to match the existing floor—a difficult job.

The solution is to find pieces of wood from elsewhere in the house. Pry out boards from a closet or from under carpeting and fill the resulting voids with plywood. To replace the damaged board, follow these steps:

1. Remove the damaged board using a drill equipped with a spade bit; bore holes across the width of the board at the ends and in the middle. Drill only through the flooring board.

2. Use a wood chisel to split the board lengthwise between the drilled holes.

3. Pry out the damaged board using a flat pry bar; pull out the old nails left in the subfloor.

4. Cut the new board to fit and test-fit it.

5. Apply flooring adhesive to the subfloor and tap the board into place. Use a scrap of wood to protect the flooring surface as you tap.

WAXING

Wax is used to seal, protect, and beautify flooring. Choose water-base finishes in the correct type of wax for the floor and its finish. Follow the wood manufacturer and finish label directions to protect the floor without producing a dangerously slick surface. Use nonskid rug pads under all runners to avoid accidents. Wax and waxlike products also are used on linoleum (not resilient types), unfinished cork, and some concrete floors. If in doubt about a product, don't use it.

SOLID PASTE WAX. Choose this old-fashioned wax in a can for unvarnished hardwood floors, true linoleum, unfinished cork, and concrete. Do not use paste wax on no-wax floors, vinyl, or urethane-finished floors. Apply by hand for a long-lasting shine. Moisten a soft, lint-free cotton cloth, such as an old T-shirt, and wring it almost dry to prevent the cloth from absorbing too much wax. Apply the wax lightly and evenly, working it into the surface following product instructions. If you prefer soft wax, use the liquid equivalent of paste wax. As the waxed surface dries, it will appear cloudy. Buff to a shine with a clean towel, an electric polisher, or a terry cloth-covered sponge mop.

LIQUID WAX OR OIL. Use these on unvarnished hardwood, linoleum, or unfinished cork. Follow the label instructions. Liquid wax is easier to apply than paste wax, but the finish doesn't last as long. Do NOT use on no-wax floors, vinyl, or urethane-finished floors. Dampen a soft, lint-free cloth, a mop, or the pad of an electric floor polisher to prevent the wax from soaking in. Apply polish evenly and lightly. When dry, buff the floor with a clean towel or a sponge mop covered with a terry cloth towel.

Find room for a **built-in china cabinet** by using space between wall studs. This shallow storage works for **glass and plate display**.

WATER-BASE SILICONE POLISHES. Apply on all floors except unsealed wood, cork, or linoleum. Use this type of polish only on urethane-finished surfaces. Apply these long-lasting polishes in several thin coats rather than one heavy coat, which takes a long time to dry. To apply, dampen a clean mop head. Pour some polish onto the mop and some directly on the floor. Spread the polish evenly to avoid bubbles in the liquid. Allow the polish to dry, then buff the floor with a clean terry cloth towel, an electric polisher, or a terry cloth-covered sponge mop. Apply second and third coats to high-traffic areas, buffing after each coat dries. Avoid splattering polish onto baseboards or walls because it stains wallcoverings and paint.

SEALING FLOORS

After several years of wear, cork and hardwood floor surfaces need to be refinished or resealed. Polyurethane finishes, both water- and oil-base, are hard and durable. Shellac, lacquer, and nonurethane varnish are less frequently used sealants; after they are applied, they take several days to dry before the surface is durable. Acrylic sealers, which are not as durable, are fine for low-traffic areas.

Before refinishing floors, thoroughly remove any wax or residue with a product formulated for wax removal. Lightly sand any rough spots or dark stains. If more extensive sanding is needed, rent a vibrating sander. Schedule this project on a warm, calm, dry day when windows can be open to avoid breathing fumes. Brush on the appropriate sealer with a foam pad, working from a corner to a doorway. Let the surface dry thoroughly before allowing traffic on the floor.

Add dining hot buttons

If you want to flip your property as quickly as possible, choose a property that has (or can be remodeled to have) the following highly sought-after features:

Functional storage. Buyers want a place to store their linens and tableware.

Display space. Most everyone has a few treasures they'd like to proudly display. The dining room is the ideal place for showing off heirloom dishware and other belongings.

Soothing color scheme. The palette in this room needs to feel welcoming to everyone who enters the space.

Dramatic lighting. A gorgeous chandelier on a dimmer switch allows homeowners to set the mood with the turn of a knob.

DINING ROOMS & EATING AREAS

Freshening woodwork

Now that the wood floors in the eating area look good, what about the wood trim? The grooves and raised surfaces in some moldings trap dust, grease, and soot. Clean dusty trim with a vacuum brush attachment, a feather duster, or a soft paintbrush. Clean dirty molding with an all-purpose cleaner; test the cleaner first in an inconspicuous spot. Mix a solution of 1 cup ammonia, $\frac{1}{2}$ cup white vinegar, $\frac{1}{4}$ cup baking soda, and 1 gallon warm water. Pour part of the solution into a spray bottle and spray and wipe small sections of molding at a time. Rinse with clear water and wipe the molding dry with a clean soft cloth.

For picture molding that has spaces for picture hooks located below the crown molding, use a new soft paintbrush or cotton swabs to remove the dust. If the space is grimy, dip a cotton swab in the cleaning solution you used for the molding, follow with a swab dipped in clear water, and finish with dry swabs. As houses settle, gaps appear between the crown molding and the ceiling; fill the space with a bead of paintable caulk (as long as the molding is already painted).

Removing years of grime, paint, and finish from stained wood trim takes a lot of elbow grease and time. Here are some tips for stripping woodwork so you can restore it to its former glory:

• Always wear protective gloves, eye wear, and a mask, and make sure the space is well-ventilated. Additionally, protect and cover all nearby surfaces.

• Apply stripping gel to small sections of trim. Gels come in toxic and nontoxic forms; nontoxic formulas tend to be less effective but are safer.

• Scoop off old paint or finish with a putty knife when it begins to bubble. For detailed areas, swap the putty knife for an awl. Stripping gel softens the wood, too, so take care not to gouge it.

• Work small sections at a time because it's even harder to remove paint or finish that has bubbled and dried.

• Throw away the rags and towels used in each session; they can't be reused.

• Depending on the age and number of layers of paint or finish, you may need to apply several treatments of stripper to reach bare wood.

• When you reach wood, sand it and apply wood conditioner so it accepts stain evenly.

• Apply stain and layers of protective finish.

How does it function?

Before you solidify your dining room and eating area decorating and design plans, take accurate measurements of these spaces and lay out the components using the room arranging kit provided on pages 238–251.

Adding stylish storage

Dining rooms don't require as much storage as harder-working kitchens and baths, but some functional storage is desirable. Prospective buyers will imagine simplified mealtimes and easier entertaining when they find that they can store linens, good china and silverware, and serving and tabletop pieces nearby.

Utilitarian storage is only one option. As one of the home's showplaces, the formal dining room benefits from open storage where favorite possessions can be displayed.

Clean windows will make your dining room or eating area appear warmer and more welcoming and will let in more clear light than dirty ones.

USE FREESTANDING STORAGE PIECES. Purchase or rent a hutch, buffet, sideboard, or other cupboard. A low sideboard is ideal if you have a large painting or mirror to cover the wall above it. If not, think tall when selecting an armoire, hutch, or cupboard. For impact, leave upper cabinet doors open to show off a display.

HANG IT ON THE WALL. No dining space is too small for vertical storage or a small wall rack. Wall-mount shelves above table height. Or encircle a room with a unifying display shelf. A plate rack, for example, offers charm when lined with vintage dessert plates.

BUILD IT IN. Built-in china cabinets or shelf-lined niches—created between the studs—turn blank walls into handsome and functional dining room assets. Or make use of dead corner space with a custom corner unit or by building in new unfinished corner units. For formal symmetry, treat corners identically.

Fitting in dining space

If your property lacks a formal dining room, be creative for the open house and stage a spot for dining. For example, a half-round table or drop-leaf table can accent a wide hallway—and also transition into a welcoming dinner-for-two spot. Or set a modest-size rectangular dining table flush against a family or living room wall or directly behind a sofa. Even a slim sofa table can serve as a dining table when you pull up a couple of chairs.

You can give bed-and-breakfast-style romance to a master bedroom by snugging a slim dining table or sofa table against the foot of the bed or in front of a window, or by replacing a nightstand with a larger table that can double for late-night snacks.

Gather in the kitchen

It's no wonder that the eat-in kitchen tops the wish list of most home buyers. A staple of older homes and a selling point of new ones, the eat-in kitchen promises good times with family and friends with its casual, back-door air—and speaks to the heart of every potential buyer. Here's how to play up this selling point:

• Use easy-care fabrics and finishes so breakfast nooks and kitchen dining areas offer a cozy and clean look.

• Repeat hues and fabrics from other parts of the room. Painted chairs, new tie-on chair cushions, and table runners can echo the palette or pattern of the kitchen tile, wallpaper, or window valance.

• Pull a table up to a kitchen window seat for dining. Built-in booths make efficient use of floor space and give the kitchen a distinctive look.

• Arrange dining pieces so they're out of the busy flow of traffic.

• Replace the switch for existing ceiling lights with a dimmer. If there are no over-the-table lights, wire in a hanging pendant or strip of track lights.

GATHERING ROOMS

Create a welcoming gathering space

Give your property a salable edge with a gathering space that anyone would love. The most sought-after gathering rooms are chameleon like, standing ready and able to serve the needs of any family, regardless of size or lifestyle.

How does it look?

You can make your home's family room accommodating to a variety of people by filling it with the right basics—classic furnishings (whether traditional or modern) and simple backdrops.

THINK SUBTLE. Neutral backdrops complement formal gatherings and cozy family get-togethers. White ceilings and window treatments, neutral-color walls, and white or wood-tone mantels and built-ins pay no allegiance to a single style but are appropriate for all.

MAXIMIZE SUNLIGHT. Minimal window treatments, such as gauzy sheers or translucent fabric shades, shed ample light by day yet still look dressy enough for nighttime entertaining.

GATHERING ROOM MUSTS:
- Like-new flooring
- Attractive windows
- Adjustable lighting
- Social seating
- Stylish decor

ENCOURAGE A FEELING OF WELCOME. Convey an instant feeling of comfort by staging your gathering areas with overstuffed versions of traditional pieces, such as a rolled-arm sofa and a pair of cushy club chairs with matching ottomans. Loosen up traditional furniture groupings with a wicker chair or wooden rocker.

ADD ARCHITECTURAL CHARACTER. Ceiling moldings and other decorative trimwork such as chair rails and door trims add interest and style without breaking a remodeling budget. Just be conscious of scale before you make your selections. If your room has an 8-foot ceiling, use a simple, narrow crown molding rather than a deep, elaborate version.

Likewise consider the style of the moldings. Ornate moldings look best in more formal, traditional houses. If the home you are flipping features period styling, such as Craftsman or Victorian, choose moldings that fit the look.

COMBINE STORAGE AND STYLE. If your pockets are a little deeper, you can transform a featureless living room into one filled with timeless elegance by lining a blank wall with a grouping of bookcases (purchase affordable ready-to-assemble ones from a home center or discount furniture store) or custom built-ins. These storage accents show potential buyers where they can store personal collections of books and electronics. They also make the gathering space seem larger by playing up its vertical and horizontal lines.

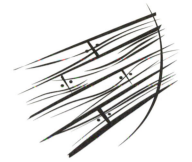

Flooring

HARDWOOD. Houses built before 1960 often have hardwood floors. Salvage this flooring if you can bring it back to its original luster through cleaning or refinishing. If the floor is in good shape but won't come clean with a damp mop, use a cleaning product specifically designed for wood floors and follow the manufacturer's instructions.

Note that wood floors typically have a hard sealant finish, such as polyurethane, or a softer, oiled finish—common in older homes in which the floors have never been redone. For advice on repairing floors with either type of sealant, see pages 67–69.

TILE. Floor tile broadly includes terra-cotta, porcelain, quarry tile, and paver tiles—glazed and unglazed. Salvage this flooring material if you can restore it to its original luster and then soften its look by adding attractive area rugs.

Each type of tile has slightly different care requirements. Glazed tiles are more impervious to stains, making them easy to maintain. Tiles without a glazed surface are more porous and tend to stain more easily than glazed tiles. Before cleaning any tile, test your stain removal technique on inconspicuous spots on the tile and grout. A nonabrasive all-purpose tub/tile/sink cleaner

Consider wood and wood-look laminate floors

Improvements in technology and manufacturing have made solid wood and wood-look laminate floors easier to take care of and less costly to install, so they're a perfect choice for a gathering room or master bedroom floor. Both of these flooring types are available in a tongue-and-groove design that snaps together, eliminating the need for nailing and gluing. For those who prefer the more solid feel of a glued-down floor, preglued, snap-together systems are also available.

For more warmth and comfort underfoot, top the wood floor with a large, neutral-color area rug, or a series of smaller rugs placed where you step out of bed and in front of seating arrangements. If you add an area rug, you can take it with you when you sell the home (for use in your next flip or your personal residence). Although you can offer home furnishing items (such as area rugs) for sale during an open house, note they often become add-ons in a buyer's offer and will not, ultimately, add anything to your bottom line.

removes most stains. If the all-purpose cleaner doesn't work, try these techniques. To remove blood stains, dab the spot with hydrogen peroxide or diluted bleach (¼ cup bleach to 1 gallon water). For spots made from coffee, tea, or juice, wash with detergent and hot water; blot with hydrogen peroxide or diluted bleach. To remove gum, tar, or wax, place ice cubes in a zipper-type plastic bag and lay the bag over the material. Once the material has been solidified, use a crafts stick to gently scrape away as much residue as possible. Remove the remaining residue with nonflammable paint thinner. To clean grease or fat stains, wash the tile with club soda and water or with a nonabrasive floor cleaner. For ink or dye, soak a clean cloth with diluted bleach and lay it over the stain; let it stand until the stain disappears, then rinse well. Dissolve nail polish with nail polish remover. If a stain remains, dab it with hydrogen peroxide or diluted bleach.

GROUT. Because grout is more porous than tile, it often collects dirt and stains more than the tile itself. To clean stained grout, use a strong bleach solution (¾ cup bleach to 1 gallon water) and scrub with a small brush or toothbrush. Do not scrub too hard because you may loosen the grout. If grout is deeply stained or discolored but is otherwise sound, paint it with grout paint, available at most home centers and tile distributors. If the grout is loose or cracked, replace it. Tile stores sell and sometimes rent tools for removing grout and also provide instructions for regrouting tiles.

Carpeting

Salvage the existing carpeting only if it is a neutral color, is stylish and there are no visible stains. If you choose to try your hand at stain removal, test your stain removal technique on an inconspicuous place before cleaning. To remove spots, use a commercial spot carpet cleaner sold at home centers and grocery stores. With plain white cotton or paper towels, blot—never rub—the area. For pet stains apply an enzymatic cleaner, available at both grocery and pet supply stores.

You can also make your own cleaner by mixing 1 cup white vinegar with 2 cups water. This works best on wine, soft drink, and juice stains. For grease, sprinkle the area with baking soda. Let it sit overnight, then vacuum up the baking soda. Follow with a commercial spot cleaner.

To determine a carpet's quality, comparison-shop among brands by looking at the carpet's performance rating. Most carpets are rated on a 5-point scale, with a 4 or 5 rating as the best for high-traffic areas. A 2 to 3 rating is acceptable for areas with less traffic, such as a formal living room or guest bedroom. Some carpets are rated on a 10-point scale with the numbers 8 to10 denoting the top-rated carpets.

Make your property look **move-in ready** with new or like-new flooring.

Performance ratings measure the way the yarns of a carpet are twisted (a tighter twist enhances durability) and the density of the tufts (the denser the better). Pile height is a matter of personal choice and does not affect durability. Heat-setting—the process that sets the twist by heat or steam—enables yarns to hold their twist over time and is important only with cut pile carpeting. Most nylon, olefin, and polyester cut pile carpets are heat-set. The fiber you choose determines how well your carpet will wear:

See how much carpet you'll need

To determine a room's square footage, simply multiply the length of the room in feet by its width. Dealers may sell by the square foot or the square yard. To obtain the square yardage, divide the total square footage figure by 9. Add 10 percent to account for room irregularities and pattern match. Provide this number to your salesperson so he or she can provide you with a cost estimate. Make sure the cost quoted includes carpet, pad, and installation. Have your retailer make final measurements to ensure that you purchase the correct amount of carpet; most retailers offer this service free.

NYLON. Nylon is the most popular carpeting material and is available in an array of colors, weaves, and textures. Wear-resistant and resilient, it withstands the weight and movement of furniture and resists soiling and staining. It is a good choice for high-traffic areas.

OLEFIN. This fiber is also durable, but it is not available in as many colors and patterns as nylon. Olefin cleans easily and resists static electricity. It is often used in indoor and outdoor installations because it is resistant to moisture and mildew. Many berber rugs are made of olefin.

POLYESTER. This synthetic fiber resembles wool in texture and has excellent color clarity and retention. Polyester also cleans easily and is resistant to water-soluble stains. Oil-base stains, however, can be difficult—if not impossible—to remove. Crushing is possible, so polyester may not be a good choice in rooms outfitted with heavy furnishings.

ACRYLIC. Acrylic feels much like wool, but it tends to look a bit glossier than wool and is prone to crushing. It cleans easily, however, it also resists static electricity, and it is moisture- and mildew-resistant.

WOOL. Wool has an excellent texture and resists soils and stains. It can be dyed almost any color, but is prone to fading when exposed to strong sunlight for long periods. Wool is somewhat more expensive than the synthetic fibers.

BLENDS. A wool/nylon blend combines the look and comfort of wool with the durability of nylon, and it costs less than pure wool. Nylon/olefin and polyester/olefin blends are also available, but their performance ratings vary.

THE CARPET PAD. The type and thickness of your carpet's cushion varies according to the type of carpet. For a cut-pile carpet, choose a pad with a maximum thickness of $7/16$ inch. A berber carpet pad should be no more than $3/8$ inch thick. If the old padding seems to be in good shape, you can use it, but keep in mind that most carpet manufacturers will not honor wear warranties if an old pad is used.

Regardless of the climate you live in, there's something enticing about a fire glowing in the fireplace.

Gathering room hot button

The fireplace

Whether home buyers live in mild or seasonal climates, most desire at least one fireplace in their home. Living rooms, family rooms, and great rooms are the most popular spaces for them. Because these areas are designed for entertaining and family togetherness, a glowing fire adds to the room's sense of warmth and welcome.

HAVE IT INSPECTED. If the home you are planning to flip already has a fireplace, you'll want to inspect it or hire a chimney sweep to inspect it and make sure it is in proper working order. As wood burns, it produces water vapor, gases, and unburned particles which is smoke. In a chimney that is clean and free of obstructions, these byproducts are quickly vented through the flue to the outdoors. However, as warm air vapors reach the upper parts of the chimney they may encounter colder air and condense, forming creosote, a black or brown residue that clings to the interior surfaces of the flue liner. This is especially true if fires are not burning at high enough temperatures—for example, if the fire is allowed to smolder and smoke, if wet wood is used, or if wood with an inherently low burning temperature, such as pine, is used regularly. Creosote is a highly flammable substance that comes in many forms. It can be as hard as glass, tarlike and sticky, or dry and flaky. If creosote is allowed to build up, it may catch fire. Flue liners for residential use must be certified by Underwriters Laboratories, an independent product testing and safety agency, to withstand temperatures of 1,700 degrees Fahrenheit. However, a flue fire can reach 2,500 degrees Fahrenheit. These high temperatures can crack brick, stone, or clay flue liners, allowing heat to reach nearby wood framing and other combustible materials such as insulation, resulting in a chimney fire.

YOU CAN DO IT. Making an inspection yourself is not difficult, but prepare to get dirty. Wear old clothes—including a hat—and equip yourself with a dust mask or respirator and a pair of safety goggles. First check the firebox for damage or cracks. In a masonry fireplace, also check for brick and mortar that is loose or missing. Defects in a firebox usually can be repaired with refractory cement—a tough, heatproof sealant available through fireplace dealers. A damaged refractory liner in a prefabricated fireplace often can be replaced without having to replace the entire unit.

Open the damper completely. It should move freely and sit snugly against the throat. Use a powerful flashlight to look up into the throat to check the condition of the damper. The damper should be sound with no cracks, severe pitting, or rusted-out sections. Over the years a metal damper often will deteriorate from the water vapor and corrosive gases produced by wood fires. Broken or corroded dampers should be replaced by a professional.

Look up inside the flue and check for broken or damaged brick or defects in the flue liner. Vertical cracking in the liner is a telltale sign of previous flue fires. Any defects should be considered potential hazards. Consult a chimney sweep or masonry contractor who is familiar with fireplace repairs. Be prepared: Fixing or replacing a chimney liner is an expensive job.

Look for any obstructions such as branches, bird nests, or other debris that can restrict airflow. Finally, inspect for creosote deposits. If creosote has built up to a thickness greater than 1/8 inch, it should be removed.

If you can't see the entire flue from below, you'll have to get on the roof and inspect the flue from the top of the chimney, which can be dangerous to do, particularly if you have a steep roof. You may wish to hire a professional chimney sweep to do this and to clean the chimney.

If you decide to do this inspection yourself, don't climb up onto the roof unless your roof has a pitch of 6–12 or less and unless you are completely confident in your abilities.

Make a safety ladder by attaching ridge hooks to the end of a ladder section. Use it by hanging the hooks over the roof ridge so the ladder lies flat and secure against the roof surface. Roof hooks are available at hardware stores and home improvement centers.

INCREASE ITS APPEAL. Once you are sure your fireplace is in working order, turn your attention to its existing facade. If it looks dated or does not match the architectural style of the home, consider replacing it with a new hearth and surround. The following options are excellent choices; all are fireproof and each has a unique visual appeal:

GATHERING ROOMS

STONE AND ROCK. Granite, marble, soapstone, limestone, and other natural stone and rock formations provide timeless styling. The surfaces, whether cut into tiles or left in their natural state, stand up to heat and bring natural beauty and color to any fireplace facing or hearth. Solid color, shiny tile finishes have a tendency to show ashes or fingerprints, so for less upkeep consider choosing stone with a mottled or honed finish. If you plan to use natural stone or rock to make up the mantel and/or overmantel, you will likely need extra structural support to bear the material's heavy weight. As an alternative, cultured stone looks and feels like natural rock but weighs only about a quarter as much.

CERAMIC TILE. Ceramic tiles make an attractive and durable hearth and surround and are available in an array of colors, styles, and sizes. To disguise fingerprints and dust on this classic surfacing choice, choose a honed finish.

BRICK. Like tile, this surfacing option is attractive, durable and a longtime favorite for the fireplace facing. A range of looks can be produced depending on the type of bricks you choose and the pattern in which you lay them. As with stone, if you use bricks to cover a large portion of

Hire a chimney sweep

If you prefer to leave the messy chore of inspecting and cleaning your fireplace and chimney to someone else, hire a professional chimney sweep. Rather then relying on the phone book listings, ask friends and neighbors for a recommendation or check with a fireplace dealer. These retailers often keep a list of professionals with good recommendations. Although the chimney sweep industry is not regulated or licensed by a government agency, many sweeps apply for certification by the Chimney Safety Institute of America (CSIA) or membership in the National Chimney Sweep Guild (NCSG). These organizations promote professionalism in the industry by testing applicants and offering continuing education on ever-changing fireplace technology and safety. To find a certified chimney sweep, call the CSIA at 800/536-0118, or visit the website at www.csia.org. Visit the NCSG at www.ncsg.org.

For $150 to $200, a sweep will give your fireplace and chimney a thorough cleaning and inspection. Some sweeps lower video cameras and lights into chimneys to provide a close look at walls and liner surfaces and to establish a visual record of the chimney's condition for the homeowner. Many sweeps are qualified to complete necessary repairs, or they will recommend a professional masonry contractor to do the job.

the fireplace wall, you may need extra structural support.

ENGINEERED QUARTZ. This material is made from crushed quartz and binders. It has a composition, weight, and price comparable to those of natural stone. Because it is nonporous and fireproof, the material requires little maintenance and makes an excellent fireplace surround. It is available in tile and slab form.

CONCRETE. Concrete fireplace surrounds are nearly as durable as granite. Hairline cracks are common but do not affect the strength of the material. Concrete can be dyed virtually any color —before it is fully cured—it can be stamped to create any sort of surface texture or appearance. Because concrete is porous, it should be sealed for protection against dirt and stains.

METAL. Fireplace surrounds made of metal may be sleek and contemporary or vintage reproductions. Options include bronze, copper, iron, nickel, or steel tiles.

Mantel options

Because a mantel doesn't have to be fireproof, material options are limited only by your imagination.

WOOD. Attractive, versatile, and easy to install, wood is the most common material choice for the mantel. New mantels can be made to resemble a vintage piece with elaborate carvings and fine-furniture detailing or left purposely plain to complement a more contemporary motif.

CARVED OR CAST STONE. Carved stone mantels are elegant and timeless. They may be made of marble, granite, limestone, or slate and be hand- or machine-carved. Cast stone versions replicate the look of natural stone but are not quite as costly.

CONCRETE. Concrete replicates the look of a carved or cast stone mantel but is lighter in weight because the material is reinforced with fiberglass. As with the fireplace facing, custom looks can be

If you'll be showing your property at night, add radiance by lighting a fire or a cluster of candles in one hearth.

achieved with different color and texture finishes.

METAL. As with metal surrounds, metal mantels can be fabricated from cast-bronze, copper, nickel, iron, or steel. Finishes for a metal mantel include an aged verdigris or gilded-look. You can find metal mantels online and at fireplace shops specializing in custom mantel designs.

PLASTER AND GYPSUM. Poured into molds, these mantels typically feature more intricate detailing than their wood counterparts. They can be painted to replicate stone, wood, or metal.

FIREPLACE INSTALLATION AND PLACEMENT. If you choose to add a new fireplace, the most economical type is a direct-vent fireplace. These can be vented through a conventional chimney or directly through an exterior wall. If you are retrofitting a wood-burning fireplace with a gas appliance, you'll need to have the existing chimney relined with aluminum or stainless steel because gas fireplaces can reach very high temperatures. Where natural gas is not available, propane may be an option. For advice on installing a direct-vent gas fireplace, visit your local fireplace retailer.

When determining the right spot for a hearth in your gathering space, take into consideration the room's views, media equipment, and traffic pattern. If the room has attractive views, orient the fireplace 90 degrees from the best vista so that the furniture can be arranged to take advantage of both focal points. If the view is less than desirable, make the fireplace the main focal point of the room by centering it on the window wall and covering the remaining windows with sheer window treatments or stained glass. Set off the mantel and surround by finishing it in a color that contrasts with the walls. Draw more attention to the mantel by topping it with oversize artwork or adding custom-made doors or a hand-forged wrought-iron screen to the firebox. To create extra guest seating and to give more prominence to the hearth, raise it anywhere from 12 to 18 inches above the floor.

Group chairs, sofas, or love seats around the hearth, and define the gathering spot with an area rug. Leave ample space between the fireplace opening and the furnishings for easy access as well as safety.

If the room will contain media equipment such as a television or stereo, consider adding custom cabinetry around the fireplace to accommodate the equipment. Or move the fireplace to the corner of a room to provide more wall space for built-ins.

Avoid placing a fireplace between doors or next to a hallway, because it makes it difficult to gather by the fire without impeding traffic flow.

If you choose to turn attention away from an existing fireplace, neutralize it by painting it the same color as the surrounding walls. Face the seating pieces away from it and leave the mantel clear of any accessories.

Gathering room lighting

Ceiling lights, ceiling fans with light kits, and pendent fixtures are excellent sources of ambient lighting. For added drama, replace a light switch with a dimmer.

Floor and table lamps can be used as a source of ambient light (especially when fitted with a three-way bulb that can match the lumen output to your individual lighting needs) or as task lights when focused on a specific area.

Use hot buttons in the gathering room

If you want to flip your property as quickly as possible, choose a property that has (or can be remodeled to have) the following highly sought-after features:

Open plan. The walls separating a gathering room from the kitchen and dining room are coming down, sometimes to expand the rooms into adjacent spaces, and sometimes to make transitions between rooms more fluid. Visual dividers—such as decorative pillars or a change in ceiling height—give the gathering area an identity of its own without completely closing it off from the adjoining spaces.

Attractive windows and doors. The windows in gathering rooms are an important aesthetic and functional asset. If the windows in your gathering space are smaller than you'd like, make them seem larger by hanging window treatments 8 to 12 inches above the glazing, and extending the rod on either side so that little or no glass is covered when the panels are open. If the room could use more natural light, consider replacing solid exterior doors with glass ones to allow in more light. Also consider replacing interior doors with glass-panel ones to filter more indirect light into the room.

Social seating. Seating in today's gathering spots is about being in the thick of things—gathering where the food is prepared. Barstools around the island will help sell the kitchen as will an upholstered chair tucked in a corner near (but not interfering with) the cooking action.

Display spaces. Glass-front cabinetry or open shelves are affordable must-have commodities in top-selling homes.

Upgraded flooring. Whether it's wall-to-wall carpeting or hardwood planks, quality flooring always makes the gathering room more inviting.

Color schemes

When it comes to choosing built-in cabinetry with an eye for resale, classic white or medium wood tones are your best bets. The cabinetry should match or complement the color and style of the cabinets in adjoining rooms, such as the kitchen or dining area.

For wall color, you'll want to choose a light, somewhat neutral hue that provides a touch of contrast against the cabinets. Warm whites and soft to medium taupes and grays are the most popular choices; they blend with most any decor.

For a more customized look, mix surfacing materials. For flooring, choose a neutral wood plank, a wood-look laminate, or a neutral wall-to-wall carpeting, again allowing the amenities found in surrounding homes to serve as your quality guide. Light fixtures and ceiling fans should blend with those found in adjacent rooms.

Avoid dark colors in a diminutive space; dark color schemes shrink an already small space and make it seem less inviting. Use soft shades and natural light to visually expand a small room.

Let wall colors and window treatments carry the eye. Treatments don't have to match, but they do have to blend.

How does it function?

If the gathering room in your home is too small to comfortably accommodate a variety of social functions, consider adding a bumpout.

A bumpout is a mini addition that extends a wall no more than 4 feet, and sometimes is only a few feet wide (such as for a bay window), but can extend the full length of a wall. The space gain can be small, but the effect is often great.

Because it does not have a foundation, a bumpout is less expensive to build than a full-blown addition. Windows and a skylight in a bumpout can miraculously transform a tight, cramped room into a joyful haven with plenty of space. Such an addition works especially well in a dining or living room, where a little extra space can make a big difference in how your room looks and feels.

In a typical remodeling, the plan removes the original wall and extends the flooring by cantilevering 2×10s or 2×12s from existing joists. (It simplifies the project if existing floor joists are running perpendicular to the exterior wall.) Joists, rather than a foundation wall or piers, support the new structure.

If more support is needed, options include adding columns under a first-story bumpout, or attaching a second-story bumpout to the house with brackets. Consider the aesthetics and consult with an architect or a residential designer to make sure such an addition doesn't look tacked on. In any bumpout (especially one built on a north wall), insulation is important because the addition will have to be properly heated and cooled.

Arrange the furniture in gathering spaces to **create an airy**, stylish attitude. Angle seating arrangements and opt for an armless chair or two; they take up **less space.**

Bumpout dos and don'ts

Do blend the colors of the bumpout with those of the original house. If you decide to use matching materials, you may have to paint the original house because paint colors fade and wear in sun and weather.

Do check with your planning and zoning commission about setback requirements. If your setback is insufficient, you may be able to get a variance. Prepare for your local zoning meeting; bring accurate information, such as the distance between your house and the property line.

Don't copy the exact cladding materials of the original house. You may be able to introduce a different type of shingle or roofing material. Think about compatibility rather than matching.

Property Ladder Lesson:

Before you solidify any makeover plans for your home's gathering room, take accurate measurements of the space, and lay out the components using the room arranging kit provided on pages 238–251.

Note that replacing built-in cabinets and making over fireplaces are the two biggest cost variables in the makeover of a gathering room. Window replacement also can be costly. Before you establish your plans for these areas, get price quotes for labor (including tear-out and installation) and materials.

Design dreamy bedrooms

Although impressive kitchens and baths are top residential real estate dealmakers and breakers, comfortable and inviting bedrooms are also a priority of buyers. The master suite, of course, is the focal-point sleeping quarter, followed by at least two (and preferably three) guest bedrooms which may eventually serve as children's rooms, dens, hobby spaces, or home offices.

How does it look?

When you step inside the bedroom door, does the space feel clean and welcoming—a place where you would like to start and end your day? If not, there's work to be done. Fortunately most bedrooms can be updated without breaking the budget.

BEDROOM MUSTS:
- Ambient lighting
- Mood lighting
- Serene, inviting ambience
- Adequate storage
- Display space

Flooring

If the bedroom has wall-to-wall carpeting, it should appear clean and wear-free. Choose a quality carpet for the master suite. Because guest bedrooms don't receive the same amount of traffic as gathering rooms, lower-grade carpeting is acceptable to use as a replacement in these rooms. (For advice on carpet grading and materials, see "Carpeting" on page 74.) To make the decor inviting for a variety of tastes, choose a neutral color in a light to medium shade.

If the bedroom has wood or wood-look laminate flooring, it should appear clean and wear-free. If wood planks are scratched or dented, have the floor sanded and refinished. If the floor is covered in a wood-look laminate, you may be able to replace scratched or dented pieces. You can find laminate flooring at home centers and flooring stores (assuming the material is still available). For more information on wood-look laminates, see page 166. Although it is tempting to cover worn wood with carpet, refinishing the wood is a better investment; you will likely recoup your costs in terms of your home's resale value.

Wall coverings

If your bedroom walls are covered in drywall, as most bedrooms are, a few coats of paint is all you will need to make them look as good as new. If nails or picture hangers have damaged a wall, fill the holes with a surface compound, then sand the area smooth.

If the walls are covered in brick, wood paneling, or another surfacing material, you'll need to weigh whether the material is an asset or a deficit to the salability of your home. (If you can't decide, poll friends and neighbors as well as local real estate agents for honest opinions.) If the material needs to go, a professional drywaller can tell you whether it would be more cost effective to cover the material with fresh drywall or tear it out.

Pulling off paneling with a pry bar is a viable do-it-yourself project, but there is no way to know how damaged the wall behind the paneling may be. If the paneling is in good shape, consider painting over it. For advice on painting over a variety of wall surfaces, see pages 156–165.

Natural and electrical lighting

Lighting provides an easy way to make a bedroom seem cheerful and inviting. Installing new light fixtures is easy and affordable. For advice on choosing and installing a variety of fixtures, see pages 200–203.

When assessing a bedroom's current lighting scheme, think about natural and electrical light.

NATURAL LIGHT

When choosing bedroom window treatments for the purpose of resale look for white or cream-color bargain-price ready-made blinds, shades, or shutters. They control daylight, complement most décors, and provide privacy. Top treatments for bedroom windows are attractive, but not necessary.

VENETIAN BLINDS AND MINIBLINDS. Available at home centers and discount stores, venetian blinds and miniblinds offer more options in light control than any other type of window treatment. Venetian blind slats measure about 2 inches wide; miniblind slats generally are 1 inch wide.

Choose slats made from warm woods or solid-color aluminums or vinyls. Measure the depth of your window frame to determine which will fit best in an inside mount. Blinds can be raised to let in the light and views, or lowered and closed for privacy. Lowered slats can also be tilted to control the light and the view. For the most privacy and light control, choose blinds that when closed have little or no space between the slats. Vertical blinds operate in the same fashion as venetian blinds and miniblinds, except that the slats open and close vertically instead of horizontally. Their popularity has waned over the last few years, so avoid choosing them for use in a property flip.

BAMBOO BLINDS. These affordably priced blinds raise and lower like other horizontal blinds, except the narrow bamboo reeds do not pivot, as do other wider-slat varieties. The blinds are available in natural and painted finishes at many home centers and discount stores. When partially open, they look more like a valance than a shade, which shows well during an open house.

PLEATED SHADES. These shades are made of pleated fabrics with varying degrees of translucency. They raise and lower in a manner similar to blinds but without the pivoting slots.

ROLLER SHADES. Affordably priced solid vinyl or vinyl-and-fabric-laminated combinations are commonplace and available at home centers and discount stores. Do-it-yourself kits for fusing decorator fabrics to solid vinyl shades are available at fabric stores. To prevent tearing when the shade is pulled, choose a vinyl covering material that is at least 6 millimeters thick. For best light control, attach the shade snugly against the inside of the window frame. Steer clear of thin, shiny vinyl shades; they can look cheap and be difficult to operate—both big no-no's in terms of salability—so plan to spend a few extra dollars for a quality shade.

BIFOLD SHUTTERS. These slatted and framed window treatments are available at most home centers. A hinge between each framed section allows the shutters to fold back vertically from the window. Slats within each frame can also be tilted to control the light and the view. Bifold shutters are typically made from stained or painted wood or solid color vinyl.

UNUSUALLY SHAPED WINDOWS
If the windows in your home's bedrooms are unusually shaped, see "Windows & Doors" on pages 136–145 for numerous treatment suggestions.

Embrace lamp lighting

Cast your rooms in a whole new light with decorative lamps. When selected and placed correctly, lamp lighting gives a room a bright, warm glow and makes tasks such as reading and working easier and more comfortable.

Lamp lighting can also enhance architectural amenities and disguise problem areas through highlights and shadows. To draw attention to a specific item, such as artwork, place an accent light at a 30-degree angle, and focus its beam on the object. Approximately three times the room's normal light level is required to spotlight an object. Similarly, spotlighting objects opposite problem areas, such as a corner with exposed piping or an ill-placed support beam, draws attention away from what you don't like and toward what you do.

To generate task lighting, choose a fixture with a shade that focuses light in one area. If the shade is open at the top as well as the bottom, it can supplement ambient (overall) lighting. For reading and writing, the diameter of the beam spread out from the bottom of the shade should be at least 16 inches.

The type of shade you choose and the light output (lumens) of the bulbs used determine how much light a lamp gives out. If you experience glare, the light output may be too high. If headaches or eyestrain occur, the light may be

ELECTRICAL LIGHTING

Supplement natural light with a blend of electrical illumination strategies: ambient, task, mood, and accent lighting.

Ambient, or general, lighting creates a uniform, overall light in the bedroom and comes from one or more, usually overhead, sources. A ceiling fan equipped with a central fixture is an excellent choice for bedrooms located in warm or seasonal climates.

Backing up this general lighting plan is task lighting. These fixtures, available at home centers, are positioned to eliminate shadows in the areas where you perform specific tasks such as reading, applying makeup, writing letters, or typing on the computer.

Mood or accent lighting provides the extra touches that make a room sparkle. You can create mood lighting by attaching a dimmer switch to an overhead fixture or by adding rope lights inside a ceiling soffit or wall recess. Illuminating a portrait or a vase of flowers, adding a tiny lamp to a bookshelf, or placing softly glowing candles atop a dresser are examples of accent lighting.

MAKEUP LIGHTS. To light a vanity dresser, add a table lamp fitted with a light color translucent shade to each side of the mirror, keeping the light source near eye level. If you are much shorter or taller than average, adjust the measurements accordingly. To maximize the lamp's reflective qualities, choose a light surface for the tabletop.

too dim. To save energy costs, find bulbs with the light output you need, and choose the one with the lowest wattage. To reduce the possibility of an electrical fire, never exceed the lamp manufacturer's recommended wattage maximum.

Lampshades spread more light if they have a pale interior or liner. Some retailers code lamps and shades to make it easy to mix and match shades and bases successfully. As a general rule, the shade should be approximately two-thirds the height of the lamp base, deep enough so that a small portion of the neck (the fitting between the lamp and the socket) is visible, and about 1½ the width of the lamp base.

Before purchasing any lamp, ask if you can see it switched on; this may help you determine if the look and light output will fit your design needs. For the most comfort, place a table lamp so that the bottom of the shade is at about eye level. When the shade is higher, the glare from the bulb can cause eyestrain; lower lamplight sheds the light onto the surface below it instead of toward the reading or work area.

For the best look, keep bases and shades in proportion to the bedside table; if the lamp makes the table appear top-heavy, choose a smaller lamp or a larger table.

BEDSIDE LAMPS. To read comfortably in bed, the bottom of the lampshade should be about 20 inches above the top of the mattress.

DESK LAMPS. For desk work such as bill-paying, recipe-copying, and letter-writing, the bottom of the lampshade should be at about eye level, and the light output from the bottom of the shade should be enough to illuminate all your necessary papers and books.

FLOOR LAMPS. Position a floor lamp above and over the shoulder for good reading when seated. Short floor lamps, 40 to 42 inches high, should line up with your shoulder when you're seated. Taller lamps should be set about 15 inches to the side and 20 inches behind the center of the book, magazine, or newspaper you are reading. Check that the lamplight fully illuminates the reading surface without shadows or glare.

How does it function?

Before you solidify your bedroom decorating and design plans, take accurate measurements of each of these rooms, and experiment with laying out the components using the room arranging kit provided on pages 238-251.

"The way to get the most value out of a master suite is to make it feel like a private retreat."

Kirsten Kemp

Finessing the floor plan

To make a bedroom seem more spacious, choose light colors and simple furnishings, and add several mirrors. See-through furnishings, such as glass-top tables, gauzy curtains, and lightly scaled furniture with exposed legs, also provide an airier feel.

Disregard the decorating dictum that says a small space requires small furnishings. On the contrary, you'll use less floor space with a few pieces in a slightly larger scale than if you choose to fill the room with smaller pieces. Select an arrangement that keeps the major furnishings parallel or perpendicular to walls; a diagonally placed bed may take up too much floor space.

Sleeping

If square footage allows, stage the master bedroom with a queen- or king-size bed, because most couples today own one of these two mattress sizes. If space is a commodity, choose a bed with a wispy scroll-like iron headboard instead of a large-scale canopy, four-poster, or sleigh bed. Bedside tables (one is acceptable; two are better if space permits) should be at least as high as the top of the mattress. For convenient bed-making, allow at least 2 feet on both sides of the bed.

Storage

Unless the bedroom has attractive built-in storage or a separate dressing room packed with efficient built-ins, include at least one storage piece in the room. If possible allow at least 3 feet of dressing space in front of a closet (or more if the door swing demands it) and 36 to 40 inches in front of a chest or dresser to allow for drawer pullout space.

Allow space for displaying treasures—add a narrow mantel shelf (available at home centers) to an empty wall or above a dresser. If you plan to add an armoire, choose one with open display spaces.

If you want to set a small master bedroom apart from those in nearby homes that are also on the market, turn a blank wall into a storage-filled focal point, *above*. This arrangement shows how you can use stock cabinetry to transform a wall into an attractive and serviceable storage zone.

Situated between a bedroom corner and the bathroom door, the tall pantrylike unit functions as an armoire. The two cabinets in the upper portion are ideal for housing bedding. To the right of the bathroom door, a base cabinet orchestrates easy access to audio equipment. Three shelves above offer display space, contrasting with the unit's closed-door storage.

BEDROOMS

Even a small bedroom can appear spacious and inviting when outfitted with versatile storage and practical furnishings.

Below the television four drawers store videos and other accessories. Above the television there's more general stow-away space.

The unit's only custom piece neighbors the television. Set at an angle, the 15-inch-wideset bank of shelves is ideal for displaying plants, photos, and collectibles. It also serves as a subtle and stylish transition to a slimmer, shallower unit that is required to accommodate a window on the adjacent wall. The slender storage space on

the right couples a typical tall upper cabinet that handles linens and clothing with four storage drawers underneath.

Seating

A cushy upholstered chair and ottoman make for an enticing spot to read or enjoy a cup of morning brew, but don't force the issue. If the room looks crowded, forgo this amenity.

Make children's rooms functional

Whether the children's bedrooms in your property are large or small, use the square footage in these spaces as creatively as possible. Outfit the room(s) with double-duty furnishings, such as a bed with drawers underneath and a wall storage unit equipped with a pull-down desk, so that potential buyers can visualize the space meeting each of their child's needs now and in the future.

Redo closets to include double rods for hanging clothes at a height that even young children can reach. Add a few pullout bins and peg racks for organizing everything from socks and belts to baseball caps and hair bows. Prop these added features with common items so buyers can immediately see the potential of the organizing tools.

Install open shelves on at least one wall, and fill an underutilized corner with a triangular-shape desk or storage trunk. Add another display shelf near the ceiling line and stage it with a few trophies and a stuffed animal or two. The more potential a buyer sees in the room, the more reasons he or she will have to make you an offer right away.

Set up a winning bath

More than one well-designed bathroom in a home is always considered a bonus for prospective buyers. These guidelines will help you make sure that every bathroom in the house looks and functions its best.

Salvage or scrap?

Cabinetry

Salvage the bathroom cabinetry based on the same criteria you used to analyze the worthiness of your kitchen cabinetry on page 46. You can also learn more about identifying cabinet quality on page 47.

It's important to keep in mind that the vanity area helps define the design of the entire bath and serves as a focal point for it (though a large, luxurious bathtub can also become the star). To get an idea of what buyers are looking for in your home's price range, visit other residential open houses in your area. Then pay attention to the comments that prospective buyers make regarding the look and function of those baths. Apply what you learn to your property's bathrooms and you'll likely increase your profit. If the master bathroom in your mid- to high-end home features only a modest single-sink vanity, for example, you probably want to consider fitting in a larger vanity equipped with two sinks.

As with kitchen cabinets, you can purchase bath cabinets in modular (stock) units or you can have them custom-designed and built by a cabinet shop. For stock units, widths start out at 18 inches and continue in 6-inch increments to 72 inches. Matching filler pieces can be used to adapt a standard vanity to fit most any space. Semicustom cabinets are similar to stock cabinets in that these cabinet lines offer standard styles and finishes, but increased size options—usually 3-inch increments—are offered.

There's no rule against using kitchen cabinets in the bath; in fact, many people find the 36-inch height more comfortable for standing. Standard vanity cabinets are typically only 29 to 30 inches high, which means that the average adult has to stoop low to wash the face or brush teeth. Similarly, vanity cabinets measure only 18 to 21 inches deep from front to back. Kitchen cabinets run a more generous 24 inches deep, which means your buyer gains counterspace and storage—a bonus that many people recognize.

When considering a larger vanity, allow enough room in the front of the vanity for the doors and

BATHROOM MUSTS:
- Sturdy, stylish storage
- Up-to-date fixtures
- Pristine surfaces
- Ample, adjustable lighting

Many home center stores have staff who can help you lay out a bath at little or no charge.

drawers to open and close without interference. There should also be enough wall space for a mirror and light fixtures. Keep in mind that a mirror that spans above a vanity from wall to wall can make a small bathroom appear larger.

Countertops

Salvage the countertops if they are a neutral tone and lack stains and obvious wear. Laminate countertops that meet these criteria are acceptable if most of the neighboring homes also feature laminate countertops in the baths. Otherwise you may want to upgrade to stone or solid-surfacing.

Here are a few stone materials you can use to upgrade bathroom countertops:

MARBLE is softer and more porous than granite. It sometimes fractures along veining and offers less resistance than granite to stains, scratches, and wear. To ensure a longer life, seal marble regularly. Costs for slabs and tiles are similar to granite.

LIMESTONE is more porous than marble. Ranging from light beige to golden brown in color, limestone is typically given a honed finish. Seal limestone properly, and keep acidic substances away from it.

Beautify the bath

If you want to flip your property as quickly as possible, choose properties that have (or can be remodeled to have) the following highly sought-after features in the bathroom:

Two vanity areas. Most buyers expect a master bathroom to function well for two people, and a vanity with two separate sinks addresses this need.

Stone or solid-surfacing countertops. High-quality countertops immediately communicate an air of elegance and good value.

Stone or ceramic tile floors. Like stone and solid-surfacing countertops, stone and ceramic tile floors are long-lasting and stylish.

Custom storage hutch. The look of freestanding furniture makes a bathroom appear more spacious and hardworking.

Large whirlpool or air-bubble tub. Surround this focal-point feature with a wide ledge for display and storage, and your buyers will envision themselves enjoying a relaxing soak.

Generously sized walk-in shower. Lined with ceramic or stone tiles and outfitted with multiple showerheads and a built-in bench, a walk-in shower can be a deal maker.

SLATE is dense and nonabsorbent and is known for its blue-gray color, though it comes in other shades. Because of its low absorption rate and density, slate is highly resistant to stains, bacteria, and heat. Clean with water and mild soap, and buff out scratches.

SOAPSTONE has a gray to green color and a silky, soapy feel. It may seem familiar—for years it has been used as a work surface in laboratories and science classrooms. Soapstone is highly resistant to acids and water. Seal this material with mineral oil and regularly reoil it to maintain a uniform dark color. Remove scratches with sandpaper and water.

STONE COUNTERTOP SUBSTITUTES

The same elements that make stone beautiful—its natural colors, the variegations in pattern, and its porous structure—create challenges when it comes to using the material in a bath. To counteract these natural limitations, stone-base products offer many desirable color options and eliminate some maintenance issues. Consider these options:

ENGINEERED QUARTZ, which is made from quartz bound together with polymers, has an appearance, composition, weight, and price that is comparable to granite. Its surface captures the crystalline sparkle and density of granite, and it is nonporous, so it requires no sealing.

ENAMELED LAVASTONE is natural stone that has been glazed with high-temperature enamel. The high heat creates a durable surface with vivid colors and a glasslike sheen. The visible pores of the lavastone and the crazing of the enamel create a one-of-a-kind product. The nonporous surface is resistant to water, oils, acids, and other substances. It will scratch, so cleaning with nonabrasive detergents and water is recommended.

LAMINATED STONE is made of thin sheets of granite or marble backed by fiberglass. It is lighter in weight and more flexible than solid stone. The 5x10-foot sheets, which start at a thickness of $2\frac{1}{4}$ inches, are appropriate for countertops as well as for walls and floors.

For a rundown on more countertop materials, see "Crash course on countertops" on page 49.

Everyone needs a quiet, **peaceful** area in the home in which to **get away** from it all. A well-equipped, nicely designed master bathroom can **inspire** prospective homeowners to **envision** your property as theirs.

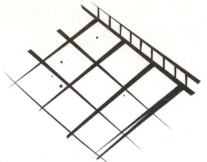

Flooring

Salvage bath flooring if it is neutral-tone material in good condition and if it echoes the bath flooring used in neighboring homes. If you need to change the flooring, the materials discussed for kitchens on pages 52–53 are also options you can consider for a bath. In addition these are other products you can use to upgrade the surfaces underfoot.

BAMBOO is an option that's becoming an increasingly popular choice for its appearance, durability, and eco-friendly nature. It looks a lot like hardwood, but it's actually three layers of grass

Expand the space

Try these tricks to visually expand the space in every bathroom:

Add light. Eliminate shadowy corners by installing overhead fixtures, downlights, or wall sconces. For more on adequate lighting, see page 109.

To increase natural light, install a skylight or simply replace an existing bath window with a larger window. Use mirrors to reflect the light you do have and to create an appearance of more square footage.

Downsize. Trade larger fixtures for smaller ones. In a powder room, for example, trade a boxy vanity for a streamlined pedestal and a protruding medicine cabinet for one that's recessed in the wall. (When substituting a pedestal for a vanity

cabinet, be sure that there is optional closet storage in the bath or in a hallway outside the bath.) You may also consider replacing a full-size tub with a roomy yet smaller shower. Be sure that the house offers at least one bathtub, however.

Tone it down. Whites, pastels, and neutrals reflect light and can make a small area feel larger. Darker shades absorb light and can make a room feel smaller. Paint background elements, such as woodwork and doors, white or in the same hue as walls to diminish their impact and visual interruptions.

Use a light color on the walls and a lighter color on the ceiling to draw the eye upward, emphasizing the height of the room.

Streamline. Clutter takes up precious space and makes a tiny room look overly full. Pare countertop objects to the minimum if you're living in the home or simply staging the space for an open house. A vanity with the appearance of freestanding furniture can also make a bathroom appear larger because you can see more flooring.

Recess shelves. Fill stud space with shelves to create recessed storage that minimizes visual interruptions. In a bathroom with a shower, install clear glass doors (or design a doorless shower) to stretch sight lines. Frosted glass creates a visual wall.

Toasty floors

Stone and tile floors can feel cold against bare feet. You can take the chill off these floors and add a tempting amenity for prospective buyers by installing a radiant heating system below your new flooring. (Avoid radiant heat beneath wood floors, however.)

These heating systems not only warm the floor, they also increase the overall temperature of the room, often eliminating the need for additional heaters.

Radiant heating systems typically have a network of electrical heating cables or hot water-filled tubes installed between the subfloor and finished floor. Most systems can be installed across the entire floor or may be confined to a specific area, such as the space in front of a tub. Like other heating systems, radiant heating is controlled by a thermostat that can be turned on or off, up or down.

You can install a radiant heating system yourself—they are available at most home centers in kit form. Or you can hire a flooring professional to install the system for you.

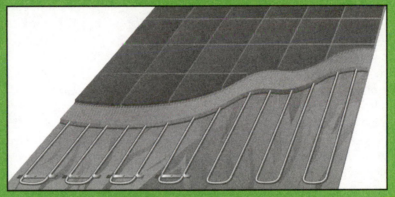

■ **Tubes of warmed water or heated cables form a serpentine pattern across a concrete floor, transforming this cold surface into a warm and comfortable base. Flooring on top of the tubing radiates the heat.**

that have been laminated under high pressure to create planks. Three coats of acrylic urethane make the surface durable and resistant to water, mildew, and insect damage. Harder than maple or oak, bamboo also expands and contracts less. Bamboo flooring comes unfinished or prefinished and is glued or nailed to the subfloor.

CORK provides a resilient, cushioned surface underfoot that is quiet, comfortable, and moisture-resistant. Made from renewable bark harvested from cork oak trees in Mediterranean forests, cork

Color scheme tip

Neutral colors create a soothing ambience and visually expand a bathroom's dimensions.

Cabinetry should be white or stained wood. Select white for sinks and bathtubs. Tile should be neutral or stone.

BATHROOMS

requires a urethane finish to ensure easy sweeping and mopping. If the old finish is sanded every few years and new urethane is applied, cork flooring can last for decades. It comes in tiles or planks that allow for each to be replaced individually should the floor be damaged; installation is similar to that of vinyl tile.

LINOLEUM, which is made from natural materials, continues to make a comeback. Often confused with vinyl, which is made from petroleum-base polyvinyl chloride, linoleum is made of linseed oil, resin, cork, limestone, and wood flour mixed with pigments, then rolled onto a jute backing and dried. Soft underfoot, it comes in tiles and in sheets of solid or flecked color and is easy to care for. As the linseed oil dries, linoleum actually becomes harder and more durable than vinyl. Although old-style linoleum tended to fade over time, today's version offers lasting color.

STONE is an elegant choice. Harder varieties, notably granite, require little maintenance and are nearly indestructible. Others, such as more porous marble and limestone, stain easily and require more care and maintenance. Some, such as slate, are prone to cracking and chipping. Like ceramic tile, stone can be cold, hard, and unforgiving so it is a good candidate for underfloor heating.

LAMINATE FLOORS IN THE BATH
Laminate flooring is suitable for a bathroom when installed correctly. (For general instructions on installing laminate flooring, see page 166.) Water is a concern, but not so much on the surface—splashes or puddles won't hurt, provided that water is wiped up promptly. However, if water seeps between the planks, around the edges,

Employ universal design

A barrier-free bath not only appeals to people with special needs, it can also be a selling point to buyers of all abilities and ages. Removing potential obstacles and difficulties from a bathroom environment means that homeowners can live comfortably in the house throughout their lifetimes and make their guests feel welcome—benefits worth pointing out to prospective buyers during an open house.

Location. Look for properties with at least one ground-floor bathroom. If the home you're considering lacks a bathroom on the main level, evaluate whether one can be installed somewhere before making the purchase. Borrowing a slice of space is worth the effort.

Door size. Plan for a clear door opening of 34 to 36 inches; larger doors are difficult to open and close from a seated position, and narrower openings make it difficult, if not impossible, for a wheelchair to make it through.

Handles. Equip entrance doors, drawers, and faucets with lever or D-shape handles. They are easier

or otherwise gets under the floor, it can cause warping and buckling, and nurture mildew.

Choose a product specifically approved for wet areas. Follow the installation instructions for the bath that are provided by the manufacturer. Expansion zones and seams between planks must be completely sealed. Silicone caulk fills the gap at the floor's perimeter. Bear in mind that it's never a good idea to install laminate flooring in a location that has a floor drain, in a subgrade location with a sump pump, or anywhere that water may stand for more than 30 minutes.

Let flooring acclimate; unopened cartons usually must sit in their destination for 72 to 96 hours before the boards are laid, to avoid excessive expansion or contraction. That's especially important for a bathroom, where humidity is typically high and you want the planks tight.

When choosing floors and countertops, look for quality products that stand up to high humidity and activity while meeting your decorative desires.

to operate than knobs, especially for young children and people with arthritis or limited mobility.

Floor space. For a typical-size wheelchair to make a complete turnaround, you'll need to leave a circular area of clear floor space measuring 5 feet in diameter. You should leave an area in front of the sink that measures at least 30×48 inches (although the clear floor space can overlap). Toilets need a clear floor space that is 48 inches square. Bathtubs need a clear floor space of 60×60 inches in front of the tub.

Shower stalls. Shower stalls are easier to get in and out of than bathtubs. Choose or build a stall with no curb or a very low one. Slope the floor toward the drain to ensure that the water stays within the enclosure. Shower stalls need to measure at least 4 feet square with an opening that is at least 36 inches wide. Include grab bars, a single-handle lever control, a handheld shower spray, and a built-in bench or seat that is 17 to 19 inches above the floor.

Sinks and faucets

Sinks

Bathroom sinks come in more sizes, shapes, and material choices than ever before. You can purchase round, oval, rectangular, or asymmetrical bowls. Each shape is available in several color choices, although white still outsells all the other colors combined. Some of the more expensive models are adorned with handpainted designs, or you can have a sink custom painted to match the decor. Still, basic white is a good choice for its broad audience appeal.

Before you choose the right sink (or two) for your bath, consider how often the sink will be used. Sinks used in half-baths and full guest baths typically receive less use, so durability and maintenance are lesser issues in these spaces than in master baths and children's baths.

In frequently used baths, choose materials to match the kind of wear and tear delivered by most potential homeowners. Choose larger, deeper sinks to reduce splashing and countertop cleanup. To ensure a good match in terms of design, consider purchasing a matching sink, toilet, and bathtub.

Materials

The most common material choices are:

PORCELAIN-ENAMELED CAST IRON. These sinks are extremely durable and easy to care for, but they are somewhat heavy and require a sturdy support system.

If you choose a pedestal sink for a **high-use** bath, hang cabinets or install **shelves** nearby.

VITREOUS CHINA. These sinks have a lustrous surface, are not as heavy as porcelain-enameled cast-iron sinks, and are the most resistant to discoloration and corrosion. Vitreous china sinks, however, can be chipped or cracked when struck by a heavy object.

SOLID-SURFACING. These sinks offer varying degrees of durability based on the material from which they are made. Sinks made from the same acrylic resin as quality solid-surfacing countertops are the most durable and require little maintenance. Polyester and cultured marble sinks share similar properties but scratch and dull more readily. Any of these sinks may be integrated directly into the countertop. Shallow nicks and scratches can be removed using a fine-grade sandpaper.

STAINLESS STEEL. Durable and unaffected by household chemicals, steel sinks tend to show hard water and soap spots.

GLASS. Glass sinks are showing up in more baths than ever before. Although they do require extra care to prevent scratching or breaking, their smooth finish is easy to clean. Frosted glass shows less spotting than its clear counterpart.

Styles

Styles of sinks fall into four main categories:

PEDESTAL. These sinks fit on top of a pedestal-shape base and are an ideal solution for a small bath, such as a powder room. The disadvantage of a pedestal sink is that it offers little counterspace and no base cabinet storage below. Before opting for a pedestal sink, be sure that a storage closet or cabinet can be located nearby.

WALL HUNG. Like pedestal sinks, these sinks have the advantage of fitting into small spaces. They have the same disadvantages as pedestal sinks with one more—there is no pedestal to hide any plumbing lines below. To make up for this, some sinks have brass legs to offer a more finished look underneath. Wall-hung sinks are often the sink of choice in universally designed baths because the sinks can be installed at any height and have a clear space underneath that allows for seated knee space and wheelchair access.

VANITY. To ensure plenty of countertop space as well as cabinet storage below, consider a vanity sink. One drawback is that vanity sinks require the most floor space of any sink style.

White is the
number one
color choice
for bath fixtures.

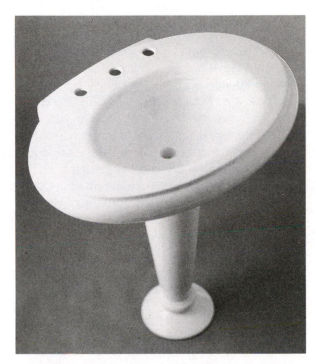

■ **A pedestal sink brings a streamlined look to a small bathroom, but it lacks the storage capacity offered by a vanity cabinet.**

VESSEL. A vessel sink looks like a freestanding bowl sitting atop—or partially sunk into—a vanity cabinet. The height of a vessel sink—like any bath fixture—should be based on what's comfortable for the user. Because you don't know who will buy your property, seek a happy medium. The National Kitchen and Bath Association's planning guidelines recommend a height of 32 to 43 inches for bath vanities. Standard-height base cabinetry at 34½ inches is common for vessel sinks, though some units are as low as 27 inches. For larger vessels, a 29-inch-high desklike cabinet is popular.

INTEGRAL SINKS are part of the same material as the vanity counter. Because there is no joint between the bowl and the countertop, these sinks are easy to clean. If the sink or counter is damaged beyond repair, the entire unit must be replaced.

A SELF-RIMMING, or surface-mounted sink sits on top of the counter. The sink is dropped into a hole large enough to accommodate the sink bowl but smaller than the outside rim of the sink. The rim forms a tight seal with the countertop to prevent leaks. These sinks are the easiest to install; the hole need not be a perfect cut because it is hidden below the rim once the sink is in place.

UNDERMOUNTED SINKS are attached to the bottom of the countertop, creating a clean, tailored look. Like rimmed sinks, they can be somewhat difficult to clean underneath the lip where the sinks and counters are sealed together. They require an exact cut for installation.

RIMMED SINKS sit slightly above the countertop with a tight-fitting metal rim joining the sink and the countertop. The rim is made of different finishes to match whatever type of faucet you select. Rimmed sinks can be difficult to clean around the seal and require a nearly perfect cut for installation.

Get in hot water

The National Kitchen and Bath Association recommends that your hot water heater be at least two-thirds the capacity of your tub. A 60-gallon hot water tank will serve a 90-gallon tub adequately, but the rest of the water in your house will be cold. The manual that comes with the bathtub will tell you how many gallons of water it will take to fill it. If your hot-water heater is too small, you can install a bigger heater, install two heaters side by side, or you can buy a whirlpool tub with an in-line heater of its own. Instead of heating water before use as with a hot-water tank, an in-line heater maintains the temperature of the water for the duration of your bath. If you plan to soak for long periods, an in-line heater is a good idea regardless of the capacity of your hot-water heater.

Faucets

As you shop for faucets, you'll see everything from traditional, two-handle models that look much like they did a century ago to the newest one-handle creations that look like modern sculpture. But don't make a selection based on looks alone; durability is the key to your buyer's satisfaction. You'll also need to make sure that the faucet set you select is the proper size and design to fit the sink. Most vanity sinks come with holes drilled in their rims to accommodate standard faucets and plumbing. These three basic faucet styles are designed to fit these predrilled holes:

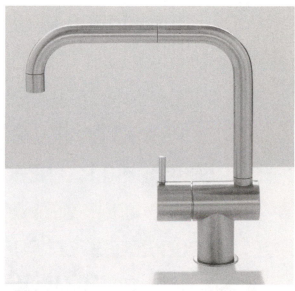

■ **This sleek, center-set faucet has a one-handle design and a pullout nozzle that makes it easy to rinse items or wash the sink bowl.**

One handle or two?

Both popular design choices, one-handle faucets are easier to use than their two-handle counterparts. With a little practice on a one-handle model, you can find the temperature you want on the first try. You can also turn the water on with your elbow or wrist when your hands are full or dirty.

Two-handle faucets, on the other hand, appear more traditional, and you can combine different handles and spouts for a custom look.

SINGLE-HANDLE FAUCETS. These faucets have one spout and one handle that controls the flow of both hot and cold water.

CENTER-SET FAUCETS. These faucets have a spout and handle(s) in one unit; they may have a single-handle or double-handle control. Most are designed for a three-hole basin, with the outside holes spaced 4 inches from center to center. Some of these faucets have a single post design that requires only one hole.

SPREAD-FIT FAUCETS. These faucets have a separate spout and handles. The connection between them is concealed below the sink deck. They can be adapted to fit holes spaced from 14 to 16 inches apart. They can be individualized

Keep in mind that a large **water-filled** whirlpool tub imposes substantial weight on floors. Locating a tub near an outside wall or perpendicular to floor joists aids in **carrying the load.**

even more if they are mounted on a countertop next to the sink. For example, the spout can be placed on a rear corner and the handles off to one side. These faucets are handy for tight installations where there is not enough room for a full faucet at the back of the sink basin. They are also ideal for whirlpool tubs, so that the handles can be comfortably accessed from outside the tub for filling.

A fourth faucet type is attached to the wall instead of the sink or the tub. These faucets were designed for unusually shaped sinks, such as vessel sinks or old-fashioned farm sinks that have been modified for use in the bath.

Tubs and showers

Tubs

There are two main reasons to replace a bathtub in your property: One is if the original tub is somehow damaged, such as when the finish is in poor condition. The second reason is if a large whirlpool tub is a popular feature in the remodeled houses of your neighborhood.

Before making such an investment, you'll need to find out if the tub you want will actually fit in the space you are allocating and whether it will fit through your existing doorways. (Getting your old bathtub out of the house may also test your ingenuity and your patience.) If the tub you want won't fit through the doors, stairwells, and hallways that connect to your bathroom, your only choices will be to downsize the tub or knock out an exterior wall.

Most bathroom floors can handle 40 pounds of weight per square foot. Extra bracing may be required for a large-capacity tub so that the floor can support it once it is filled with water.

If you're installing a whirlpool, you'll also need to provide access to the pump (typically installed near one end of the tub) in case repairs are necessary. To make your whirlpool bath more appealing to buyers, choose a pump that is quiet and offers a wide range of massage options.

Whirlpool and standard bathtubs come in four basic designs:

RECESSED TUBS. These tubs have one finished side called an apron. The tub fits between two end walls and against a back wall. Models are available with a drain at either end to fit plumbing needs.

CORNER TUBS. Space-saving corner tubs fit diagonally in one corner and, like standard apron tubs, have only one finished side. Other corner options are also similar to apron tubs, except the tubs have a finished side and end.

FREESTANDING TUBS. These bathtubs are finished on all four sides and can be placed anywhere in the room.

PLATFORM TUBS. These tubs have no finished panels, can be dropped into a platform, and can be placed anywhere, depending on the platform's design: into a corner, against a long wall, or in the center of the room.

Materials

ENAMELED CAST IRON. Durable and solid, these tubs are made from iron molded into a bathtub shape and finished with enamel in a variety of colors. They are thicker than the others and retain the heat of the water. Cast-iron tubs are heavy, so

Salvage or scrap a vintage claw-foot?

If you've purchased a property to flip that features an original claw-foot tub, but the finish is stained and peeling, is it worth saving? The answer is: Maybe.

If home buyers in your area are seeking an older home loaded with vintage character, then you may want to salvage the old tub. Though reproduction tubs are available, nothing beats an original, plus you'll save money.

Fortunately the refinishing process is relatively straightforward and involves only some short-term inconvenience. The reward

will be a spacious cast-iron tub with timeless charm that's sure to capture the attention of your prospective homeowners.

Start by checking the phone book or online for the names and phone numbers of bathtub refinishers in your area. Call several companies to obtain estimates and ask for references you can contact.

The actual refinishing process should take about three days. The professional refinisher will scrape off the old paint, prime the tub, then spray on a new coat of enamel that is as tough as automobile paint.

After that, the tub will have to dry at least 24 hours. The job should cost about $400—compare that to a new reproduction claw-foot tub.

The new homeowners should maintain the surface with a mild detergent, and avoid using anything caustic or abrasive, such as bath salts, which could scratch or stain the enamel. Suction-cup bath mats inside the tub are a no-no unless the mat is removed after every use. The suction cups exert enough pressure to pry the enamel off the surface of the tub, causing bubbles or peeling.

you may need to reinforce the floor below the tub.

ENAMELED STEEL. These tubs are produced by spraying enamel onto molded steel and firing the tub at a high temperature. Less expensive and not as heavy as their iron look-alikes, these tubs do chip more readily and have fewer color options. The tubs can also be noisier when being filled with water.

FIBERGLASS. Fiberglass backing material is finished with a layer of polyester to create this bathtub. Wood or metal reinforcement is then added to make the tub feel solid. These tubs are low cost and lightweight and come in a wide choice of styles and shapes. The polyester finish is not as durable as acrylic and the tubs do not retain heat well.

ACRYLIC. Sheets of acrylic are heated and formed in a mold, then reinforced with fiberglass and a wood or metal backing. These tubs are available in a wide choice of styles and shapes, and are lightweight. More inexpensive than fiberglass, they hold heat better if properly insulated, but the finish can still scratch.

CAST POLYMER. Solid-color polymer-base materials are used to create these tubs, which are often made to resemble natural stone such as granite or marble. Thicker than acrylic, these tubs hold heat well. Covered in the same polyester gel as fiberglass tubs, they are not as durable as acrylic or enameled cast-iron tubs.

Showers

SHOWER STALLS

If you have the space and budget, include a separate tub and shower in the bath. With separate fixtures, two people can bathe at the same time—an added value that buyers recognize. Shower stalls are also easier to enter and exit and are simpler to clean than tubs. If space and budget are too limited for a separate tub and shower stall, you can make a combination unit safer by selecting a nonslip bottom and grab bars. There are three basic types of separate shower stalls:

PREFABRICATED STALLS. Available in a variety of shapes and colors, these stalls are available in one-piece, two-piece, or three-piece versions. The most common material for these units is fiberglass with a finish surface of acrylic or a polyester gel coat. Tempered glass combined with fiberglass stalls is also available. Sizes range from 32 inches square (not large enough to meet some local codes) to 36×48 inches. One-piece versions are typically reserved for new construction and new additions. Like a bathtub or whirlpool, one-piece stalls are large and can be difficult to get into the room. Two- and three-piece models readily fit within most door openings. Doors (or curtains) are typically sold separately. Some come with their own pan, or flooring piece; others require a separate pan.

Prefabricated stalls are commonly available in four shapes that are designed to fit against a wall or neatly into a corner. Corner—or neo-angle models, as they are sometimes called—have two sides and a diagonal front. The walls of the stall need to be attached to standard wall framing for support.

PREFABRICATED SHOWER PANS. These molded flooring pieces are available in a range of materials, from plastic to stone. They can be combined with prefabricated shower stalls, or custom-made plexiglass, solid-surfacing walls, or tiled walls.

CUSTOM-MADE STALLS. These stalls offer the most design flexibility; there's no limit on the size or the style of a custom-made shower. Any waterproof material can be used for the walls including tile, stone, solid-surfacing, tempered glass, or glass blocks.

SHOWERHEADS

More and more showers are being equipped with a combination of showerheads as opposed to one solitary wall-mount unit. All showerheads are rated according to flow rate, or the number of gallons of water they spray per minute (gpm). Water-consuming showerheads deliver as many as 8 gpms. Low-flow models use just 2.5 gpms. Today's low-flow models do just as good a job of cleaning as their water-consuming counterparts. Your property's water pressure is also a factor. Some models of either showerhead type can be adjusted for a spray that varies from fine to coarse and a water action that ranges from a gentle pulsation to a vigorous massage.

■ **ABOVE and RIGHT If your bath is equipped with a special showerhead, let prospective buyers know by pointing it out in a folding "features" card placed atop the bath counter, much like those you see in fine hotels.**

Following are some of the types of spray heads that are available:

STANDARD WALL-MOUNT SHOWERHEAD. These heads are the most economical and can be adjusted slightly by moving the shower neck. Models that offer varying spray types fit the needs of most users.

TOP-MOUNT SHOWERHEAD. These showerheads work well in areas where the ceiling is too low to accommodate a wall-mount head.

HANDHELD SHOWERHEAD. These clip-held showerheads are attached to a 3- to 6-foot-long flexible hose that enables you to easily move the spray of water where you want it. The gooseneck hose adds versatility for washing your hair or rinsing off. And when it comes time to scrub down the shower enclosure, handheld sprays get the job done more efficiently.

Find fast, affordable fix-ups

When your budget doesn't allow for new cabinetry, try these low-cost, quick makeover strategies to boost the beauty of a dated bath:

Paint the vanity cabinet. Although you can sand and restain worn wood cabinetry, you may be able to achieve an improved look more quickly with paint. Follow the steps on page 197 for professional, durable results.

Change out hardware. Something as small as scruffy knobs and pulls, or ones with dated finishes, can make a bath appear "dirty" and unattractive to prospective buyers. Trade old hardware for new versions in current finishes.

When replacing pulls, find ones with the same screw span to match existing pilot holes, if possible. Otherwise you will have to fill old screw holes in the cabinet with wood filler, let dry, sand, paint, and redrill to accommodate the new hardware. An alternative is to purchase decorative backplates that are designed to position behind the new pulls and conceal the old screw holes.

Trade countertops. Unusually colored or damaged bathroom countertops require replacing. If you're a skilled do-it-yourselfer, you can make and install new laminate countertops yourself. Otherwise take precise measurements to a home improvement store and have laminate countertops cut to fit. For odd-shaped countertops, trace a template onto brown kraft paper and take it to the home improvement store. You can remove the old countertop and install the new one yourself.

Install new sinks and/or faucets. Whether your bathroom requires new countertops or not, you can change out the old sink and faucet for updated models. If you replace the sink (or sinks), buy one to fit the countertop opening, or plan on

replacing the countertop too.

If the sink and countertop are in good condition and are neutral colors, installing a new faucet can lend sparkle and style for not a lot of money and effort. See page 184 to learn how to install a kitchen faucet—a task that's similar to bathroom faucet installations.

Update lighting. Lighting from the 1960s, '70s, and '80s can make your bathroom less appealing. Trade old fixtures for new following the basic step-by-step instructions on page 202.

SLIDING-BAR SHOWERHEAD. These showerheads slide up and down on a bar mounted on the wall. Because the height of the spray is extremely easy to adjust, this type of showerhead is a good option when there is a significant variation in the heights of the people using the shower.

BODY SPRAY AND BODY MIST SHOWER SPRAYS. These heads or sprays are installed in vertical rows on opposite or adjacent walls, creating a crisscross water massage between the knee and shoulder levels that allows users to quickly wash up without getting their hair wet.

BODY SPA SHOWER PANELS. These panels are installed against one or more walls of the shower stall and are equipped with water jets arranged vertically from knee to neck level. Similar to those in a whirlpool tub, the water jets pump out and recirculate large quantities of water for a powerful massage.

Before you show your home, hang fresh white towels to convey a pristine, **hotel-like** ambience.

Toilets

A toilet may be utilitarian, but that doesn't mean it can't be stylish. Design choices range from classic two-piece models to sleek, low-profile single-piece models.

Choose a toilet that fits the look you are trying to create. Whether you are purchasing all new fixtures or just one, make sure the unit you select matches the color and the style of the other fixtures in your bath. (Again, white is the preferred color choice for its wide appeal.)

Models with an elongated bowl are more comfortable and more expensive than standard round toilets. Toilet heights range from the standard 14 inches up to 17 inches high. The taller toilets are more comfortable for tall people or people with disabilities.

The lowdown on low-flow

By law, toilets manufactured after January 1, 1994, may use no more than 1.6 gallons of water per flush. Models manufactured before this date use 3.5 or more gallons per flush. Unfortunately many of the low-flow models introduced in the mid 1990s did not work well. Because of this, they often have to be flushed twice to get the job done, so they don't save much water.

Today's low-flow toilets work much better than those early models. There are three types of low-flow toilets:

GRAVITY FLUSH. The least expensive low-flow option, these toilets work using the same principles as models produced before the low-flow mandate. The weight of the water flowing down from the tank clears the bowl. The water pressure in your neighborhood affects how gravity-assisted toilets work. Most manufacturers recommend 25 pounds per square inch to work best. (Your water pressure can also fluctuate with household activities, such as turning on the lawn sprinklers.) Relatively easy to install, these models do not discharge waste as effectively as the other two options.

Help that half-bath

A bare bones powder room with a standard-size toilet and small wall-mount sink could conceivably occupy as little as 12 to 15 square feet. However, to leave a more comfortable clearance between fixtures and provide what designers call "turnaround" space, a realistic minimum space might be 5×7 or 6×6 feet.

With a bath that small, a door that opens into the room greatly reduces floor space and makes entering and exiting tricky. Consider having the door swing out or installing a pocket door.

When choosing a location for your powder room, remember that no matter how small the space, it still requires adequate ventilation, either through an operable window or an exhaust fan.

Property Ladder Lesson: Dollars and sense

Not only does every square inch of a bathroom need to work hard, the overwhelming number of choices in adding or revamping a bath can make it seem as though every square inch requires a different choice that gobbles up the budget. To balance the budget, you may have to cut costs in column B to get what you want in column A, but this approach helps keep the task manageable. Some basic construction costs may be less flexible. Items such as running new plumbing lines, replacing windows, and building walls will lead the budget. Determine the must-have items from the start. One sure way to keep your costs in check is to keep plumbing fixtures in their original locations.

PRESSURE-ASSISTED. When this toilet is flushed, pressurized air created from a vessel hidden in the toilet tank forces water into the bowl and down the drain. The most effective low-flow option, these toilets are noisier than gravity-assisted and are more expensive to repair.

PUMP ASSISTED. These toilets eliminate waste with the assistance of an electric pump that propels water into the bowl and down the drain. These toilets are the most expensive of the three. They work nearly as well as pressure-assisted toilets and don't make as much noise.

Lighting

Well-placed artificial lighting puts your renovated bath in the best light. Here are some guidelines:

INSTALL VANITY LIGHTING—the kind of light fixture needed for shaving and applying makeup—at eye level on both sides of the mirror, if possible. Using just overhead lighting creates less-than-flattering shadows.

CHOOSE A WHITE COUNTERTOP if overhead lights are the only option so that the upward light reflection will reduce the shadowing. For accurate skin coloring, choose incandescent bulbs; avoid bulbs that cast a golden glow.

ILLUMINATE OTHER AREAS in the bath with recessed or track lighting, which is unobtrusive yet highly functional.

PROVIDE SEPARATE CONTROLS for recessed lighting and vanity lighting. Give each a dimmer switch. This allows homeowners to control the lighting level so they can see to clean or create a relaxing mood for a soak in the tub.

Exhaust fans

Proper ventilation keeps a bath free of mildew and moisture damage. Install overhead fans and operable windows to let air in and moisture out. Choose a ventilating fan that exchanges all the air in the room eight times or more per hour.

Before an open house or a private showing, flip on all the lights so prospective buyers can see how well the bath is lighted.

BONUS ROOMS

Optimize extra space

Bonus space in your property can include a loft, a finished attic, or even a garage that has been converted. Your buyers can probably imagine using this "extra" square footage for all kinds of functions. But you can help them envision the options by spotlighting the space's potential with appropriate furnishings and "props." Some possible functions of bonus spaces include a home office or a hobby room.

Home office

In the past decade, home offices have increased in popularity from a "hope-for" to a "must-have" in moderately and high-priced homes. In more modest homes, potential buyers typically request that these spaces serve dual purposes, such as an office that doubles as a guest bedroom.

This real estate trend follows along with the vast increase in the number of people who work full- or part-time from a home-based office. Consequently home offices and dens, when it comes to selling your home, are more important than ever before.

BONUS ROOM MUSTS:
• Sturdy, stylish storage
• User-friendly workspace
• Adaptable furnishings
• Adjustable lighting

Double-duty rooms

If the home you are flipping has just two or three bedrooms, you'll want to stage one of these rooms to appear as a versatile, multipurpose space.

• Consider a daybed. Perfect for an at-home worker's time-out spot, as well as for guests to sleep, space-saving daybeds come in all furniture styles, from country to traditional to contemporary.

• Look for an armoire outfitted for a computer. These look good and buyers see how a computer or television might fit into the space.

• Think modular. Modular office components can make efficient use of guest space, transforming it into a hardworking area, and can easily move from house to house (or flip to flip) as long as the pieces are not attached to walls. Invest in a desk, tables, and chairs equipped with rollers so that they can be moved quickly and easily.

• For a small room, consider an L-shape glass and metal desk that can be tucked into a corner.

Office storage

Whether the office in your property doubles as a bedroom or not, ample, versatile storage is a requirement. Built-in bookcases are a natural fit; choose ones with adjustable shelves and be sure to point out this feature via a pretty folded card displayed on the shelf. To make the most out of available space, choose tall pieces. For a more expansive look, enclose only a few shelves with doors; leave the other shelves open.

Crunch the numbers

Measure existing office space before you shop for furnishings.

Standard desks are 30 inches high. Look for pieces with adjustable work surfaces and legs so they can fit a variety of configurations, such as adjacent to a wall or under a window.

File cabinets come with 15x29-inch letter-size drawers (legal-size drawers are 3 inches wider). Hanging-file and specialized drawer inserts can convert ordinary chests into attractive office storage.

Every home office needs to accommodate a computer. Predrilled holes in work surfaces are ideal for computer cords.

Modular storage units come in a range of dimensions, from stackable cubes to shelf units that you can customize with optional shelves, doors, and drawers.

If you want to keep office remodeling costs down, consider stand-alone storage pieces, such as armoires and freestanding shelf units that can be moved to your next flip. Credenzas designed for hanging files and other office essentials are a popular and convenient choice.

In a kitchen home office, install a combination of full-height and glass-front cabinets to provide storage that can hold everything from books and papers to off-season serving pieces.

You can carve out office space in a master bedroom by sliding a writing table into a corner, beneath a window, or at the foot of the bed. Think beyond traditional furnishings—a slim sofa table topped with a stack of books, a writing tablet, and a container of pens conveys a new sense of usefulness. Depending on the room's available storage, you can even claim a closet as a spot for a desk and storage shelves or add a wall of modular bookcases that includes a flip-down desk. For more suggestions on putting unused space to work, see page 113.

Make great impressions

When furnishing a home office, create a clean, uncluttered appearance by choosing furnishings that match the existing woodwork.

For an even sleeker look, add desk accessories in the same finish as the desk, then brighten the desk with a bud vase and a fresh flower. Cover reference books, such as the phone book and dictionary, with colorful fabrics or a wallpaper remnant.

Use pretty containers for workaday items—flea market bowls for corralling stamps and sticky notes, and fabric-covered boxes for incoming mail and stationery.

Office lighting

For paper and computer work, you'll need ambient (overall) lighting and localized (task) lighting. Ceiling lights and hanging fixtures are excellent sources of ambient light. To create a shadow-free work surface, choose fixtures that are bright enough to illuminate the work area but not so bright that they cause glare. White-shaded lamps (white shades reflect light without absorbing it) and light color hanging pendent fixtures are excellent sources for surface light, as are table lamps and recessed spots.

Floor and desk lamps can be used as a source of ambient light (especially when fitted with a three-way bulb that matches lumen output to your individual lighting needs) or as a task light when focused on a specific area.

Highlight the value of a bonus space by furnishing the area to illustrate the room's possibilities.

Hobby rooms

If the previous owners of your property had a special room designated for a hobby, such as sewing, woodworking, or gardening, glorify its existing functionality by staging it for as many uses as possible.

If your home has a utility sink near a side or back entrance, for example, fill the counter next to it with a few potted plants and a pretty watering bucket. Stage a backyard shed to appear as a gardener's paradise or a handyman's workroom by adding a few potted plants and tools, or a work bench, a peg board and hooks.

If you have a sewing machine, set it up in a corner and drape a pretty fabric by it as though you might be in the midst of a sewing project.

For advice on making the most out of mudrooms and laundry rooms, see pages 116–121.

Attics

The potential uses for these upper-level rooms are what make them most enticing to potential buyers. As a seller, transforming these treetop spaces into enchanting living areas makes economic sense because you can boast additional square footage and increase your asking price.

Does it measure up?

As spacious as an attic or a loft may seem, you'll need to evaluate several key areas before you begin renovation plans.

CODES. Attic living space must be at least $7\frac{1}{2}$ feet high over 50 percent of the floor area. To meet that percentage, sidewalls must be 4 to 5 feet high, according to most local codes. Sidewall to sidewall should measure at least 5 feet. For affordable ways to gain more attic space, refer to the information about dormers on page 114.

HEADROOM. Walk toward a wall until your head reaches the sloping ceiling. Extend your arm toward the wall. The point of farthest reach is the point where usable space begins.

BEAMS. If your roof is supported by a series of W-shape trusses, your attic isn't an easy remodeling candidate. If horizontal collar beams stretch across open space below, then you're in luck. (You can often raise low collar beams safely with the advice of a professional remodeling contractor.)

RAFTERS. Most attics will require shifting rafters or adding spaces to create niches for insulation.

STAIRWAY. Most codes require a minimum width of 30 to 36 inches. If the attic has no stairway, deduct a 3×13-foot rectangle from your usable floor space for steps. A circular staircase requires a 5-foot-square area, but local building codes may put limits on its use.

FLOOR. Most attic joists hold the ceiling up but don't have enough strength to bear weight from above. Local codes require that the floor bear a minimum load of 50 pounds per square foot.

CEILING. The minimum ceiling height for reasonable use is usually 48 to 60 inches. Headroom in the room's center should be at least 8 feet to satisfy most codes.

EXITS. Each attic bedroom needs an emergency exit. A 2-foot-wide egress window of at least 5½ uninterrupted square feet satisfies the code (unless it's a double-hung window, in which case only half the window qualifies). The sill cannot measure more than 44 inches from the floor.

Put underused spaces to work

Most homes have quirky little underused spaces. Make them selling points with some imagination and sweat equity:

Turn a wide stairway landing into a mini retreat with a window seat and a reading light. Or group two chairs and a small table for conversation and coffee.

Dead-end hallways are prime spots for well-organized computer workstations. If there isn't a window, build in a desk and storage. To maximize light from a window, consider a variety of modular pieces that will allow you to customize and organize the space around the window frame.

SUNLIGHT. To allow for adequate natural light, make the volume of glass in an attic at least 10 percent of the floor area. If possible, plan windows at eye level or above. Windows that are too low to see the horizon create uncomfortable viewing angles. Windows placed higher than eye level are fine—they gather interesting views of the sky and afford natural light and privacy.

WINDOW EXTERIORS. Look at window placement from the outside too. The style and placement of your windows should be in harmony with the home's architecture.

shed dormers

Dormer strategies

You can increase the amount of headroom and living space in your attic by adding dormers. Choose from two basic structural styles. Gable dormers, below, offer traditional good looks, but shed dormers, above right, are easier to build and yield more space.

Dormers change the appearance of a home's exterior dramatically. If they are well-proportioned and harmonize with the existing structure, they become a visual asset. Build dormers that are large enough to be worth the remodeling time and expense, but not so large that they look out of proportion with the rest of the home's exterior. The front walls of gable and shed dormers can sit back from the main house wall or align with it. Align and style windows within dormers to match the existing windows beneath them. For more advice on updating the exterior of your property, see pages 132–135.

■ **ABOVE** Your house will look balanced when dormer windows align directly above windows or doors below them or are strategically lined up with the spaces between the windows beneath them.

gable dormers

■ **LEFT** A common strategy used to increase attic headroom is to add gable dormers facing the front of the house and a shed dormer facing the back of the house.

"Dormers will add value if done correctly. Be sure to use an architect, and have a plan before you start your bonus project or you might find a surprise." *Kirsten Kemp*

standard gable

standard shed

hipped gable

deck gable

eyebrow gable

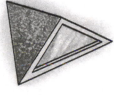

segmental gable

arched gable

inset gable

■ ABOVE Structurally speaking, all dormers are gable or shed, but they can be finished in an array of forms. Choose a style that's consistent with the exterior features and architecture of your home.

■ RIGHT You can build a dormer with walls of any height or none at all. Dormers create intriguing architecture in the living spaces beneath them. Consider letting the ceiling beneath your dormer follow the new roofline. Doing so adds to the drama and character of the space.

gable dormer with sidewalls

gable dormer with short sidewalls

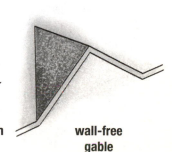

wall-free gable dormer

Make a clean start

Ensuring your property has an organized space for a washer and dryer can be a deal maker and can significantly increase the value (see Nicole Posca's case study beginning on page 12 as one example). A mudroom or space where one could be created is another big bonus with prospective buyers. Here's how to make the most of a laundry room or mudroom.

How does the laundry function?

If you have a choice, deciding on location is the first step to planning a laundry center. Consider where the laundry is most often located in homes in your area. Near the kitchen? Close to the bedrooms? Or is it most often in the basement or garage?

Locating the washer and dryer in the basement means extra steps, but this arrangement frees up valuable upstairs space. Spills, splashes, or an overflow normally do less damage in a basement location. Upstairs a leak could damage walls, flooring, and the ceiling below. Including an emergency shutoff valve on the washer plumbing connection can reduce this concern.

LAUNDRY ROOM & MUDROOM MUSTS:
- Washer/dryer hookups
- Durable, easy-care surfaces
- Storage
- Countertop and sink
- Ample lighting
- Direct access to the outdoors or the garage

If the property you purchase lacks a laundry room, the resale potential could fall. Perhaps a large existing closet could neatly accommodate the hookups and appliances behind folding doors (see page 119). A smaller closet might hold a stacked washer and dryer. Have a plumber and an electrician make the necessary connections and install shelving at the top of the closet as a place to stash laundry supplies.

Plumbing and wiring

Even a small sink can be used to soak grimy clothes. If you have the room, opt for a deep bowl, which doubles as a place to rinse off garden tools or wash the family pet.

Washers require a drain and hot and cold water lines. Gas dryers need a gas supply line and no more than 50 feet of venting to the outside. Electric dryers require a 120-volt circuit. Some models condense moisture into a drip pan without venting. Washers and gas dryers require 220-amp small-appliance circuits. Units must be on independent, grounded circuits.

Storage

Install shelving near the future location of the washer so the buyer sees a place for keeping supplies handy. A wall-hung rack for hanging clothes for drip-drying is another feature that increases perceived value.

Enclosed cabinetry hides the sink plumbing and conceals detergent bottles and other laundry necessities. If you have room for an extra cabinet or two, consider adding a slide-in hamper and a pullout wastebasket. Including a generous length of countertop offers a place to fold clothes, do

Fit in a mudroom

Mudrooms come in many shapes and sizes—20 square feet is enough—so finding a place to fit one into your property may be easier than you think, especially if you keep these concepts in mind:

Start by the door. Your quest for a mudroom begins near an entryway. It's almost effortless to drop gear by the door and pick it up again when leaving, so it makes sense to position mudrooms in proximity to entries. Doing so also confines dirty shoes and gear to one easy-to-clean area.

Try small spaces. Even tight areas, such as large closets, wide hallways, and ample foyers, make fine candidates for mudroom-type storage. A few hooks or a built-in bench with storage beneath the lid can be helpful. Devoting a single wall to shelving, cubbies, cabinets, or locker-style compartments enhances storage and organization in this space.

Check the porch's potential. Porches and sunrooms on the back of older homes qualify as good locations for conversion to mudrooms because they're near the yard and garage.

projects, arrange flowers, or wrap gifts. If the laundry room is located off the kitchen, consider matching cabinetry and countertops for these adjacent spaces.

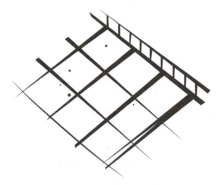

Flooring

Select flooring materials for the laundry room that are extremely durable, easy to clean, and moisture-resistant. Here are a few options to consider:

• Ceramic tile is durable and water- and stain-resistant and comes in a wide choice of colors, designs, textures, and shapes. Tiles can be mixed for border treatments and field accents to give the laundry room a hint of style. The downside of tile is that it can be cold and can be hard on the feet. Glazed tiles can be slippery when wet. Moisture and dirt may collect in grout joints, and unsealed tiles stain easily.

• Vinyl is available in sheet and tile form. Sheets up to 15 feet wide eliminate seams in most laundry rooms. Vinyl is flexible, comfortable underfoot, water and stain-resistant, and easy to install—especially tiles. Vinyl is also easy to clean, and the

GFCI breakers

Electrical codes require ground fault circuit interrupters (GFCIs) on receptacles within 6 feet of a water source. GFCIs detect stray current, shutting off receptacles to prevent shock.

polyurethane finishes eliminate waxing. There are a large number of designs available, and tiles can be mixed to create custom patterns or color accents. A disadvantage of vinyl flooring is that it dents and tears easily. With vinyl tiles, moisture and dirt can get into seams between the squares.

• Linoleum is considered chic again because of its design flexibility, lower cost to value, environmentally friendly ingredients, and durability. Linoleum floors don't release harmful gases, or VOCs (volatile organic compounds). And because the linseed oil in linoleum is constantly oxidizing, it retards the growth of bacteria. (The recipe for linoleum includes linseed oil, crushed limestone, wood shavings, and pine resin tapped from living trees.) The fact that linoleum actually hardens over time is yet another plus. Linoleum is available in a dazzling array of colors and is flexible enough for you to cut it into original designs. One unfavorable aspect of linoleum is that it tends to be much more costly than vinyl.

• Rubber is less known but a good option for the laundry room or mudroom. Available in more than a hundred colors and a variety of patterns and textures, rubber features color that wears consistently, and the material is comfortable and quiet underfoot. Rubber comes in sheet form or in 24×24-inch or 36×36-inch tiles. It is a long-wearing, slip- and stain-resistant, and antistatic material. One drawback is that the textured patterns can hold dirt. In addition, special cleaners must be used to avoid removing protective wax and oils. To care for rubber flooring: After installation, follow the manufacturer's instructions for the first cleaning and wax application (though some floors offer a built-in wax). After that, clean

regularly with a product formulated for rubber floors and recommended by the manufacturer. Mop up excess cleaning solution. To avoid water spots after cleaning the floor, put a towel under your feet and "skate" to dry the surface.

Lighting

Uniform, glare-free lighting is important to thoroughly inspect, sort, and fold clothes. Compact fluorescent bulbs illuminate without adding heat. Some wall-mount ironing boards include a task light. When the laundry room or mudroom includes wall and base cabinets, tuck fixtures beneath the upper cabinets to provide task lighting for the countertop.

A multipurpose mudroom

Especially prized in snowy or wet climates, a mudroom handles muddy boots and grimy fingers with wipe-clean surfaces. Locate the mudroom near a back entrance or between the garage and kitchen. To handle all the dirt that is tracked in, choose durable flooring, such as ceramic tile, stone, vinyl, linoleum, or rubber.

A mudroom can handle more than just mud. The planning stage of a family room, kitchen, or garage—whether it's an addition or a revamped space—is an ideal time to work in a service area that performs a number of valuable functions.

STORE GEAR. Plan storage where prospective homeowners could imagine organizing winter wraps and summer sports equipment. There should be storage for boots and shoes. Shelves, racks, hooks, and pegs provide storage and keep items from being strewn throughout the house. Include one tall cabinet to accommodate anything from hockey

Make the laundry room and mudroom appear more efficient with **moistureproof surfaces**, plenty of storage, bins for sorting laundry, and surfaces for folding.

Incorporate a laundry center

Don't despair if your property lacks a laundry room. These options make it possible to fit this workhorse into minimal space:

Narrow, stackable washer/dryer combos in 24-inch widths require less floor space than standard side-by-side 30-inch models.

Tuck-under washers and dryers fit underneath a counter. Available in standard widths, these front-loading appliances have controls on the front panels. You can also stack them.

Condensation dryers make it possible to install appliances in rooms and closets without venting them to the outdoors. The dryer discharges moisture into the washer's drain line.

Cabinet-top dryers make room for many levels of air drying on top of the appliance surface, eliminating the closet-laundry conundrum of finding a place to lay or hang just-washed delicates to dry.

Create this organized laundry-in-a-closet, *right*. You need a 6×3-foot slice of space—less for a stacked washer and dryer. Fit the closet with a 4-foot fluorescent lighting fixture and a shelf to hold detergent and other laundry necessities. You will also need hot and cold water supply lines, a drainage

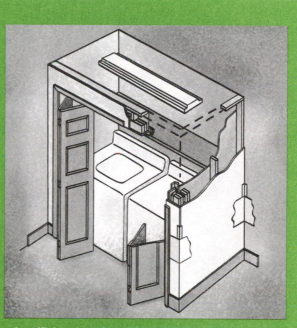

■ An efficient laundry with a side-by-side washer and dryer as well as storage can fit neatly into a closet as small as 6×3 feet. Add bifold doors, as shown here, to keep any messes out of sight and to allow full access to the space.

system, and electrical outlets. An exterior wall usually works best so the dryer can be vented to the outdoors, or install a condensation dryer. A floor drain to handle overflows or leaks is necessary.

An ironing board that **folds down** out of the wall adds **convenience** and saves on **storage space.** Purchasing a wall-mount rod for hang-drying clothes makes the space **more efficient.**

sticks to long-handle brooms and mops.

LAUNDRY HOOKUPS. A service area located beside the kitchen is often a good location for the washer and dryer. If your property doesn't include the necessary connections for a washer and dryer, have them installed. For increased perceived value, include a fold-down ironing board. A bank of cabinets with a countertop is ideal for storing washday supplies and serving as a folding surface.

SPACE FOR HOBBIES AND HOUSEHOLD BOOKKEEPING. Additional countertops and storage in a mudroom can easily serve a future homeowner as a place for enjoying hobbies or wrapping gifts. Consider including a desk area that can double as a sit-down hobby surface or as a close-to-the-kitchen office space. Many buyers want the home office out of the kitchen and relocated to the mudroom in order to keep clutter corralled and out of sight.

MULTIFUNCTIONAL MINISHOWER. For more added value, consider installing a small shower in one corner of the mudroom. Equipped with a drain, waterproof surfacing, a handheld showerhead, and a hanging rod, this shower area can serve as a place to rinse off muddy feet, groom the family pooch, or hang-dry clothes.

Hang shelves and cabinets

Your property's laundry room and/or mudroom will have the appearance of a hardworking space with the addition of shelves and cabinets. Any shelf system—be it simple boards or a cabinet with doors—must be hung on a wall properly. If it is not anchored into wall studs, it probably will come loose when weight is put on it. If it is not plumb and level, it will look shoddy and may even prove unsafe.

As you plan shelving for your property, decide the following:

Will the shelves be supported at the ends (by the side of the shelf unit or cabinet) or from the back?

Do you want the shelves adjustable or fixed? Adjustable shelving offers design flexibility.

It may seem time-consuming, but it's wise to draw a detailed plan of your shelf or cabinet system. Without a plan, it's difficult to buy materials and easy to overlook hard-to-correct design flaws.

Unsupported shelf ends should extend no more than one-third the distance between the shelf standards.

Select the hardware that suits your purposes best:

Rigid pressed-steel angle brackets hold medium-weight loads. For heavier loads, choose brackets reinforced with triangular gussets. Mount with the longer leg against the wall. Check that upper screws are fastened firmly.

Brackets that clip into slotted standards are a good way to achieve adjustable support when you want to mount shelves from the rear. Choose from 8-, 10-, or 12-inch brackets.

Pin-type clips that pop into predrilled holes let you create adjustable shelves with a finished appearance. The clips are relatively inexpensive, but the holes must be drilled precisely.

End-mount adjustable standards and clips are strong but not as attractive as the pin-type clips mentioned above.

Light-duty wire brackets are among the many accessories you can mount on perforated hardboard. Measure the thickness of the pegboard before you buy it; $\frac{1}{4}$- and $\frac{1}{8}$-inch perforated hardboard require different bracket types.

Capture subterranean space

Typically the greatest concern a prospective home buyer has about a property's basement is that it be not clean and clutter-free and moisture free, with no signs of instability in the foundation walls. When an unfinished basement is dry and the walls are sturdy, a potential buyer then considers the available headroom: Is the ceiling high enough to convert this subterranean square footage into comfortable living space?

Scrutinizing a basement

Before you buy a property to flip, use these guiding principles to see how the basement ranks.

Foundation inspection

Soil movement and settling around the foundation of your property exerts pressure on even the sturdiest basement walls, causing cracks. Although minor cracks do not generally threaten the integrity of the foundation, they could indicate drainage problems around the house that you should correct. Cracks can be a source of moisture or radon gas leaks. If you've already purchased a property with cracks in

UNFINISHED BASEMENT MUSTS:
- No signs of moisture
- Stable walls
- Adequate headroom to allow for future finishing as living space
- Clean, free of cobwebs and creepy crawlies
- Good storage opportunities
- Ample ambient lighting

the foundation walls, use the guidelines that follow to help you fix any drainage problems around the perimeter of the house. This should relieve pressure on foundation walls and prevent further cracking. Existing cracks then should be sealed from inside using hydraulic cement.

Homes with severe bowing of basement walls should be avoided. However, if you've already purchased a property with this problem, it may require steel bracing installed inside the walls. Consult a licensed remodeling contractor who specializes in this type of basement repair. Find these professionals in the business listings of a phone book or via an Internet search engine under "foundation contractors" or "waterproofing contractors." Before choosing a contractor, always ask for references and check them out.

Dry, dry, dry

You'll want to make sure that the basement of the property you're considering is dry. Some problems are obvious—wet or damp walls or telltale moisture stains on floors are sure signs that corrective measures will be required.

Water is particularly tricky to control and can invade a basement in a variety of ways: excess rainwater in the surrounding soil forcing its way through foundation walls, rising water tables permeating unsealed concrete floors, and condensation forming on pipes. Many moisture problems originate around the exterior of the property and can be fixed with preventive maintenance or drainage systems. Others require professional expertise. For more about moisture-related maintenance, see "Preventive Maintenance," *opposite.*

Remove excess humidity in the basement by plugging in a portable dehumidifier.

By the book

Most building codes require a finished basement room to have a minimum ceiling height of 7 feet. However, boxed-out obstructions, such as ductwork, beams, and plumbing, can drop as low as 6 ½ feet. Measure the distance between the floor and the bottom of the ceiling joists to determine if there is enough room to create a new living area. Be sure to allow for the thicknesses of the finish materials you plan to install on the ceiling and floor.

Most codes also dictate that rooms designed for living areas (as opposed to bathrooms or laundry rooms) must have at least 70 square feet of space, with no wall less than 7 feet long.

A bedroom in a finished basement must contain an egress window, which is usually an operable window measuring at least 20 inches wide and 24 inches high that can serve as an emergency escape. To make it readily accessible, the lower edge of the window opening must be no more than 44 inches from the floor.

Preventive maintenance

The most common cause of basement moisture problems comes from rainwater and melted snow gathering in the soil around the foundation. Reduce the chance of problems from rainwater runoff by ensuring that water flows away from the foundation. Grade the soil around the foundation so it slopes away from the house at a rate of 2 vertical inches for every horizontal foot over a distance of at least 3 feet. This ensures that most water ends up beyond the porous backfill soil. Fill low spots with dirt for proper drainage.

Debris collecting inside the gutters can dam downspouts, causing water to overflow and end up next to the foundation. Make sure all gutters are cleaned out, straight, and sloping gently toward downspouts. Sagging gutters ruin the curb appeal of your property, trap water in low spots, and cause overflowing. Downspouts should extend at least 5 feet from foundation walls. Lengthen short downspouts or place concrete splash blocks beneath downspout openings to direct water away from foundation walls.

Another way to help keep a basement dry is to install a sump pump. A sump pump sits in a reservoir below the level of the basement floor. There are two types. A pedestal-type pump has a motor that sits on top of a long pipe. The pipe extends to a base in the bottom of the sump pit. When water enters the pit, it moves a float that engages the motor. Water is then pumped from the pit. A submersible sump pump sits entirely inside the pit. A float attached to the pump signals the motor to switch on, removing the water. A submersible sump pump is considered the more reliable and effective unit.

Both pumps remove water through a discharge pipe to the outside of the house. The exit location should be treated like a downspout, with proper grading of the surrounding soil to drain water away from foundation walls.

One concern about sump pumps is that when they are needed most—for example, during a heavy thunderstorm—that's exactly the time when electrical power may be lost. For this reason consider installing a battery-operated backup system for the pump. In the event that electrical power fails, the battery takes over, running the pump for several hours.

To the finish

Once you are certain that your property's basement is dry, consider these ideas for upgrading the space for everyday living:

Flooring facts

Almost all basement subfloors are concrete. You can apply many kinds of flooring products over concrete for an attractive, durable finish underfoot.

Most concrete slabs have small cracks and other imperfections. You can install some floor coverings, such as carpeting and laminate planks, directly over cracks less than $1/4$ inch wide. Other materials, such as vinyl sheet flooring, require the subfloor to be free from imperfections. Cracks wider than $1/4$ inch may indicate foundation problems, so consult a foundation contractor before installing a floor covering.

Level any uneven floors or sloped concrete subfloors with concrete-base leveling compound. Follow the directions for applying the product. When cured, the compound will be smooth and level and will provide a good base for many types of flooring.

Remember that concrete slabs are in constant contact with the ground beneath them, so they tend to remain cool. If you want to "sell" the basement as a warm and cozy living space, select a flooring material that separates your buyer's feet from the chill.

Install a plywood subfloor

For comfort underfoot or to span an uneven concrete slab, you can install a wood subfloor. In a typical installation, $5/8$- or $3/4$-inch exterior-grade plywood sheets are nailed to a grid of "sleepers"—pressure-treated 2x4s laid flat to help keep the finished height within the building code requirements. Correct any unevenness in the concrete with shims placed beneath the sleepers. Fill spaces between the sleepers with rigid foam insulation before nailing the plywood in place. The result is a smooth, even subfloor that will accept most types of flooring.

Conceal structural supports by building them into partition walls or by framing around them to form a decorative column.

Painting foundation walls

To give the basement a low-cost facelift, paint the masonry foundation walls. Keep in mind that paint won't hide such defects as cracks, chips, holes, and missing mortar. Even if defects are patched, the repairs may appear through the paint.

For best results, prepare wall surfaces thoroughly, applying paint only to surfaces that are free of dirt, dust, and grease. It is especially important to correct any moisture problems and allow wall surfaces to dry before painting.

Prepare walls using a wire brush to remove loose dirt and old mortar. Check walls for efflorescence—a powdery white deposit that sometimes appears on concrete or concrete block walls. Efflorescence is caused by salts in the concrete that, over time, make their way to the surface. Although efflorescent deposits are harmless, remove them before walls are painted for a cleaner look. Use soap and water and a stiff brush to scrub off the deposits. Be sure to rinse thoroughly with water and allow the walls to dry completely. If efflorescence remains, consider using a phosphoric acid masonry cleaning product.

Paint prepared walls with a good-quality latex paint. Be sure to read the manufacturer's recommendations about painting basement walls. During the painting process, have a portable dehumidifier running to keep humidity levels low and to help the paint dry completely.

Some types of paint are made specifically to seal walls against moisture. Called "waterproofing paint" or "masonry waterproofers," these tough coatings contain mixtures of synthetic rubber and portland cement. They are designed to seal the pores of cement and cement block, reducing the penetration of moisture due to capillary action. Although not a true waterproofing system, this kind of paint can stand up to the kinds of moisture that could cause regular latex paints to blister and peel. It is available in standard colors or can be tinted to a desired color.

Finesse foundations walls

Foundation walls usually are made of poured concrete or stacked concrete block—not the most attractive surfaces. Fortunately you often can cover basement walls quickly and inexpensively to make your property even more appealing. Attaching wood furring strips to flat, dry masonry walls, then covering the strips or studs with drywall, gives the walls a smooth, even surface that accepts any type of finish material. You can paint, wallpaper, or tile to complement the main-level decor. Add moldings and/or wainscoting to increase interest. (For information on how to install crown moldings or wainscoting, turn to pages 172–183.)

To make the basement more energy-efficient (a good selling point when energy costs are high), fill the spaces between the furring strips or studs with rigid insulation or batts. Installing this type of wall system offers the opportunity to add electrical outlets, cable, speaker wire, and telephone lines.

Ceiling options

Basement ceilings can be difficult to finish because often there is an array of obstructions, such as pipes, ducts, and wires, all attached to the underside of the overhead joists or running between them. You usually can move wires and water supply pipes, but finding acceptable new routes for ductwork or drain lines often is difficult. One option is to disguise or box obstructions within a wood framework, then cover the frame with finish materials.

The three primary options for finishing a basement ceiling are painting, installing a suspended ceiling, or covering the joists with drywall or wood.

PAINT. One particularly low-cost finishing option is to leave all the elements in the ceiling exposed, and camouflage the overhead tangle with a coat of paint. Painting everything a single color makes the different elements blend together, and they become less noticeable. A paint sprayer will coat everything evenly— including the sides and much of the upper surfaces of various elements. Paint the joists, the underside of the subfloor, wires, pipes, and ducts. Light or dark colors work well. Dark colors disguise the many

FINISHED BASEMENT MUSTS:
- No signs of moisture
- Gloom-free
- Updated finishes for walls, floor, and ceiling
- Good storage
- Ample ambient lighting

Update with partition walls

Because partition walls have no structural responsibilities, they are easy to construct and install in any basement location. This versatility makes them ideal for camouflaging posts and other obstructions that can't be moved. Typical stud wall construction is sufficient for partition walls, but don't rule out flights of fancy. Curved walls or walls made of glass block are simple ways to enhance a basement.

elements better, whereas light colors help make the space brighter.

CEILING SYSTEMS. A low-cost, low-maintenance solution is to install a ceiling system. Options include planks or tiles that secure directly to the joists and thus retain headroom, or panels that fit into a suspended grid and allow quick access to plumbing and wiring. Today's ceiling systems are more attractive than they were in the past. Be sure to browse the Internet as well as the aisles of a home center to see the various styles and products available.

DRYWALL. To give a basement the sense of being part of the main living area and to create a smooth, even finish, install a drywall ceiling. Use drywall to box in large obstructions such as ducts and pipes. Although such obstructions are unavoidable, careful planning will ensure that any boxed-in elements become an integral part of your basement design scheme.

Bathroom basics

You may consider adding a bathroom to the basement of your property to improve resale value as long as the space has the headroom required by local building codes. Keep in mind that it can be tricky to add the drain necessary for a shower or a toilet. The installation of either of these fixtures means connecting to an existing main drain. This may determine the location of the bathroom and require cutting and removing concrete to splice into the existing line—a potentially messy and expensive job. One solution is to elevate the new bathroom (provided you have the headroom) to create underfoot space in which to conceal new

Banish gloom

If you've purchased a property with a gloomy basement, consider installing window wells and larger windows to improve natural lighting. Good artificial lighting will help make the below-grade space more cheerful during evening hours.

If the basement of your property is already finished, select wall colors to brighten the outlook. Also consider staging the space for an open house using vibrant-hued upholstered furnishings, glass-top tables, and airy wicker pieces to further enliven the below-grade space.

You can make a cold basement appear more cozy by installing a new gas fireplace. (For more on fireplaces, see page 76.)

Radon alert

Before you purchase your property, it's wise to check radon levels in the basement. Radon is an odorless, colorless gas that occurs naturally in many types of soil and is often present in negligible amounts in basements. Because radon has been linked to lung cancer, however, high levels of radon are considered a serious health threat. Most hardware stores or home improvement centers have do-it-yourself kits that you can use to measure the approximate radon level in a basement. For best results, precisely follow the directions that come with the kit.

plumbing lines and a drain. You may want to seek the advice of a qualified plumbing contractor.

Lighting

Basement rooms rely heavily on good artificial lighting. Make sure you provide adequate sources of overall, or ambient, illumination. Recessed fixtures are a good choice for a finished basement because they don't interfere with headroom. If you do opt for track lighting in a finished basement, install it around the perimeter of the room.

Bring comfort to an outdoor room

Sunrooms, porches, decks, and patios have become cherished gathering spaces for families. Properly furnishing and accessorizing these rooms is as important to selling your home as is the staging of any interior space.

How does it look?

When you step outside your home's patio door, what do you see? Is the outdoor space as comfortable and inviting as your indoor rooms? With the right mix of furnishings and accessories, you can make your outdoor spaces as much of a selling point as your indoor spaces. Approach decorating an outdoor room—whether it's a screen porch, a concrete patio, or a corner of yard—as you would an indoor living space. With a few simple luxuries, a comfy chaise lounge, a gentle fan, or a quilt for crisp evenings, an open-air space can become a peaceful oasis for resting, relaxing, cooking, dining, and entertaining family and friends.

Comfortable living

Make the most of your alfresco rooms by taking advantage of any attractions that nature has afforded you. Purchase a few comfortable outdoor furnishings and arrange them in cozy groupings that take advantage of the view, whether it's of a nearby lake, a garden of rose bushes, or a 100-year-old tree.

Color palette

Choose an outdoor color scheme in the same fashion as you would an indoor one. Consider colors that complement your home's exterior siding or trim, patio umbrella, awning, or even your garden flowers.

If your outdoor space has some architectural detailing, such as an alcove or outdoor fireplace, set it off by painting it a color that is a few shades darker or lighter than the house.

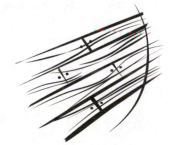

Flooring

If your outdoor room has a concrete or stone floor, give it a fresh look by scrubbing it clean with a power hose. If the floor is made of tile, clean it to look like new by following the instructions listed on page 73–74.

To give a wood deck a new look, scrub it clean using a power hose and let it dry thoroughly, then repaint or stain it, and top it with a sealant specifically designed for wood decking.

Walls

Give the vertical surfaces in your outdoor living area a fresh look with another coat of paint. Deck trim, posts, and pillars should match the trimwork on the main portion of the house.

Strategically placed bushes and ornamental trees can help define outdoor rooms.

Outdoor lighting

Today the choices for outdoor lighting are as numerous as they are for indoor lighting. At home centers and at retail stores specializing in outdoor furnishings, you can find outdoor-rated electric ceiling fans, chandeliers, and sconces, candlelit chandeliers, lanterns, and torches; and battery-operated lamps and canister lights.

Add outdoor accessories

To be a well-dressed room, an outdoor living space requires the same finishing touches as an indoor room. Use under-eaves space to display weather-resistant artwork such as a mosaic tile picture or decorative sconces made from terra-cotta pottery. Items made from wire, redwood, and powder-coated metals also work well. Be sure to choose pieces that are sturdy enough to withstand a swift breeze. Fill empty corners with potted plants and plant stands, then incorporate additional accessories such as decorative rocks, fountains, and colorful watering cans. Shelves are ideal for displaying potted arrangements and shapely architectural salvage.

Firelight

A blazing fire under the stars is one of the most appealing, alluring aspects of outdoor living and can extend the length of the warm season by a month or more. This luxury is now quite affordable thanks to portable fireplaces and fire pits. And because the units are portable, you can take the appliance with you when your property sells.

Affordably priced freestanding units are available at home centers and at department and outdoor specialty stores. Note that some municipalities have banned their use due to air quality control and nonburn restrictions, so check with your zoning authority before investing in one.

How does it function?

To underscore the usefulness of your flip's outdoor living spaces, arrange outdoor furnishings to accommodate tasks and entertaining. For example, use furnishings to divide a long, narrow patio into three functional areas—one for cooking, one for dining, and one for lounging.

Activity-center design

To make cooking and dining outdoors more comfortable, place an outdoor console near the grill to hold spices, marinades, and serving platters.

For dining, choose comfortable chairs with colorful cushions. During an open house, bring color to the table with runners, colorful linens, and attractive dinnerware. For the lounging area, consider adding footstools and chaises that encourage relaxation.

SUNROOMS, DECKS, PORCHES & PATIOS

Material matters

To withstand the elements, all your outdoor furnishings should be made of treated woods, rustproof metals, or heavy plastics. Soften the look of these functional furnishings with cushions, pillows, and throws made of fabrics that withstand moisture and sunlight.

For open, unprotected patios choose a synthetic fabric rated for all-weather use. All-weather acrylic is an excellent choice because it is mildew-resistant and can withstand 1,000 sunlight hours without fading. Similarly, all-weather polyester vinyl repels moisture, resists mildew, and can withstand 500 hours in the sun. For cushion filling, look for mildew- and moisture-resistant fills that dry quickly.

In protected areas, such as on a three-season porch, sturdy natural fibers such as treated canvas make viable covering options, but for increased longevity you'll want to bring these items in during rainy periods.

Sturdy stairs and railings

Make sure patio and porch stairs and railings are safe and sturdy and meet building code regulations. Although regulations vary from region to region, most include these basic requirements:

- Decks and porches located more than 30 inches above the ground must have guardrails at least 36 inches high.
- Stairs more than 30 inches high must have guardrails at least 34 inches high.
- Guardrails must have rails, posts, or other ornamental fill that will not allow objects 4 inches in diameter (such as a 4-inch ball) to pass through.

Increase indoor/outdoor connections

Outdoor access and light rank high in priority for home buyers. If your home lacks a connection to the outdoors, you can increase its salability by simply replacing a solid-panel door with a French door or patio doors. Your interior will reap the benefits of instant fresh-air access and more light. Indoor spaces with a strong outdoor connection also seem larger than their actual square footage, giving you more impact for your remodeling dollar.

Consider pouring a small concrete patio outside your new entrance, and staging it with a few potted plants and a comfortable lounge chair, and you will have an outdoor living space for a modest expense.

- The height of stair handrails must be between 30 and 38 inches.
- A stairway that has more than two risers must have a handrail on at least one side.
- The minimum depth of treads in 10 inches.
- The maximum height of a riser is 7¾ inches. (Note: A riser 6 inches high and a tread 12 inches deep is recommended for outdoor stairways.)
- The dimensions of treads and risers cannot vary by more that ⅜ inch from step to step.

All-season rooms

A true sunroom is characterized by fully insulated walls and ceilings and heating and cooling system controlled by thermostat. If your property has such a space, you'll want to highlight it in your sales flyers and newspaper ads. If you are considering adding a sunroom, note that it is the most expensive option a homeowner can consider when adding a porchlike environment.

Sun and heat control

You can help control sun and the heat it generates in mostly glass rooms by installing shades or blinds and opening doors and windows when possible. Fan-assisted ventilation can also help ensure that the air temperature remains comfortable.

Windows and window glazes

Glass windows and doors are primary components of any sunroom. If any of the windows are damaged or worn and need replacement, you can reduce costs by combining fixed windows, which are lower priced, with windows that open. To reduce costs further, use stock sizes rather than custom sizes wherever possible. You'll want to choose the same framing material for the replacements that is used on the original windows, whether it be wood, vinyl, aluminum, or wood-clad. If the room tends to overheat, you can reduce heat transfer from the sun by choosing replacement windows with high R-values, which measure a building material's resistance to heat transfer. Glazing with high R-values is a better insulator than glazing with low R-values.

Note that safety glass is required by most building codes for skylights, large glass doors, windows within 18 inches of the floor, and windows installed on walls that incline 15 degrees or more.

Let **landscape elements**—such as the flower colors in the garden—**serve as the inspiration** for the color scheme of an outdoor room.

Capture curb appeal

Like it or not, curb appeal can mean the difference between prospective buyers stopping for an open house or driving right on by. Making sure the exterior and surrounding yard of your property appears well kept, updated, and welcoming should hold equal priority with updating the interior. After all, if the house and yard look as though they need work, buyers will assume that the inside needs help too. Shaping up the exterior can mean the difference between a fast flip and one that languishes on the market.

How does it look?

One of the best ways to determine objectively how your property sizes up is to drive around the neighborhood and take note of the properties that have instant appeal. You should also find out which homes sold the quickest in your area and study the exteriors and yards of those properties.

What color are these houses? What kinds of amenities do they offer, such as a three-car garage or a charming courtyard leading to the front door? Are they heavily landscaped? Do they boast an abundance of flowers, or are the plantings lower maintenance?

You can find all the clues you need by touring and studying your neighbors' properties

EXTERIOR MUSTS:
- Siding and windows in good condition
- Freshly painted siding and trim in neutral tones
- Shutters and gutters in good condition
- Garage door in good condition
- Welcoming front entry
- Orderly, updated landscaping

and learning what prospective buyers expect to find outside the best of them. Take pictures of these houses and bring them back to your own. Now you can analyze where yours might fall short and make changes that will transform it into an eye-pleasing neighborhood landmark.

Enhancements

ENTRYWAYS

Entries serve one main purpose—to lead visitors into the house. As simple as that sounds, to function at its best a good entry should designate where to enter, provide a bit of shelter for guests waiting outside the door, and enhance the architectural style of the house. Keep these tips in mind to design a pleasing entry.

CONSIDER THE APPROACH. You don't want guests tripping over cracked concrete or winding through thorny shrubs to reach the front door. Should the entry be moved for better function? Once the location of the entry is established, plan an easy, attractive route to reach it.

DIRECT TRAFFIC. Install landscape lighting along the path to the entry and add cheery lights on both sides of the door.

OFFER SHELTER. If the current entry doesn't feature an overhang, portico, or porch to protect the door, consult an architect or other design professional for options that integrate with the existing design.

STUDY THE STYLE. Unless you plan to overhaul the entire exterior of your property, select entry details that coordinate with or enhance the existing architectural style. When you tour the neighborhood, note details that enhance similar house styles.

SIDING

Observe the siding all around your property and determine whether a fresh coat of paint will suffice or if new siding is in order. If you decide to re-side, here are some considerations:

SITE SPECIFICS. If your property needs new siding, regional or local differences in climate and environment greatly influence the choice of siding. Metal and vinyl provide little insulation value, and in extreme temperatures vinyl may become brittle or warped. Airborne salt or pollutants may alter the appearance of metal. Wood must be maintained to withstand pests, sun, and moisture damage. Note the characteristics of your locale and shop accordingly. If you live in a wind-prone area, look for a siding and installation system that has been tested to resist strong winds—some siding can withstand gusts of more than 150 miles per hour. If you prefer wood but live in a damp climate, consider a vinyl product manufactured to mimic the look of real wood.

GETTING IT DONE. Vinyl, metal, and wood are lightweight, easy to install, and usually readily available. Stone and masonry-cast veneers may also be installed quickly, often in any season. This inevitably saves money, except when special

Siding tip

Metal and vinyl sidings are sold in strips or squares and offer quick, inexpensive installation, but they may produce seams that disrupt an exterior's visual flow. Look for extra long strips to minimize joint lines.

Update the entry

Don't have the cash or time to revamp the entire exterior? Enhancing the entrance by adding a few details is the quickest way to infuse curb appeal.

Accessorize. Sweat the small stuff when it comes to accessories. A decorative mailbox or new address numbers are instant updates. Consider a piece of art, a chair, or a potted plant to provide a welcome change. Bored with the door? Replace the hardware—coordinated doorknobs, hinges, kick plates, and doorbells can make an entryway shine. Don't forget lights—a well-placed fixture illuminates the entry and radiates style.

Landscape. The entrance is more than just the front door—it includes the walkways and surrounding flowerbeds. Resurface damaged concrete with tile or flagstone, and ensure pathways are easy to follow. Don't overlook the landscaping—a flowerbed or bush does wonders to liven up a property.

Refresh. If accessories and plants don't add enough oomph, it may be time for some minor structural changes. Perhaps all you need is a brand-new front door. Or consider what columns, an awning, or a portico might add.

details, such as cedar shakes, require expert installation. Stone and brick are durable and attractive, but their individual placement and heavy nature require extra labor, expertise, and a great deal of time. To keep costs in check, consider manufactured stone, masonry-cast siding, or stucco. Each offers bricklike benefits without weighing down the budget. Along with an organic appearance, these materials are resilient and easier to handle than natural stone. If you're set on the real thing, a design specifying partial walls of stone paired with another siding material is a cost-conscious option.

MAINTENANCE AND REPAIR. Vinyl and steel siding require little upkeep aside from the occasional cleaning, but scratches, fading, and dents may be tough to hide. If you live in a sun-drenched area and want vinyl siding, look for a brand that features fade-resistant protection for 25 years. Wood, stucco, and masonry readily accept fresh coats of paint and are quickly patched. If stucco siding requires repair, make sure to determine and fix the cause of the problem, or it will likely reoccur.

ROOFING

Though your inspection team should let you know the condition of the roof before you purchase a home, it's a good idea to assess it again before tackling the exterior transformation. Fortunately you don't have to risk your life by climbing a ladder and crawling out on the roof. Instead simply scan the roof from all sides through binoculars, paying special attention to problem areas.

INSPECT RIDGE SHINGLES FIRST. Look for cracks and wind damage. In the case of asphalt shingles, the mineral granules may be worn away. A leak here can show up anywhere inside.

LOOK AT ROOF VALLEYS—another place where deterioration causes problems. Make sure any flashing is sound. Shingles should lie flat on top of the flashing. If leaks occur during windy rainstorms, the shingles that lie on the flashing may not be cut correctly; ask a pro.

CHECK OTHER FLASHING TOO. It should be tight, rust-free, and sealed with pliable caulking or roofing cement.

LOOSE, CURLED, OR MISSING SHINGLES leak moisture, which weakens sheathing and harms walls and ceilings. If individual shingles have been

Affix gutters, downspouts

Make sure that all gutters and downspouts are securely affixed to the fascia boards and that they are without rust, free of holes, and clear of peeling paint. Clean out all gutters and downspouts to ensure that rainwater is directed away from the foundation.

Consider a **small fountain** near a patio. The sound of running water is pleasing and can **mask street noise.**

Sit a spell

Encourage prospective buyers to linger near a garden or the front entrance by carving out a spot to sit.

Create a greeting place. Even beneath a small entry portico, it's nice to have a chair or two in case you or your visitors wish to sit and chat.

Build a bench. Turn to page 213 for a bench you can easily build anywhere in the yard.

damaged by a falling branch, replace them singly. If shingles show general wear and tear, it's time for a reroofing job.

A LARGE QUANTITY OF GRANULES in the gutter signal that the roof is losing its surface coating. Expect problems soon.

WATCH DURING HEAVY RAIN to see if gutters are freeflowing. Flooding can work up under lower shingle courses.

LANDSCAPING

Fences and small structures, such as an arbor or trellis, can provide an attractive backdrop for exuberant new plants while enhancing the curb appeal of your property.

Curving walkways lined with plants and flowers add charm and can give the exterior a cohesive look. Provide places where buyers can envision themselves entertaining or relaxing. For example, top an existing concrete-slab patio with flagstone, creating the perfect setting for an outdoor dining area.

Universal design

If you know that your property is located in a neighborhood that attracts older residents, you may want to consider making the entry more accessible. Making your property's entry welcoming and accessible to everyone isn't difficult, but it does require smart planning. Steps and thresholds should be no more than ½ inch high. Ideally the front door can be accessed without climbing steps at all. Include a covered entry to protect visitors from the elements. Equip the front door with an easy-to-use lever instead of a knob; consider an electronic lockset instead of a key. Exterior door openings should be at least 32 inches wide; 36 inches is better. Doors with swing-clear hinges allow full use of the doorway.

Windows and doors

Ensure that all windows and doors are freshly painted and in good working order. Replace missing screens on windows and repair broken screen doors. If windows are rotted or in poor working order, replace them too.

Select window and door fashions

Are you wondering which treatment will work best for the windows in your home? Find the illustration on the following pages that best matches your window design and check out your options. Note that for property flips, window treatments are most important in rooms where privacy and light control are issues. In gathering spaces, they serve as decorative accents and can be a worthwhile investment if the window is the room's primary focal point. If your side or backyard view is less than inviting, you may want to disguise it with sheer panels or light-filtering shades. If the window itself is unattractive, the right treatment can make it a selling point instead of an eyesore.

Single windows

If you're dressing a single window, will it be more attractive if you make it appear larger and more noticeable or have it fade into the background? Add fullness with flowing curtains or tiebacks, as shown in Figures A, D, and E. If the window's scale matches the other elements in the room, use a top treatment as shown in Figure C, or a simple panel as shown in Figure B. If you don't want to draw attention to your window, treat it with a simple shade or blind in a color that matches the walls or woodwork in the room.

Multiple/matched series

A series of identical windows invites sunlight into your home's interior. These windows offer a variety of decorating options. To keep the focus on the view and the architecture of the window, use a top treatment as shown in Figure F. If you need a treatment that offers more privacy or light control, mount shades or blinds inside each window's moldings as shown in Figures G and H. Individual interior mountings offer a crisp, tailored look. If you prefer a fuller treatment, fabric options range from to-the-floor draperies as shown in Figure I to draperies topped with cornices or valances as shown in Figures J and K.

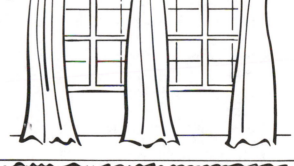

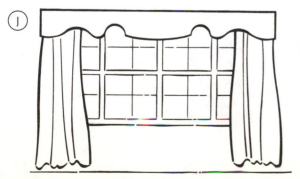

Corner windows

As shown in Figures L through P, mirror image window dressings allow you to treat corner windows separately but achieve the effect of a single design. Be sure draperies or vertical blinds draw to the outside and blinds raise and lower without clashing. In small spaces, avoid fabrics with busy patterns and contrasting colors; instead match treatments to wall color to blend them into the background and expand the room.

Bay and bow windows

Like the corner window, the windows within a bay or a bow may demand separate but equal treatments as illustrated in Figures Q through U. To keep things trim and tailored, use shades, blinds, or shutters as shown in Figures Q and R. To draw more attention to your treatment, add a swag or valance as shown in Figures S and T. For a formal look, install framing draperies across the front of the window alcove, as shown in Figure U. For a curving bow window, use a flexible rod that can follow the curve in one sweep.

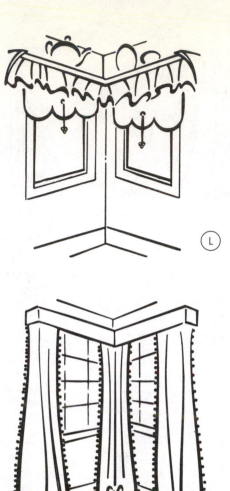

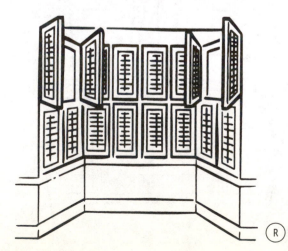

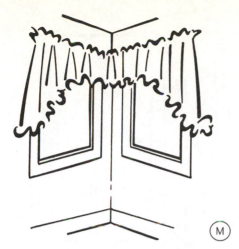

M

N

P

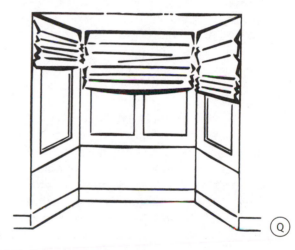

Q

T

U

(V)

Sliding doors

Sliding doors present a unique decorating challenge. Because they are doors, your covering must allow them to open and close freely. Yet, like windows, they require a dressing that enhances their appearance and provides adequate privacy and light control. Blinds, fabric shades, draperies, and sliding panels are all options to consider as illustrated in Figures V through Z. Make sure they mount at the ceiling line and draw totally to the side so the walkway will be clear. To control light throughout the day, use a layered treatment of draperies over blinds.

High windows

The goal in treating high windows is to visually enlarge them with long treatments or make them appear purposeful by placing a piece of furniture beneath them. If the room is full of horizontal elements such as beds and dressers, add visual interest with a vertical to-the-floor treatment, as shown in Figures 4 and 5. To make windows appear larger, install a row of fixed shutters below the windows and operable shutters on the actual panes as shown in Figure 2.

(Y)

(2)

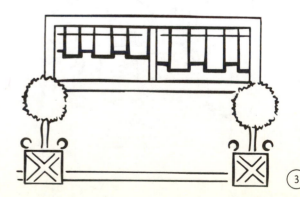

(3)

W

X

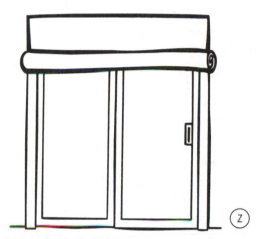

Z

1

4

5

Casement windows

Standard casement windows open in or out and can be treated similarly to single windows as shown in Figures 6 through 10. Newer windows offer fold-down cranks that do not interfere with window treatments. If your window has a full handle crank, your covering should mount to the outside so that it falls clear of the window's cranking mechanism. Swinging rods as shown in Figure 6, or fixed curtain rods as shown in Figure 7, offer solutions. If you choose tiebacks, dress each window in a drapery panel that draws to the outer edge of each window where tieback hardware is installed. For inward-swinging casement windows, you'll need a treatment that doesn't interfere with the window's operation. Inset the curtains or blinds far enough above the windows' molding so that they can be raised high enough to allow the windows to open freely.

French doors

French doors, as shown in Figures 11 through 15, combine the challenges of outfitting inward swinging casement windows with those of covering sliding glass doors. There are two basic solutions for these doors: Affix your treatment to each individual door panel or opt for a treatment that clears the doors by drawing completely to the side or top. For a look that won't interfere with the architecture, mount blinds or shades on each door. If your decorating style calls for a softer touch, consider shirred lace panels or door-mounted tiebacks. If you prefer traditional drapery treatments, make sure the rod extends well beyond the frame so draperies can be drawn out of the way of the doors. If your French doors are topped with transoms, leave the upper windows bare, or treat the doors and windows as one, with the rod installed at the ceiling line.

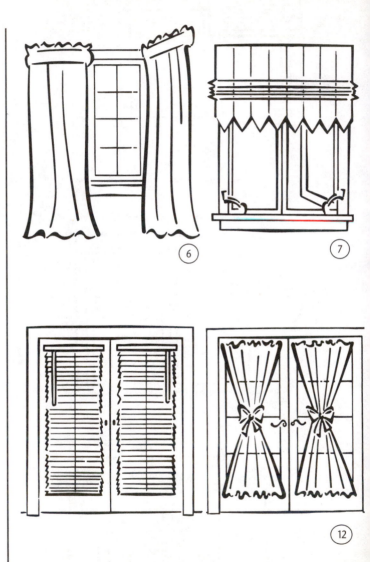

When dressing a casement window with **a full crank handle,** choose a treatment that **mounts** to the outside.

Shapely windows

The trick to treating windows with sculptural curves and unusual shapes is to flow with the shape of the opening. Where privacy and light control are needed, use custom-fitted shades, blinds, or even shirred fabric. Palladian-inspired half-round windows are most spectacular when minimally dressed. For example, in a bedroom add a privacy treatment to the lower part and leave the top half-round bare for maximum natural light.

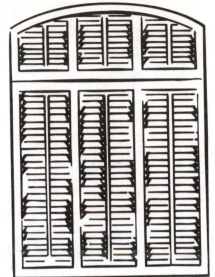

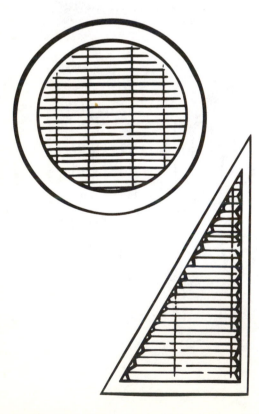

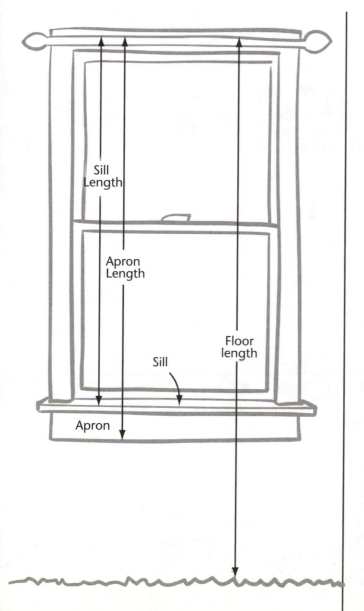

Sill Length

Apron Length

Sill

Floor length

Apron

Measuring guide

The key to purchasing ready-mades or made-to-order draperies, blinds, or shades is learning how to measure your windows accurately. To ensure accuracy, use a quality steel tape measure. Decide whether you want your treatments to fit inside the window (an inside mount) or to cover your window (an outside mount). Measure accordingly.

INSIDE MOUNT

For an inside mount, measure the opening width at the top, middle, and bottom, recording the narrowest measurement. Do the same for the length, recording the longest measurement. Round to the nearest $\frac{1}{8}$ inch.

OUTSIDE MOUNT

For an outside mount, measure the opening width and add at least 3 inches to each side of the window opening if there's room. Measure the opening length and add at least 2 inches in height for hardware and any overlap.

DRAPERY MEASUREMENTS

To measure the drop for draperies, measure windows from where you intend to install the rod to where you want draperies to fall. For width, measure the full length of the rod. To calculate the length of a scarf or a single fabric piece, measure the distance from the bottom of the drapery ring or the top of the rod to the desired length of the scarf. Multiply that measurement by 2 and add 10 inches to each side if you want the fabric to puddle on the floor. Measure the width of the area to be covered and add that figure to the length for the total yardage needed.

CHAPTER 3: HOW TO
MAKEOVER
magic

Here's the help you need to decide which jobs to do yourself and which to hire out. Discover how to weather the process and get step-by-step instructions for popular projects.

Should you hire the pros?

Have you witnessed this all-too-common scenario? A new real estate investor gets excited about an ambitious project and tears into walls or floors. Once the demolition is finished and some initial work is done, however, it becomes difficult to keep up the energy level. After a long day of work, the TV and the armchair are much more appealing than the tool belt. So the house remains an unfinished mess for weeks or months longer than was originally proposed in the remodeling plan. If the investor is living in the house, life can become even more stressful with the chaotic clutter of renovations.

Remodeling always takes longer and is more difficult than new construction because you run into many obstacles. This is especially true of older homes with plaster walls.

Remodeling always takes longer and is more difficult than new construction.

To gauge whether you are really ready to take on a large project, first try some modest repairs or installations. Once you are convinced that you have the needed skills and can complete projects in a timely manner, it is probably OK to attempt a more serious job.

Work safely

Home improvement projects can be dangerous. Many tasks call for sharp tools or power tools that can cause injuries. Follow these rules for safety:

Before using a power tool, read its instruction manual and follow the precautions. Tighten adjustments; check that the guard works before you operate a tool.

Keep power tools dry and plug them into grounded outlets. Take care not to cut the cord.

Keep fingers well away from a power blade. Clamp small pieces of wood before cutting them, rather than holding them.

Wear work gloves when handling rough materials, but take them off and roll up your sleeves if operating a power tool.

Wear eye and ear protection when cutting with a power tool.

Unplug a power saw before changing the blade.

When working on wiring, shut off the power to the circuit first. When working with plumbing, shut off the water first.

When working on a ladder, don't lean out to either side. Keep your body weight between the sides of the ladder. It may take longer to get off the ladder and move it to reach farther, but it is well worth your time. Falls are one of the most common causes of injuries in the home.

Avoid physical strain

You may not be accustomed to physical construction, so it is quite possible for you to strain muscles or joints while engaging in remodeling work. Often you feel fine while doing the work but wake up the next day in pain. Don't take chances. Follow these guidelines to avoid injury:

Don't overexert yourself when lifting heavy objects or when repeatedly lifting lighter loads. Get a helper to do some of the work and take plenty of breaks.

Working in an awkward position can put a strain on your back and other areas of your body. Take the time to move or arrange things so that you are as comfortable as possible.

Lift with your legs, not your back. When picking up a heavy object, keep your back as upright and straight as possible. Bend your knees to reach the object you want to pick up.

Professionals often charge what look to be astronomical rates. However, before you decide to save money by doing it yourself, consider all the factors: A pro can probably do things much more quickly than you. If you can make extra money by working overtime or taking on extra work in your field, chances are it will be easier to do so and hand over the remodeling project to a pro.

Some contractors are willing to lower their prices if the homeowner/investor agrees to perform certain tasks. This sort of "sweat equity" arrangement can be beneficial, but only if the terms are clearly spelled out. The contract should state precisely what you will do and when you will do it. Ideally there should be a clear division between the contractor's work and your responsibilities. For instance, you might agree to

MAKEOVER MAGIC

STRATEGIES

In remodeling, it's all small stuff and it's all worth sweating.

install moldings and paint the walls, or install the flooring. (Step-by-step instructions for all these projects are on the following pages.)

Determine whether the contractor carries insurance. Every contractor's insurance should cover property damage, liability, and workers' compensation. If the contractor is not covered, you could be liable for hefty fees in case of an accident. Ask to see a certificate of insurance.

Writing the contract

Once you've chosen a bid, negotiate a contract. It should have the following important elements.

• An itemized list that details all work to be done. Specify the type and brand of materials and

finishes to be used. Include a specific timetable. You may want to work in a penalty for late completion, or a reward for early completion.

• A fixed-price contract that specifies the total cost of the job. A cost-plus contract should specify the cost of materials and labor. Payments should be dependent on work completed.

• A right of rescission permitting you to back out of a contract within 72 hours of signing it.

• A certificate of insurance guaranteeing that the contractor is covered. Include in the contract a warranty ensuring that the labor and materials are free of defects for at least a year.

• An arbitration clause that delineates the method for resolving disputes.

Find and hire a great contractor

To achieve a happy relationship and professional results, follow these steps to find and hire a pro:

Get the names of several contractors by asking friends for recommendations. Take a look at examples of their work to see if it meets your expectations.

Obtain rough estimates from the contractors who interest you. This

information will help you narrow the field of candidates and enlighten you about how candid they are about money matters.

For a major job, get at least three bids. Give a contractor a week or so to produce the bid. Read the bids closely; they should detail the materials to be used. If one contractor is much lower than the others, check that he or she is truly

capable and experienced.

When accepting bids, find out how long the contractor has been in business—the longer the better. Ask who finances the contractor's company (usually a bank). Ask the bank about the contractor's solvency. You don't want a contractor to go bankrupt during your project.

Survive your remodeling

If you plan to live in your house while you remodel it for resale, brace yourself. As bad as you may think the house looks now, just wait until you see it with exposed studs, dangling electrical wires, and decades-old insulation flopping to the floor. Your mental and emotional health will fare much better if you're confident about the results.

For that reason, take plenty of time to assess your needs and craft a design. Hire an architect and contractors you trust to do the job right, or be certain you can finish the job yourself in a timely manner and with professional results. It's a good idea to visit other work sites so you can see what a remodeling job in process really looks like.

Sweat the small stuff
In remodeling it's all small stuff and it's all worth sweating. The key is to sweat about it during the planning stages and not while standing in the middle of a construction zone at 2 a.m.

You can save yourself a gallon of perspiration by packing away anything that has value to you— sentimental or otherwise—to avoid breakage.

Remember nature will call
The most important rule of living in a remodeling? Maintain at least one functioning toilet and faucet in the house at all times. If you must shut down all of the toilets for an extended period, plan on staying someplace else. The cost of the hotel room will seem cheaper with every flush.

Plan for cooking and cleanups
When deciding whether to overhaul the kitchen, your first concern likely will be cost. Your second concern should be how to feed yourself and others who live in the household. Set up a temporary kitchen in another room, complete with refrigerator, microwave oven, and several small appliances. Keep in mind that if you don't invest in paper plates and plastic utensils, you'll likely be doing at least some of the dishes in the bathroom sink or the bathtub. Also stock up on convenience foods, such as squeeze-bottle mayonnaise and precooked bacon.

Protect the children
Kids and power tools don't mix. Nor do kids and stacks of lumber, kids and exposed electrical wires, or kids and construction workers with jobs to do. Perhaps your most difficult task may be finding ways to keep young children safe. Simple preventive measures, such as shutting doors and asking the workers to put their tools away, can eliminate obvious dangers. Diversion tactics can take care of the rest. Swimming lessons, trips to the park, and weeklong stays at Grandma's can keep kids away from harm.

Keep it clean
Construction dust is maddeningly fine. Plan to seal off the work areas from the rest of the house with plastic sheeting (replacing it for each step in the process— demolition, construction, drywall, and painting). Also set up a back entrance so workers can come and go as needed without disturbing the hanging plastic or tramping through the house. Still, you can expect a certain amount of drywall dust to filter into the rest of the house.

To head off postconstruction dust, clean the rest of the house as frequently as possible during the project. Try to go over the house regularly with a vacuum and damp mop, regardless of whether debris is visible.

Tool talk

To complete basic do-it-yourself projects, you may find the following tools handy to keep onsite:

Basic tools

- Work surface (such as a pair of sawhorses topped with a 4×8-foot sheet of plywood)
- Tape measure
- Chalkline
- Plumb line
- Carpenter's level
- Framing square
- Power mitersaw
- Jigsaw
- Coping saw
- Keyhole saw
- Utility knife
- Miter box and backsaw
- Electric drill
- Router
- Electric screwdriver with assorted phillips and slot tips
- Hammer
- Nail set
- Pliers (locking pliers, side-cutting pliers)
- Adjustable wrench
- Flat pry bar
- Adjustable clamps
- Assorted files (rasp, wood file)
- Stud finder
- Drywall taping knives
- Caulking gun

Also familiarize yourself with the tools your local rental store may have available, such as a compressor equipped with a nail gun, paint sprayer, tile saw, or drywall lift. If you know that you will use expensive equipment only once or twice, it can be more economical to rent rather than buy.

Working up to code

Most likely a local building department in your city or county has the authority to determine how all new buildings must be done in your locale. (Some rural areas have no building department; ask county authorities what to do in this case.)

A building department has exhaustive and detailed lists of regulations (codes) covering remodeling projects, including wiring, plumbing, roofing, structural framing, and the installation of permanent appliances (such as air conditioners).

Though dealing with it may seem a hassle, your building department is there for your protection. The regulations are not arbitrary but are based on decades of experience. A project that is built to code will likely be safe and durable; a project built without observing codes may be dangerous and flimsy. When it comes time to sell, you could be in legal trouble if it is found that significant work was done on the house without an inspection.

Follow regulations

The consequences of ignoring these regulations can be harsh. You may be required to have the work professionally checked or you may be ordered to tear out the work and start again. Personnel at insurance companies may balk at paying a claim for damage done to your house if you have not followed regulations.

As a general rule, the building department and its codes come into play whenever a new permanent structure is built or when new electrical, plumbing, or gas service is installed.

So, for instance, you probably do not need a permit to replace an existing toilet, sink, tub, or

Though dealing with it may seem a hassle, your building department is there for your protection.

light fixture. However, if you run new electrical cable or new pipes in order to install fixtures where there were none before, then you need a permit. A sand-laid patio (rather than one that involves a concrete slab), a simple storage shed with no wiring or plumbing, or a small deck that is not attached to the house may be exempt from inspections. However, always check with the building department to be sure.

Most codes are based on national standards but may be modified to suit local conditions. For example, construction techniques required for earthquake-prone areas are different from those for other areas, and construction in areas that are consistently wet may require weather-resistant materials in outdoor applications.

Create detailed drawings

Whenever you're undertaking home improvements, make sure you know what local building codes apply to your project. In addition, be aware that codes may vary significantly from town to town—even within the same county.

Working with a building department involves several steps. First go to your local building department and ask for general guidelines for the project you are proposing. They may have copies of regulations for common projects or they may direct you to reference works.

Second, make a detailed, neat drawing of the project, including a materials list, and show it to an inspector in the office. The inspector may ask for changes and clarifications.

Finally, once your plans are approved, one or more inspections will be scheduled—typically one inspection for the rough installation and one for the finished project.

Working with an inspector

Some inspectors are friendlier than others, but they are all there for your protection. Treat the inspector with respect, and you will likely have a mutually beneficial relationship.

• Go to your inspector with a plan to be approved or amended; don't expect the building department to plan the job for you.

• To avoid wasting the inspector's time, find out as much information as possible about your project before you talk to the inspector. Consult the building department's literature, national codes, and how-to books.

• Draw plans that are close to professional quality. Everything should be to scale and should be drawn clearly. You may need to make a bird's-eye view and one or more other drawings.

• Never argue with an inspector. Always be courteous. Follow instructions. Assume the inspector knows more than you do. Inspectors are wary of homeowners, because many take on projects beyond their abilities. Show the inspector you are serious about doing things the right way.

• Be sure you clearly understand when you need to have inspections. Do not cover up any work that needs to be inspected.

• If you are hiring a contractor, it is usually best to have the contractor, not you, deal directly with the inspector.

Most homes built after World War II have walls made of drywall, which is a fairly durable material.

Identify a bearing wall

One of the first things people often consider when buying a house—whether it's one they plan to live in for a while or to fix up and resell—is whether to remove a wall or two and create larger, freeflowing rooms that are ideal for entertaining.

Every wall fits one of two structural categories—bearing walls, which support a load above, and nonbearing walls, which support only themselves. If you remove a bearing wall or make a big opening in a bearing wall, you could literally bring down the house.

To determine whether a wall is bearing or not, do some sleuthing in the basement or attic—wherever there are exposed joists or rafters. If the joists run parallel to the wall in question, you can be sure it's not a bearing wall.

However, if the joists are perpendicular to the wall, you can reasonably expect that the wall is bearing a load.

If you cannot see the joists, use a stud finder to locate them and determine the direction they run.

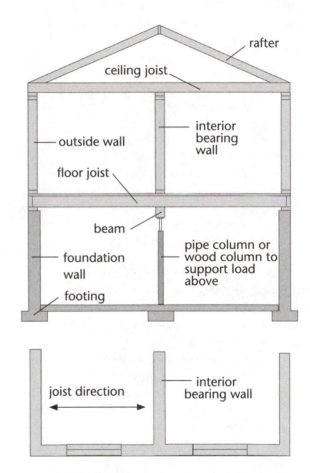

■ Inspect joists to see which direction they run. If the joists run perpendicular to the wall as shown, the wall is likely bearing a load.

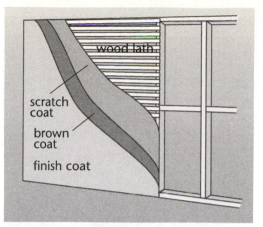

■ Plaster over wood lath

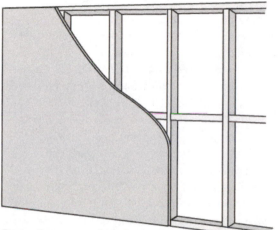

■ Drywall over wood studs

Know your home's walls

It's wise to find out what type of walls your property has before you buy. (Check out Tristen Moffett's experience with plaster-and-lath walls on page 43.) These illustrations show some possible options that you might discover. No one wall type is necessarily better than the other, but drywall can be easier to repair and more readily accepts the addition of tile and other materials.

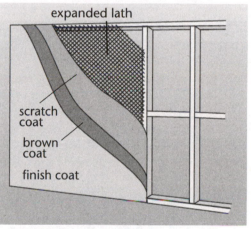

■ Plaster over expanded lath

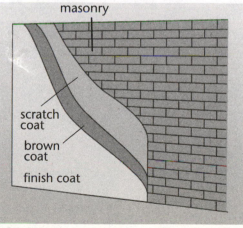

■ Plaster over masonry

Freshen every room with paint

Probably no other decorating tool is as effective for its price as paint. For about $20 a gallon, you can completely transform a room from dull to vibrant. Follow these guidelines for achieving professional results.

Prepare the room

Although getting a room ready to paint may take time and energy, all the steps noted here are necessary for a successful project. The work you do to prepare a room correctly prior to painting will be well worth it.

To begin, remove anything from the room that is breakable, including small items such as knickknacks, and move all furnishings to the center of the room. Cover the furnishings and floors with drop cloths to protect them from paint splatters. Using a screwdriver, remove all outlet and switchplate covers, as well as anything else attached to the walls. To avoid losing the screws that accompany the outlet and switchplate covers, tape them to the back of the covers.

Unless you are painting on new drywall, you may need to smooth out any blemishes with 80-grit sandpaper or fill in any imperfections with surface compound (see *opposite* for more detailed information). Once the compound is dry, sand it smooth. When you finish sanding, sweep or vacuum any lingering dust to prevent it from sticking to the wet paint. Wipe down all moldings, including baseboards and casings, with a lint-free cloth to remove dust and debris.

Remove popcorn ceilings

Highly textured ceiling surfaces, often called "popcorn" or "cottage cheese" texture, seem to be universally despised by homeowners, but they are also everywhere. (The Bernal-Martyns, see page 20, and The Moffett Group, see page 36, decided to remove this texture.)

Before attempting to remove ceiling texture, find out if it contains asbestos. Though a contractor usually can tell what the material is made of, don't rely on a visual inspection. Instead look in the phone book under "Asbestos Removal" to find a qualified expert. If your ceiling contains asbestos, it should be removed by a firm that specializes in the procedure.

Homes built since the 1970s are more likely to have ceiling texture made of painted cellulose. You can remove this material, but it is a dusty, messy job. Wear a dust mask and lay down disposable coverings—dampened cellulose will dry and stick to anything.

Working in one small area at a time, use a hand pump sprayer or a roller to wet down the ceiling with warm water. Using a stiff, wide putty knife, carefully scrape off the dampened texture. Avoid gouging the surface and you will spend less time later spackling. When you finish scraping and touching up, sand the ceiling. Then apply primer and top coats.

Repair the walls

Make sure the time and effort you have spent painting will pay off in a great return on your real estate investment. Repair any dents, cracks, or peeling spots on the walls before you paint them. This will give you a smooth surface on which to paint, resulting in an even application. Regardless of which type of repair you have to undertake, make sure you prime the area before painting.

CRACKS

To patch plaster cracks, first undercut wide cracks to make them broader at the bottom; this helps lock in the filler materials. Blow out any loose plaster. Wet the crack with a sponge, then pack compound into it with a putty knife. Use patching plaster to fill any large holes and cracks. After 24 hours, wet the area again with a sponge, and level it off with a second coat of patching material. When dry, sand and prime.

DENTS

To fill dents in drywall, clean any debris out of the depression and sand lightly to roughen the surface. Pack the dent with surface or joint compound; use surface compound for large dents because it shrinks less. For deep depressions and holes, affix fiberglass tape to the damaged area before applying the compound. Let the patch dry overnight, then sand with 150-grit sandpaper or smooth by wiping with a damp sponge. Then prime the surface.

FLAKING OR PEELED SPOTS

If there are flaky or peeled spots on your walls, oil-base paint that turned brittle over time could be the culprit—or the original surface may not have been properly dulled or cleaned, causing poor paint adhesion. Scrape off loose paint, then sand. Clean interior surfaces with water and a mild household detergent; rinse. Fill any gaps or holes with filler or caulk. Prime. Paint that is older than 20 years may contain lead. If you suspect that the old paint contains lead, never sand it and try not to disturb it. The best solution may be to simply paint over it. If the paint is peeling or otherwise unsound, contact a company that specializes in lead abatement.

WALLPAPER

Although you can successfully paint over wallpapered walls (See "Painting special surfaces," page 164), it is usually best to remove wallpaper before painting. There are many excellent wallpaper strippers in gel and liquid forms available at hardware and home improvement centers. Follow the manufacturer's instructions for the product you have chosen. For a natural solution, mix 1 part vinegar to 1 part water. Put the solution in a spray bottle and spray onto the wallpaper; peel or scrape away as with commercial products.

PAINTING GUIDE

Protect with tape

Apply low-tack, quick-release painter's tape to moldings to protect these surfaces from paint and to avoid gaps between the wall and molding that would reveal the old wall color. Although painter's tape is more expensive than regular masking tape, it won't leave a sticky residue. You can tape drop cloths to the baseboard to help protect the floor.

■ **Shop the paint supplies aisle of any home improvement store to find a large assortment of tape options. Different widths are available, so you can easily protect trimwork around the room.**

■ **Select the best brush for the job you're doing. Angled brushes are ideal for cutting in or trimming edges with paint where walls meet the ceiling and abut trim.**

Choose the best brush

For basic painting, all you need are good-quality synthetic- or nylon-bristle brushes with flat and angled bristles, a roller and roller cover, and a paint tray. When shopping for paintbrushes, choose high-quality ones. Although they may cost more, they are more durable, and you'll be pleased with the results of your labor. What makes a quality brush? If more than two bristles come out when you tug, it is poorly constructed. Look for a brush with flagged bristles (which look like split ends of hair and hold more paint) and a sturdy,

Preparation is the key to professional results when painting. Always give this step first priority.

noncorrosive ferrule (the metal band wrapped around the bristles and handle). A quality brush measures half again as long as its width: A 2-inch wide brush should have 3-inch long bristles. Also find a brush that is comfortable to hold.

Buy a variety of brushes ranging from 4 inches wide for walls and ceilings to 1 inch wide for mullions, although a 1½-inch and a 2½-inch brush are appropriate for most painting jobs. Tapered, or angled, brushes are perfect for painting narrow areas of windows, doors, and molding. The shaped bristles allow you to paint clean edges against trim. These brushes have long, thin handles that you hold like a pencil.

Use only synthetic-bristle brushes with latex paint. Natural-hair bristles will frizz if exposed to the water in the paint. You can use natural- or synthetic-bristle brushes with alkyd (oil-base) paint, although natural bristles provide a better finish.

Rolling along

Use short-nap rollers for smooth surfaces and long-nap rollers for rough surfaces. A quality roller will quickly return to its original shape. If you separate the nap on the roller cover, you shouldn't be able to see its cardboard core. (If you do, it might not be dense enough to deliver a smooth coat.) As with brushes, use synthetic rollers for water-base paint and synthetic or natural-fiber rollers for oil-base paint.

Search for smart buys

Choose a variety of quality paintbrushes for your projects. Flat brushes work for general painting, whereas angle-bristle, or tapered, brushes are ideal for trimwork. Store brushes in their original, protective plastic covers to help the bristles maintain their shape.

You may find that these additional products can simplify the job of painting:

Specially designed roller covers with the nap running around the end can allow you to paint into corners.

A paint mixer attachment for a power drill makes mixing cans of paint quick and easy—and eliminates the need for wood and plastic stir sticks.

Reusable paint can covers help reduce mess and waste when you pour paint from the can into a paint tray.

Plastic liners for paint trays and small paint buckets are inexpensive and make cleanup a snap: These disposable liners can be thrown away after use, eliminating the need to scrub paint from a tray or bucket.

Primer pointers

Whether the room you are painting has never been painted or you are painting over a wall that has already been painted, consider using primer before repainting. Here are tips for success:

• Primer is necessary on new or weathered wood or on other raw surfaces. It is wise to use primer on an uneven or deteriorated painted surface or on a stripped surface.

• Primers and sealers come in latex and alkyd (oil-base); your primer and paint should always have the same base.

• Some primers are formulated for special circumstances, such as stain-blocking, drywall, and metal primers.

• If there are ink and crayon marks or water stains on the surfaces to be painted, use a stain-blocking primer on the walls prior to painting. This will prevent marks and stains from bleeding through the paint finish.

• For more complete coverage, have primer tinted the same color as the paint that will be applied over it.

Estimating paint needs

So that you don't waste your budget, buy only the amount of paint you will need. For help in estimating your paint needs, turn to page 234.

Selecting paint

When purchasing paints, you will find numerous brands at various prices. Think quality: Premium paints contain more paint solids (pigments and binders) and less liquid. They are more durable, adhesive, fade-resistant, and uniform in color and sheen—often requiring fewer coats for complete coverage. Premium paints are a better long-term investment because they generally require repainting in 10 years; less expensive paint may need recoating in four years.

When you browse the paint aisle at a paint, hardware, or home improvement store, in addition to various brands you will no doubt see latex and alkyd (oil-base) paints. Keep in mind that water-base paints are safer to use than oil-base paints and cleanup is a snap with water and mild soap. Regardless, oil-base paints have advantages over latex in some circumstances.

Low-odor, fast-drying latex paints have a water base (quality paints have no more than 50 percent water content). Compared with alkyd paints, the color in latex paint is less likely to fade, chalk, crack, or grow mildew. Recent technological advances have made latex paints as adhesive as and longer lasting than oil-base paints; they also resist cracking and chipping better than alkyd paints. Besides general interior painting, latex is the best choice for exterior wood, new stucco, and masonry, or weathered aluminum and vinyl siding.

Oil-base paints are made of petroleum distillates, pigments, and resins; most of the liquid portion is petroleum solvent. The best paints have no more than 30 percent solvent. Oil-base paints are often more durable than latex paints, but they can be more difficult to use. Although oil-base paint has

Tinting primer with your top coat color may help you avoid a second or third coat.

excellent adhesion and fair durability, it's more likely to harden, become brittle, and yellow over time. It has a strong odor (requiring that you use it only in well-ventilated areas) and must be cleaned with mineral spirits or other solvents, including paint thinner, and its drying time is long (from 8 to 24 hours). Alkyd paint is your best choice for exterior surfaces with heavy chalking or when you repaint a surface over four or more layers of old oil-base paint. Do not use oil-base paint on fresh masonry or galvanized iron—it fails quickly.

You can paint latex over oil-base paint, although you must use an oil-base topcoat if you are painting over four or more layers of old oil-base paint. Avoid painting oil-base over latex because the latex underneath is flexible and will expand and contract, causing an oil-base top coat to crack. To test which paint you have, rub mineral spirits on the surface; oil-base paint will generally dissolve, whereas latex will be unaffected by the solvent.

Choose the best finish

Paint—both latex and oil-base—generally comes in four finishes: flat, eggshell, semigloss, and gloss. Paint finishes are measured in degree of gloss, or sheen. The finish has nothing to do with the actual color of a paint—just how much light it reflects. When selecting a finish, keep in mind that the higher the gloss, the more durable it is. If you are painting over an already painted surface, you can paint gloss paint over a glossy surface, but you must first dull the surface with sandpaper so the top coat has something to hold on to.

Flat paint has no glossy finish. As the least reflective of all finishes, flat paint is dull and hides imperfections. Modern flat paint is easier to clean than in the past, but it won't withstand repeated washing and wear. Use flat paint on ceilings and walls in living rooms, bedrooms, and dining rooms. As a rule it offers easier, better coverage than other finishes and costs less.

Eggshell finish, also known as satin and low-luster, is between a flat and semigloss finish. Use this sheen where you would use flat but want easier cleanup, such as in kids' rooms.

Semigloss is more reflective than eggshell and should be used on kitchen and bathroom walls that will be exposed to moisture. Keep in mind that a semigloss or gloss sheen may appear a shade lighter than your paint chip because of the way it reflects light.

Gloss is the most durable and stain-resistant sheen of all. This finish is best for high-traffic and dirty areas, because it is easiest to clean, but it is also most likely to highlight surface imperfections. Use semigloss or gloss on trim, doors, and cabinets.

PAINTING GUIDE

Applying paint

Now that you have prepared the room for painting, gathered the best tools, and selected the right paint, you can begin painting.

Work in a well-ventilated area to reduce adverse affects from paint fumes (even latex paints have an odor in a small enclosed space). Open windows and turn on fans. Consider wearing a dust mask and goggles to prevent lung and eye irritation.

Mix paint well with a paint stirrer or a mixing attachment for an electric drill. Stir from the bottom of the can to mix the clearer layer at the top with the heavier pigmented material that often settles to the bottom.

■ **To evenly cover the wall, start by rolling the paint on in a W pattern as shown. Fill in with long floor-to-ceiling strokes.**

If you are painting the ceiling, paint it before doing the walls. Use a 2½-inch angled brush to outline the ceiling. This technique is known as "cutting in." Paint the ceiling with a roller and an extension handle to avoid standing on a ladder. If the ceiling is textured, you may need to use a paint sprayer, which is a power tool that lets you spray paint onto a surface with a hose and nozzle. (See "Remove popcorn ceilings," on page 156.)

Decide on paint additives

These products that can help with common painting problems:

Paint extenders and conditioners. If you have problems with brush marks showing, add a paint extender, which conditions the paint and improves brushability and workability.

Mildewcide additive. If you are painting an area that has a tendency to become wet, such as walls near a bathroom shower, in the basement, or around the kitchen or laundry room sink, you may want to use a mildewcide.

Mildewcide is a chemical additive that prevents mildew from growing on paint, although it doesn't kill existing mildew. It usually comes in liquid form and can be added to paint—use extreme caution when adding and mixing. Paint that already contains mildewcide mixed in by the manufacturer is more effective than a mixture you've made yourself; check paint labels to see if the paint you have chosen contains the additive.

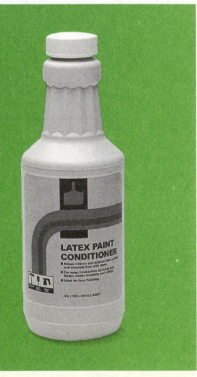

LATEX PAINT CONDITIONER

■ For a clean edge use an angle-bristle brush when cutting in. Leave an "airy" edge, which allows the cut-in stripe to blend in when you paint the entire wall; a crisp line can be more difficult to cover.

■ Holding a brush correctly is one of the keys to successful painting—and it reduces hand fatigue.

Cutting in

As with ceilings, you will need to cut in all walls. Cutting in is used for sharp edges around windows, where a wall meets the ceiling and other walls, and around moldings. Use an angle-bristle brush for this purpose to ensure a clean edge in areas that may be difficult to reach with a roller.

To paint, dampen the brush slightly with water if using latex paint, paint thinner if using oil; blot off any excess. Load the brush by dipping one-third of its bristles into the paint. Lift the bristles out of the paint, then gently tap them against the paint can's rim to remove excess paint (paint should not drip from the bristles as you paint). Cut in around all the walls and openings; let dry. Cut in again for a second coat if necessary; let dry.

Rolling on

After the second coat of trim paint has dried, it is time to fill in the outlined area with a roller. Dampen the roller slightly if using latex. Dip the roller in a tray full of paint and roll it up the tray's ramp until the cover is saturated but not dripping. Paint strokes in a W pattern for even coverage and distribution of the paint, *opposite top*. Once a wall

is covered with diagonal strokes, use long floor-to-ceiling strokes to fill in any uncovered areas. As you roll the paint on, be sure to overlap still-wet areas to prevent visible roll marks. After each wall is painted, let dry. Make sure surfaces are dry before applying a second coat. A premature second coat could lift up the first coat.

Finishing up

As soon as you are finished painting, peel away the painter's tape from the molding and trim. This will allow you to clean up any smears on the molding while they are still wet.

Before cleaning up and storing your tools, take a step back and evaluate your work. If you see splotches on the ceiling, for example, or areas that didn't receive even coverage, touch them up now.

Defeat drips

If a paint drip has hardened on a wall, sand or scrape it down. If it's still tacky, press a piece of masking tape gently over the flaw, then pull it off. Once the paint is dry, sand smooth and touch up with fresh paint.

PAINTING GUIDE

With proper preparation, you can renew almost any surface in the house with paint.

Painting special surfaces

Almost every home contains surfaces other than drywall or plaster that could benefit from a fresh coat of paint. You can may be surprised that you can paint these surfaces:

CONCRETE. Thoroughly clean the concrete using a scrub brush. If there are any oil spots, apply a degreasing solution according to the product directions; let dry. Use epoxy paints, which dry to a hard finish and come in water- and oil-base formulas, or cement paints. To prevent backaches from bending over when painting a concrete floor or patio, use a roller with an extension handle.

LAMINATE COUNTERTOPS. Painting these surfaces should be considered a temporary measure because of the high wear they typically receive. For longest wear use a special laminate paint, or use epoxy paint or a bonding primer beneath wall paint.

MASONRY. You can paint brick (such as on a fireplace), stucco, and concrete block using the same procedure as for painting concrete. First use a stiff brush to remove dirt and chalk. You can also thoroughly clean the surface with a trisodium phosphate (TSP) cleaner (available at home improvement stores) and a wire brush. Avoid painting masonry less than 30 days old. If you must, wet it down and brush on acrylic sealer while the surface is still wet (remember this isn't necessary for masonry older than 30 days). When the surface is dry, paint it with a high-quality latex floor paint.

TILE. Choose epoxy paint for maximum adhesion to nonporous surfaces such as ceramic tile, or use a bonding primer beneath gloss or semigloss latex paint. Painted tile is more likely to endure on a wall than on a countertop or entryway floor. For even coverage, paint the grout and the tiles rather than attempting to paint just the tiles.

VINYL FLOOR. First prepare the floor with a trisodium phosphate (TSP) cleaner; this will take the gloss off the vinyl surface and help the paint to adhere. Apply a stain-blocking primer and then paint with an extremely durable acrylic paint. On vinyl flooring use wall paint or porch-and-deck paint topped with several coats of clear polyurethane. An additional top coat every couple of years will ensure its durability and cleanability.

WALLPAPER. If you can remove the wallpaper and paste, do so. If not, wallpaper can usually be painted over with good results. First spot-test the wallpaper in an inconspicuous area to make sure it won't loosen when covered with primer and paint. Repair bubbles by slicing them open, then gluing them down. Flake off peeling edges and feather with surfacing compound. Use a stain-blocking primer to ensure that the wallpaper color does not bleed through the paint; use latex or oil-base paint.

WOOD FLOORS, PATIOS, AND DECKS. Some manufacturers make latex or oil-base paints formulated for floor surfaces. Many floor paints come only in factory colors, so if you want a custom color, use wall paint topped with layers of clear polyurethane. To paint outdoor projects, start with two coats of stain-blocking primer tinted to match your paint color, add any decorative painting you desire, and seal and protect wood from outdoor elements with a coat of varnish.

WOOD PANELING. Remove dirt or wax buildup with a high-strength household cleaner; rinse. Dull the glossy surface with sandpaper. Wipe with a damp rag to remove residue. Coat the surface with a stain-blocking primer; let dry. For the top coat use latex paint in a flat, satin, or semigloss finish.

WOOD VENEER. If the veneer is securely adhered to the substrate, you can paint the surface. Remove dirt or wax buildup; rinse. Use fine sandpaper to dull the surface so the paint will adhere. Wipe with a damp rag. Apply a stain-blocking primer tinted to match the paint color; let dry. Finish with latex paint.

Clean up

Clean and store your tools after you finish painting. Remove as much paint as possible from brushes or rollers by drawing a brush comb or wire brush through the bristles. Then work the bristles back and forth across newspaper. When using latex paint, wash the brush under running water, bending the bristles back and forth in the palm of your hand to work out all traces of paint. Always let the water run from the handle down to the bristles. For oil-base paint, dip brushes in paint thinner. Hang brushes and roller covers to dry completely, combing the bristles so they are straight. When dry, wrap brushes and roller covers in their original sleeves.

If you keep the leftover paint, tightly seal the can and store it upside down to prevent a top skin from forming. If you want to dispose of leftover latex paint, remove the lid from the can and let the paint air-dry away from children and pets. To speed the drying process, add cat litter. Discard dried paint with normal trash. If you have empty cans, clean them and put them in a recycling bin. If you have leftover oil-base paint, take it to a toxic waste drop-off center or to a household materials recycling center where unused paints are recycled.

Evaluate the colors

When you're choosing the color or colors for a room, remember these facts:

Drying time changes color. Paint usually dries darker than it appears when wet. For a more accurate view of what the color will look like when dry, paint a sample board of the same texture as the wall.

Light changes color. Move the sample board around the room, observing how it appears near natural and artificial light in the day and evening.

Sheen changes color. A flat, matte paint differs in look from the same color in a shiny, glossy finish. The shinier the color, the lighter it will look.

Texture affects color. Smooth surfaces reflect light, so a heavily textured wall will appear darker than a smooth wall that's the same color.

Colors affect one another. Move the sample board around the room, close to various furnishings or other elements to see how the paint color will "fit" in the room.

Install a laminate plank floor

For rooms in your property that need a quick facelift, there are few better updates than a laminate plank floor. In a weekend, even beginning do-it-yourselfers can transform the appearance of a room with durable flooring that offers the look of virtually any wood or stone surface—a feature most prospective buyers will appreciate.

TOOLS
- Pry bar
- Tape measure
- Circular saw or handsaw
- Jamb saw
- Hammer
- Nail set (to reinstall trim pieces)

MATERIALS
- Laminate flooring
- Underlayment (one roll covers approximately 100 square feet)
- Laminate floor installation kit (available at home centers and specialty retailers)
- Finishing nails (to reinstall trim pieces)

■ **Laminate planks successfully mimic the look of real hardwood flooring and other natural materials.**

Plan the project

Laminate flooring planks are manufactured with no actual hardwood or stone. Instead they feature a digital image of oak, maple, marble, or another natural material printed on paper. They are sandwiched between a protective coating and a core material that gives the plank the heft of a light board and lets it connect to adjoining planks.

Laminate flooring came to the North American market from Europe in the early 1990s and quickly caught on. The reason? Beauty and convenience. Fast, easy installation is a key attraction, but a laminate floor will charm your buyers with a look that closely mimics natural materials without all the maintenance. Be sure to point out to buyers that laminate

floors resist scuffing and denting, and they will never need to be refinished—unlike a real wood floor.

These floors are installed most often in kitchens and entryways, but they work well in other areas of the property—even bathrooms. If you choose laminate flooring for a bathroom, especially a kids' bath with lots of splashing, consider using a

Step-by-step

1. Acclimate the flooring to the room.

Flooring should sit in the room for at least 48 hours prior to installation, giving it time to expand or contract in relation to the room's temperature and humidity. This prevents buckling and other problems after installation.

2. Remove existing base molding.

Pry the molding off the wall and set it aside to reinstall later. Remove old flooring if needed.

3. Lay underlayment.

Installing foam underlayment helps the floor feel more "lively" and deadens sound. Make sure the floor is clear of staples or nails left from any flooring you tore out, then roll the underlayment out into the appropriate spaces (Photo A), preventing the edges of adjoining strips from overlapping.

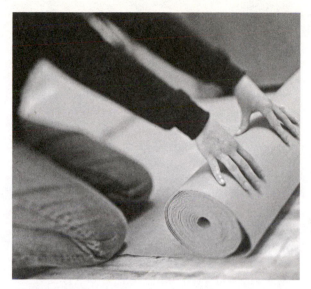

■ PHOTO A

4. Plan the layout.

To decide which direction to lay the planks, consider which wall provides the longest and straightest starting point, how sunlight will strike the floor, and where the room's focal point is. It's important to plan ahead so you don't end up with a very narrow strip of flooring against the far wall.

---

product with planks attached by glue. This creates a more water-resistant floor than planks that snap together without glue.

. Installing the floor requires accurate measuring and a variety of saws. Prep time is minimal because you can install laminate over most existing surfaces. There are two kinds of flooring that should be removed

before laminate goes down: carpeting and wood floors bonded to concrete. Many sources say you can install laminate over carpeting with a nap shorter than ¼ inch, but the safe route is to remove carpeting. If you're installing laminate over a concrete floor, always lay down a vapor barrier first. A wood floor left under the vapor barrier will probably rot over time.

Laminate's simple installation process makes it a hit with do-it-yourselfers. Manufacturers design planks to connect with a wide variety of tongue-and-groove systems, and many products require no glue. For this project, the light maple floor costs about $2.99 per square foot and uses a glueless installation.

The last plank should be at least 2 inches wide. If you measure across the room (figuring in a ¼-inch gap at each wall) and have a remainder that is less than 2 inches, add that value to the width of a full plank and divide by 2. This will be the width of the first and last planks.

5. Cut the first piece.

Depending on your calculations from Step 4, you may have to rip the first plank to width. When cutting laminate planks with a power saw (whether ripping or cutting to length as shown in Photo B), cut with the finished side down. When using a handsaw, cut with the finished side up. If the wall has an irregular contour, cut the first plank to reflect the contour.

■ PHOTO C

6. Install the first row.

Install the first row of planks with the tongue side facing the wall. Some manufacturers recommend cutting the tongue edge off planks facing walls. Connect one plank to another by connecting the tongues and grooves. You may be able to snugly connect the planks by hand, or you may need to use either a pull bar from an installation kit to pull them tightly together (Photo C) or a tapping block to tap the joints together (Photo D).

■ PHOTO B

7. Allow an expansion gap.

Always leave a ¼-inch gap between the planks and the wall. Even acclimated floors subtly expand and contract during their lifetime. Most installation kits include spacer chips you can wedge between the wall and planks to create the proper gap (Photo E).

8. Cut the last plank to length.

When you reach the end of a row, cut the last plank to length.

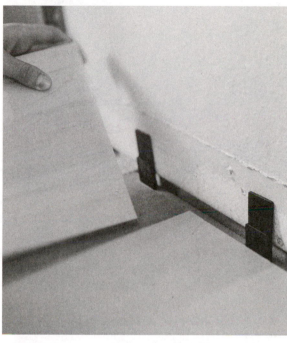

■ PHOTO E

■ PHOTO D

Leaving a **gap** between the wall and flooring allows the **planks to expand** and contract.

■ PHOTO F

Measure carefully

Don't rush your measuring. Take your time and
double-check your work. Adopt the carpenter's
maxim, "Measure twice, cut once." No matter
what measuring device you use, get comfortable
with it and learn to read it accurately. Many a
board or laminate plank has met its ruin because
someone couldn't distinguish a ¼-inch mark
from an ⅛-inch mark. Once you've made a
measurement, don't trust your memory. Jot down
the figure on a piece of paper or a wood scrap.

9. Install additional rows.

As you snap on new rows (Photo F), allow at least
12 inches between the seams in adjoining rows.
You can start a new row with the scrap from the
plank you cut at the end of the previous row, but
don't use pieces shorter than 12 inches.

10. Install the last row.

There should be only ¼ inch between the last row
and the wall, so you will probably need to slide the
planks into position at an angle, then gently pry
them into place with a pry bar.

11. Cut around door casings.

For a professional appearance, don't try to cut
planks to fit around door casings. Instead use a jam
saw to cut the door casings about 1/16 inch above

■ PHOTO G

■ **PHOTO H**

the height of the laminate flooring, giving planks room to slide under the casing. You can achieve the proper height by using a piece of the flooring with underlayment at the casing as a spacer. Rest the jamb saw on the top and cut the casing at the appropriate height (Photo G).

12. Install the trim pieces.

After all the laminate planks are in place, reinstall the base moldings (Photo H). Then install shoe moldings over the expansion joints, and use transition strips to connect the laminate floor to adjoining surfaces such as carpet. Laminate floors are designed to "float," so nails used to attach trim should never pass through the flooring. If you're installing the floor in a bathroom, keep water out by laying a bead of 100 percent silicone caulk around the entire perimeter before you install the shoe molding.

Waterproof silicone caulk, applied to the perimeter of the floor, keeps moisture from migrating into the substrate, which could warp the planks.

CROWN MOLDING

Create architecture with new crown molding

Lend interest and style to a plain, boxy room with the addition of crown molding at the ceiling. It's a fairly easy-to-add detail that resonates so strongly with today's buyers, it is worth the investment of time and money.

■ **Crown molding draws the eye upward and makes most any room seem grander.**

TOOLS
- Paintbrushes
- Pencil
- Miter box and saw
- Tape measure
- Stud finder
- Coping saw with spare blades
- Small flat and round files
- Fine-grit sandpaper
- Drill
- Hammer
- Nail set
- Pneumatic finish nailer with air compressor (optional, but helpful in place of the hammer

and nail set listed above; available at rental stores)
- Putty knife
- Caulking gun (for painted moldings only)

MATERIALS
- Paint or stain and sealer
- Finishing nails
- Extra blocks for practice cuts of similar pieces
- Patching compound or wood filler
- Caulk

Add molding and trim

Make your house stand out from the open house crowd with rooms made memorable by adding moldings and trim. Along with paint color and window treatments, moldings represent the simplest way to add style and definition to any room. Crown molding bridges the junction between walls and ceiling, a prominent location where the architectural accent can shine.

Home centers offer a variety of premilled molding materials. For a distinctive traditional look, or if you plan to stain the trim, the solid wood trim available in many species is the best choice, but it is also more expensive than painted molding. If you plan to paint your molding, consider finger-jointed wood, wood composite, or urethane trims to keep costs down. Urethane molding trim offers additional flexibility: It's lighter in weight, can be installed with just construction adhesive, and generally allows you to use heftier profiles.

Tips for success

For the best results, follow these suggestions:

- Keep a consistent scale from floor to ceiling. Although it's tempting to install an impressive wide crown molding and skimp on the base or casings, molding sizes should be balanced throughout the room.
- Think ornate and layered for more formal or traditional rooms. To create a more contemporary look, use fewer, simpler profiles and clean lines.
- Never assume that two surfaces meet at a true 90-degree angle; adjust cut angles to eliminate gaps in the corners.
- Invest in the proper tools to get good results; molding requires precise cuts regardless of the style or type. As a general rule, painted moldings make it easier to camouflage imperfect fits. It's a good idea to make practice cuts on some short sacrificial stock before you cut the longer pieces.
- Use corner pieces, plinth blocks (decorative corner pieces), and other transition pieces where possible. They make for simpler installation than miter cuts, and joints tend to stay closed despite seasonal changes in humidity.

Step-by-step

When it comes to installing moldings, there's no substitute for learning by doing. Still, it helps to have a working knowledge before you get started. If this is your first attempt at installing crown molding, start with something simple—a modest-size room with four walls and square corners.

Here are the standard steps to follow:

1. Take rough measurements.

Measure the width of each wall along the ceiling.

2. Prefinish the molding.

Paint or seal, stain, and varnish the molding before installing; let it dry.

3. Locate concealed framing.

Moldings should be nailed to studs or ceiling joists rather than directly to the drywall, so scan the walls and ceiling with a stud finder, and make light pencil marks to indicate the studs and joists. Mark a few inches away from the wall-ceiling joint so you can still see your marks after you put the molding in place.

4. Determine the installation sequence.

Work from one point around the perimeter of a room. That way, you'll have only one "closer" piece that must fit precisely against adjacent moldings on each end.

CROWN MOLDING

■ **PHOTO A**

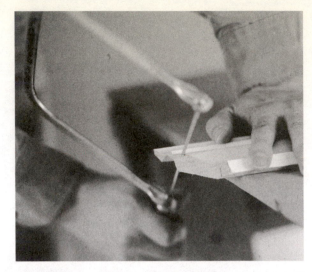

■ **PHOTO B**

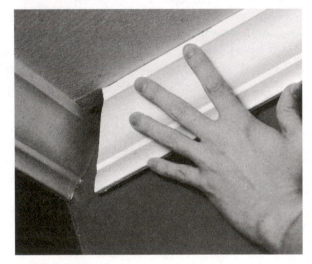

■ **PHOTO C**

5. Decide on the type of corner joint.

When two molding pieces meet at an outside corner, use miter cuts (cutting the pieces at 45-degree angles) at the meeting end of each. When moldings meet at an inside corner, irregular wall surfaces usually create a poor fit if you use mitered ends. Instead cut one molding with a square end and the other with an inside 45-degree miter (Photo A). Then use a coping saw to cut along the contoured edge of the mitered molding, removing the exposed end-grain stock (Photo B). File and sand the cut until the contour fits snugly against the adjacent molding (Photo C). Use extra blocks of molding to practice first, and make repeated test fits and trim cuts until you get it right. Touch up with caulk and paint or stain after you finish.

6. Start driving, slowly.

Nail each piece in place, but don't countersink the nails yet. If you're power-nailing with a pneumatic finish nailer, drive in only enough nails to hold the molding securely. That way you can remove the molding, if needed, with little or no damage to the pieces. If you're using a large crown molding, install a hidden nailer strip behind it to provide more surface area to nail into.

Practice mitering and coping skills on scrap crown molding to **avoid costly mistakes**.

7. Splice long runs.

When a long wall forces you to create a joint between two pieces of molding, cut a scarf joint (overlapping 45-degree beveled ends) for a less conspicuous joint. The exception to this is large crown molding. Making angled cuts in this stock is difficult, so pieces will likely fit better with square cuts butted against each other, creating a butt joint. If possible always start by precision-cutting one end of the molding and leaving the other end about ¼ inch too long, then position it in place to mark the precise length to cut (Photo D).

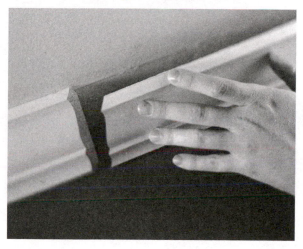

■ **PHOTO D**

8. Tidy up the details.

After all molding pieces are fitted properly, finish driving and countersinking the nails (Photo E). For nails near ends, drill pilot holes to prevent

splitting the wood. Fill nail holes with wood filler or patching compound, then sand. Use caulk or wood filler for small gaps at corners (Photo F). Touch up

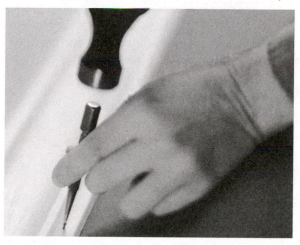

■ **PHOTO E**

■ **PHOTO F**

Build your own

Look closely at an elaborate piece of installed molding. You might discover it's not one piece at all but several layers stacked for a more complex profile. An old trick, the idea makes larger moldings more affordable. Start with a base platform of dimensioned stock such as a 1×4 or 1×6. This increases the profile size and provides a nailing base for the smaller pieces you add. The examples shown here give you an idea of the design possibilities.

Experiment right in the store aisle, stacking lengths of molding to achieve a custom look for less.

4-piece profile

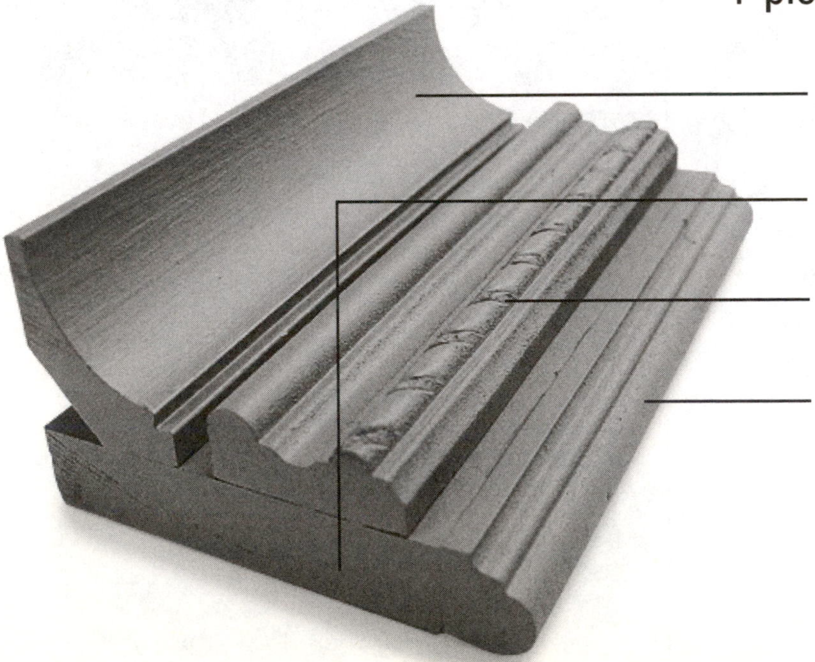

- 2-inch cove/crown
- ¾×3½-inch pine
- ⅝×1½-inch rope MDF
- ¾-inch bead-and-cove

5-piece profile

¾-inch bead-and-cove ————————————

¾-inch cove ————————————

2¼-inch colonial casing ————————————

¾×¾-inch pine ————————————

¾×3½-inch pine ————————————

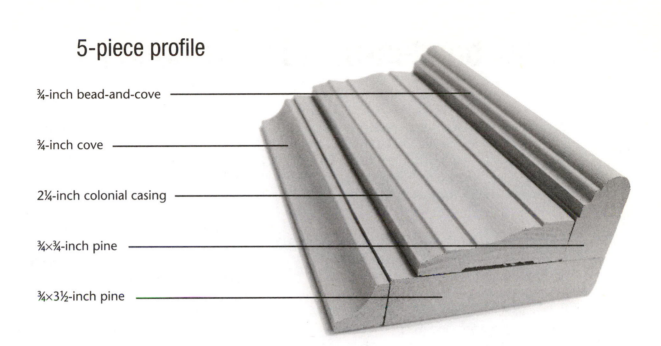

5-piece profile

———————————— 1×2-inch poplar

———————————— ¾-inch cove

———————————— 1×2-inch poplar

———————————— ⅝×1½-inch egg-and-dart MDF

———————————— ¾×5½-inch ogee base

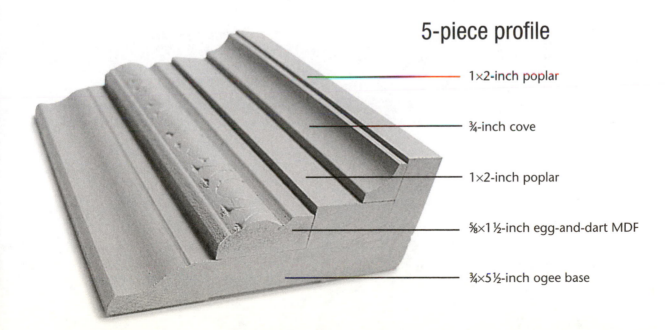

Install beaded-board wainscoting

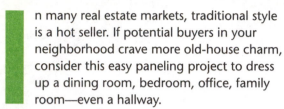

I n many real estate markets, traditional style is a hot seller. If potential buyers in your neighborhood crave more old-house charm, consider this easy paneling project to dress up a dining room, bedroom, office, family room—even a hallway.

Step-by-step

1. Follow instructions; think safety.

First a couple of reminders: You should always follow manufacturer recommendations when installing any product and use proper safety equipment at all times. The information presented here gives you a general overview of the project, but the manufacturer may offer specific instructions for the product you choose.

2. Determine the desired wainscoting height.

Although there are plenty of rules of thumb, there are no hard-and-fast rules when it comes to choosing wainscoting height. To generally maintain room proportions, wainscoting can be installed at one-third or two-thirds the total height of a wall. (Usually the one-third rule results in a measurement from 28 to 36 inches high.) Wainscoting can also be used as part of a chair-rail installation at approximately one-half the total wall height. (To actually protect walls from being bumped by your chairs, the rail height would be determined by the height of the chairs.)

Win with wainscoting

When you're trying to flip your property in only a matter of weeks, adding wainscoting is an ideal way to achieve a quick and dramatic update for walls without much effort or expense. You can also point out to potential buyers that the material is practical too, providing a durable coating that prevents dings and dents in heavy-traffic areas.

One of the most popular materials to use for wainscoting is beaded board, named for the rounded beadlike strip that camouflages the edges between individual planks of wood. Placed side by side vertically, these panels create a repeating pattern of wide and thin vertical lines. Beaded-board wainscoting adds style and visual interest while it protects the walls.

The vertical lines add visual height to a room, so beaded board is also perfect for small spaces such as powder rooms or informal entryways. To increase vertical impact, you can cover two-thirds of the wall with the material and paint the upper third.

Cost in time and money depends on the area to be covered, as well as the products and materials used. If you are reasonably handy and feel confident in your abilities, you should be able to cover a 10×10-foot room in a weekend, give or take

■ **Wainscoting lends charm and architectural interest to a plain room.**

a couple of coats of stain or paint. Assuming a 32-inch plank height, traditional beaded board made from pine or poplar costs approximately $12 per linear foot of wall, whereas panel products that achieve a similar look cost approximately $8 per linear foot at 32 inches high.

Traditional beaded board can be sealed and left the color of the natural wood, stained, or primed and painted. If you choose a beaded-board-look product made from medium-density fiberboard (MDF), it will require priming and painting.

Panels that simulate beaded board are easier to install than individual planks and are sometimes available finished in white—a real time-saver when you want to sell your property in the shortest amount of time possible. Other panel types can be stained or painted.

Although some panel products arrive cut to wainscot height, full-size panels can be cost-effective. (Do the math: 96 inches divided by 3 equals 32 inches, so you could get three 32×48-inch pieces of wainscoting out of one standard 8×4-foot panel.) Some potential buyers may fault the panelized products for looking less crisp than actual beaded board, but you can't beat the ease of installation.

Consider other materials

Practically any hard-wearing material can serve as wainscoting. If you're feeling creative, sheets of laminate, rolls of sisal or bamboo, or corrugated-steel panels could be pressed into service as unusual installations. You could also simply install a chair rail molding one-third of the way up the wall (about 28 to 36 inches above the floor) and paint the lower third a different color than the upper two-thirds of the wall. Or, install wall covering below the molding and paint the wall area above. If your neighborhood tends to attract young families with toddlers and you are updating a family room, playroom, or child's bedroom, consider using chalkboard paint below the chair rail.

3. Acclimate the product.

Bring the panels into the house a couple of days before starting your project to let them acclimate to the house, preventing expansion or contraction after they are attached to the walls. Stack them horizontally with thin blocks of wood between each sheet to allow air to circulate. While you wait for the product to lose excess moisture it might have picked up in the warehouse, you can begin planning your project and prepping the walls.

4. Prepare the wall.

Even if you have just installed new flooring, it may not be level. Installing the wainscoting from a level line on the wall will help hide imperfections. At one point on the wall, measure the desired height of the wainscoting (cap molding above the wainscoting panel will add slightly to the finished height). From that point, use the level to draw a horizontal line (Photo A), then extend it around the room. It's much easier to extend a level line

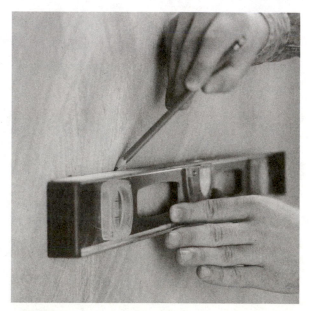

■ PHOTO A

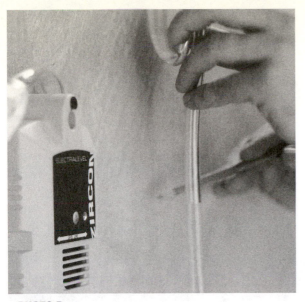

around a room with a water level (Photo B) than with a carpenter's level. Water levels, which are available at home centers, use long tubes filled with water. They make it easy to mark points throughout the room at exactly the same height. Use a chalkline to connect the points (Photo C).

The line you marked around the room is the top of your panel installation. The base molding installed toward the end of the project will cover the bottom edge of the beaded-board paneling, so even if your floor rises or falls, the visual presentation of your wall will appear level.

If you're working on a wall that already has base molding, remove that now. You'll replace the base molding as one of the last steps.

5. Cut and prepare the panels.

After the panels have acclimated, cut them to the desired height. Measure the positions of any outlets, light switches, or other boxes on the wall, then transfer those measurements to the back of the panel. Using a jigsaw or keyhole saw, cut out the holes (Photo D). Later you'll need to install a box extender at each electrical point to ensure that wires are properly contained.

■ PHOTO C

■ PHOTO D

6. Paint the panels.

Consider painting the panels before installing them to minimize paint drips inside the house. You also can paint the panels after hanging them on the wall. In either case, brush on one coat of stain-resistant primer, and apply two coats of satin-finish latex paint using brushes or rollers.

7. Glue and nail the panels.

Squeeze a zigzag bead of construction adhesive on the wall side of the panel (Photo E), then using nails along the edges as indicated by the manufacturer, attach the panels to the wall. Using adhesive will help anchor the field of the panel. If you're hammering the nails by hand, use a nail set (Photo F) to recess the nail so it can

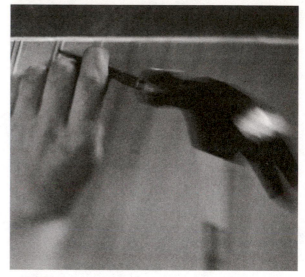

■ **PHOTO F**

be covered with wood-color or paintable putty. Panels should be spaced and overlapped according to manufacturer recommendations too. This allows for expansion and contraction caused by temperature and humidity changes.

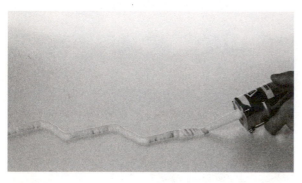

■ **PHOTO E**

Construction adhesive and nails secure the panels to the wall.

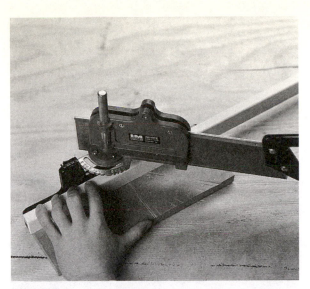

■ PHOTO G

8. Install cap and base molding.

Using brads, nail the cap molding (sometimes referred to as chair rail) at the top of the wainscoting panels. Use a miter box (Photo G) to cut the angled joints where walls meet. Using brads, install new base molding or reinstall your previous molding (Photo H).

■ PHOTO I

9. Putty holes and fill gaps.

Fill any visible nail holes with putty (Photo I), and caulk any gaps as necessary. When the putty dries, lightly sand the filled spot. Touch up the filled spot with matching paint.

■ PHOTO H

SINKS & FAUCETS

Update with a new sink and faucet

I nstalling a sparkling new sink and stylish faucet can do wonders to freshen a kitchen for little investment in time and money. Shop any home center and you'll discover a wide variety of styles, options, and finishes that will help make your property's kitchen appear up-to-the-minute and ultrafunctional.

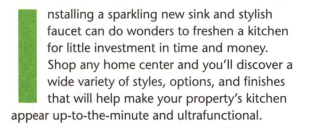

TOOLS
- Basin wrench
- Water pump pliers
- Crescent wrench
- Screwdriver
- Jigsaw (if you need to enlarge the opening in the countertop)
- Putty knife
- Flashlight
- Bucket and towel

MATERIALS
- Sink
- Faucet
- Strainer set
- Plumber's putty
- Silicone sealant

■ **If you're not replacing the countertop, purchase a sink that's sized to fit the opening for the existing sink. Otherwise cut an opening in the new countertop, using the template that comes with the sink.**

Refresh for a quick sale

A complete kitchen makeover may not be in your budget, but you likely can afford a new sink and faucet. These two components can be enough to give the work core an updated look that prospective buyers will notice. Replacing both fixtures at once not only provides the most thorough visual boost,

it also saves you the sometimes maddening task of disconnecting an old faucet from a sink.

Because kitchen sinks and faucets long ago evolved from simply functional tools into major kitchen fashion accessories, manufacturers provide seemingly endless component choices. For this

project, choosing a drop-in sink and a top-mount, single-handle faucet yielded quick results.

When making your own selections, keep a couple of factors in mind: Although most drop-in sinks are available with various numbers of faucet holes, you should know how many holes your faucet

Step-by-step

1. Shut off the water supply.
The copper lines that supply hot and cold water to the sink often have shutoff valves under the sink. Turn them off (Photo A). In some homes you may need to turn off water elsewhere, such as at the lines in the basement that lead to the sink. Once the water supply is off, turn the faucet on to let water and pressure drain from the lines.

2. Turn off the power.
If you have a garbage disposal, turn off the breaker panel switch that provides electricity to the kitchen and unplug the disposal's power cord.

■ **PHOTO A**

requires. Is it a single-handle unit, or does it have separate handles for hot and cold water? Do you want a separate sprayer or soap dispenser? Even if you do wind up with differing setups, such as the one-hole faucet and three-hole sink used for this project, you can make it work because faucets typically include a plate, called an escutcheon, that covers unused holes in the sink.

Measure the width of the base cabinet in which the sink will be installed. A sink should be 4 inches narrower than the cabinet to allow enough room for a mounting that doesn't require modifications of the cabinetry.

To install this new enameled cast-iron model, the old sink was simply detached and lifted out of the hole in the countertop and the new sink set in its place. (If your new sink is larger than your old one, you'll need to enlarge the countertop hole.) The faucet shown here features a pullout sprayer.

3. Disconnect the existing sink and faucet from the plumbing.

Use a crescent wrench (or a basin wrench if the nuts are difficult to reach) to disconnect the faucet from the supply lines (Photo B). Then disconnect the sink from the drainpipes using water pump pliers (Photo C). Keep a bucket and towel handy to clean up the water that inevitably will spill from the pipes as you disconnect them.

■ **PHOTO B**

■ **PHOTO C**

■ **PHOTO D**

4. Disconnect the garbage disposal.

Disconnect the disposal from the sink by loosening the ring that attaches the disposal to the sink flange. The best way to do this is to insert a long screwdriver into the lugs on the ring and twist (Photo D). When the disposal is loose, lift it off the drainpipe. You also must remove the disposal's mounting bracket from the bottom of the sink drain; you'll need to attach the disposal to the new sink. To remove the mounting bracket, pry the retaining clip off the drain flange (Photo E), then loosen the screws on the bracket.

■ **PHOTO E**

5. Remove the old sink.

Many sinks are secured to the countertop by clamps under the countertop. To remove the clamps, loosen their screws. Loosen the sink by inserting a putty knife under its edges. Lift out the sink, keeping in mind that you may need help because many sinks are quite heavy.

6. Measure the countertop opening.

The new sink's packing box should include a template that shows how large the countertop opening must be. Use it to check the existing opening. If your new sink is the same size as the old one, use the existing opening. If the new sink is larger and the countertop is laminate, enlarge the opening with a jigsaw.

■ **PHOTO F**

■ **PHOTO G**

7. Install the faucet on the sink.

It's easiest to install a faucet on a new sink before the sink is put in place. Follow the installation instructions for your specific faucet. The process typically involves laying a gasket on the sink and then setting the faucet on top of the gasket with its tailpieces extending through the sink's holes (Photo F). Tightening a nut on the underside of the sink secures the faucet to the sink (Photo G).

8. Drop in the new sink.

Confirm the sink's fit by grasping the sink through the drain holes and setting it into the new hole. Then lift the sink out and apply silicone sealant around the edge of the opening (Photo H), leaving no gaps. Set the sink in place again (Photo I) and press on the sink to set it in the sealant. If the sink requires clamps to secure it to the countertop, attach those now. Use a damp cloth to wipe excess sealant off the countertop. Let the sealant cure for 30 minutes before proceeding.

■ **PHOTO I**

9. Install the new strainers.

You could use the old strainers in the new sink's drain holes, but shiny new ones will look better with a new sink. You often need to purchase these separately from the sink. Apply plumber's putty to the underside of each strainer flange and set the strainers into the holes.

■ **PHOTO H**

■ **PHOTO J**

10. Reattach the plumbing.

On the sink's underside, attach the gaskets that came with the strainers to the strainer flanges. Then attach the drainpipes to the strainers and tighten the nuts (Photo J). (You may need to adjust the lengths of the drainpipes if your new sink's shape is different from the old one's.) If you have a garbage disposal, reconnect it to the sink flange, insert its drainpipe, and plug in the power cord. Reconnect the faucet by reversing the steps you took to disconnect the water lines. Turn on the power to the kitchen.

11. Turn on the water; check for leaks.

For a few days after you finish the installation, keep a close eye on the plumbing because small leaks are almost certain to occur. Be ready to tighten fittings and add sealant or putty as needed.

Plan at least a **half day** to cut a hole in the **kitchen** countertop, install the sink, and **hook up** the faucet.

Make it easy to install

These tips can simplify installing a new sink and faucet:

If the sink you buy doesn't come with a template and you have to cut a hole in the countertop, flip the sink upside down on the countertop where you plan to cut. Trace the outline of the sink, remove the sink, then draw a line that is an inch or so inside of that outline. Erase the first line to make sure you do not cut it.

The most difficult part of installing a new faucet is getting at the parts underneath. You may need to remove any cabinet doors that are in your way, hook up a work light to eliminate shadows, and make your work area as comfortable as possible.

If you are installing a sink at the same time as the faucet, consider attaching the faucet to the sink before you install the sink.

Often even penetrating oil won't loosen old locknuts. You may have to knock the nut loose with a hammer and screwdriver.

Tile a backsplash

To a prospective buyer, tile—whether it's ceramic, stone, granite, or marble—is nearly always perceived as a quality material that adds value to a house. Installing tile on a backsplash is a smart option for upgrading the look of a kitchen, bath, or laundry room.

■ Color, texture, interest—you get them all when you add a tile backsplash to a kitchen, bath, or laundry.

TOOLS
- Level
- Sandpaper
- Tape measure
- Straightedge or framing square
- Pencil or felt-tip pen
- Mastic trowel
- Scribing tool
- Safety goggles
- Work gloves
- Snap cutter
- Rod saw or tile nippers
- Tile spacers
- Rubber-blade float
- Rubber gloves
- Tile sponge
- Plastic pails
- Small stiff-bristle brush
- Soft, dry cloth

MATERIALS
- Drywall or surfacing compound
- Mastic
- Ceramic and tumbled-marble tile
- Grout mix
- Grout sealer
- Masking tape
- Caulk

Treat it with tile

Unlike finishes installed in large sheets or panels, which often require off-site fabrication and a crew of professionals (all of which can cut into your real estate profits), tile can be installed a few pieces at a time with just some basic skills. Thanks to the ever-expanding range of colors, textures, shapes, and designs offered by tile manufacturers, you can create interesting one-of-a-kind tile patterns simply by mixing and matching the pieces and playing around with various patterns. And tile will give your budget a break, because it's easy to get a stylish look for a relatively low cost. In the kitchen shown *above*, a tile backsplash is less expensive than a solid-surfacng one and introduces visual variety.

As you shop tile showrooms and building centers, one of the first things you'll notice is that tile varies widely in price—from $1 per square foot for basic

Step-by-step

1. Check wall surface.

Lay a carpenter's level or a long, straight board across the wall horizontally and vertically to see how level the surface is. Fill in low spots with drywall or surfacing compound; let dry. Sand the wall smooth before applying mastic.

2. Locate baselines.

Use a tape measure to locate the wall's center. Then, using a level, draw horizontal and vertical guidelines with a soft-lead pencil or felt-tip marker (Photo A). Plot out your tile pattern and, starting at the midpoint, arrange a single row of tiles in each direction to see how they fit. Adjust the spacing as needed to minimize cutting and waste. The best spacing may require straddling the center row of tile on the vertical or horizontal guidelines, in which case your actual baseline will be slightly off-center. Be sure that tiled areas stop short of

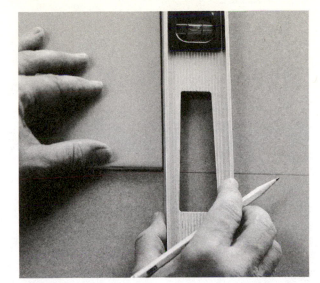

■ PHOTO A

electrical boxes or extend beyond them; cover plates shouldn't overhang the outer row of tile. Using a level or a framing square, mark the final baselines.

3. Apply mastic.

Spread mastic on the wall with the smooth edge of the mastic trowel, then use the notched edge to

ceramic-finish clay tile to $30 per square foot for solid-stone tile. The pricier versions—such as granite and marble—tend to be extra durable and offer more appealing surface coloration. However, durability and good looks are also available in less expensive versions—such as porcelain

ceramics.

Tiles also vary widely in size. Today's designers favor 6×6-, 8×10-, 12×12-, and even 24×24-inch sizes rather than traditional 2×2- or 4×4-inch pieces. Larger tiles deliver a sleeker look but are more difficult to fit into tightly defined areas (such as

backsplashes). They may involve trickier cuts and more waste. In this kitchen, cuts and waste were minimized by choosing 6×6-inch field tile. For low-cost visual punch, random accent tiles and a border of 1×1-inch mosaic tiles were added.

■ **PHOTO B**

5. Measure and mark for cuts.

To mark a tile for cutting to the right fit, lay it faceup directly on top of the whole tile it will adjoin. Next butt another whole tile against the edge you're cutting to and overlap the tile to be cut. Using a scribing tool, scribe the face of the first tile along the edge of the lapped one, making sure to etch through the glaze; this will help minimize chipping when you cut the tile. When cutting tile, wear safety goggles and work gloves.

6. Cut tiles to fit.

For straight cuts, lay the tile faceup on the bed of a snap-cutting tool. Position your scored mark under the scoring wheel and lock the tile into place with the tool's adjustable brace. Apply firm, steady pressure as you draw the scoring wheel across

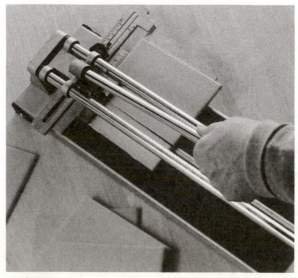

■ **PHOTO C**

cut a series of V-shape furrows. Apply just enough mastic to set one or two short rows of tile at a time so that you can adjust the spacing before the mastic hardens. Avoid covering the baselines with mastic until you're certain that the horizontal and vertical spacing is working out according to plan.

4. Test mastic.

Before pressing a whole group of tiles into place, press in a single tile, then pry it off and check the backside to see if the mastic is evenly distributed (Photo B). Voids or extra-thick deposits of mastic can weaken the bond. Repeat this test each time you apply a fresh layer of mastic.

If you have **many cuts** to make in the tile, rent a wet saw to make the job **go faster**.

the tile. After scoring, park the wheel in the slot above the tile and exert firm downward pressure on the lever arm (Photo C). The tile should snap neatly apart along the scored line. A few tiles will break no matter how careful you are, so expect to redo some cuts. For irregular cuts, use a rod saw or a pair of tile nippers. Before using either tool, practice on a piece of scrap to get a feel for the technique, then proceed cautiously.

■ **PHOTO D**

7. Add spacers.
If your wall tile doesn't have built-in spacing lugs (nubs that protrude along the edges), add temporary spacers to keep the tiles from shifting before the mastic hardens (Photo D). It's important to use spacers between the countertop and the first row of backsplash tile in order to leave room

for caulking. Field tile often comes with built-in spacers, but specialty tiles (such as decorative accent inserts) usually don't. You can buy small bags or flat sheets of spacers from a retail tile supplier or discount building center.

■ **PHOTO E**

8. Mix and apply grout.
Allow the tile to set at least 24 hours before grouting. For joints ⅛ inch or less, use unsanded grout; for larger joints, use sanded grout. Follow directions on the package for mixing the grout, then apply immediately with a rubber-blade float, holding the tool at an angle to help work the grout into the joints (Photo E). Repeat until all the tile is grouted. When grouting, wear rubber gloves to protect your skin from irritants.

BACKSPLASHES

Use **flexible caulking** to fill the gap between the tile backsplash and the **countertop**.

■ **PHOTO F**

9. Remove excess.

Wait about 10 minutes for the grout to firm up, then wipe off excess with a tile sponge (Photo F). Rinse the sponge in a pail of water after each pass. After the last sponging has dried, remove the final haze with a soft cloth, or scrub it off with water or a solution of water and white vinegar. Dump the rinse water outdoors; grout deposits can clog waste lines.

10. Seal and caulk.

Grout is porous and will stain easily if left unsealed. As soon as it has dried thoroughly (usually about three days), apply one or two coats of grout sealer with a small stiff-bristle brush (Photo G). Use a soft, dry cloth to remove excess sealer from the tile itself as you work; some sealers can discolor tile finishes. Where the tile meets the countertop, run a double strip of masking tape along the joint, then fill the joint with caulk and smooth it with a wet finger. When the caulk dries, peel off the tape.

■ **PHOTO G**

Give cabinet doors a makeover

Replacing kitchen cabinets can gobble up a huge chunk of your rehab budget. Consider a refresher for cabinet doors instead and use the money you save to upgrade appliances or flooring.

Pick a style

Take a trip to any home center and you'll discover aisles full of materials that you can use to dress up existing cabinet doors. Molding, tiles, glass, wallpaper, or other decorative elements can be used to transform a door from dull to dynamic.

Here are some ideas to jumpstart your imagination:

1. Wood onlay

Glue molding and a carved appliqué on a door, then layer on an antiqued paint finish for an elegant look.

2. Stencil

Paint a background color, then stencil on a design. (See page 197 for step-by-step instructions for achieving a professional-quality finish with paint.)

3. Wallpaper panel

Flip through a few wallpaper books and find a design you like. Glue wallpaper into place on the cabinet doors and spray on a polyurethane finish to protect against mishaps and moisture.

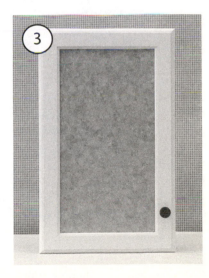

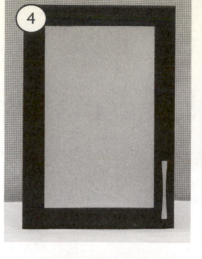

4. Stainless steel

Most metal fabrication shops will cut stainless-steel panels to fit your doors. Use contact cement to glue panels in place.

5. Textured glass

This door has a Victorian look, but glass panels come in many styles, such as frosted glass or glass with leaf patterns.

6. Plastic laminate

In an active household, plastic laminate may be the best choice. Laminate gives you a wealth of color and pattern choices, and it's a material that can take a beating.

7. Walnut veneer trim

For an Arts and Crafts-style kitchen, dress doors with ³/₄-inch preglued walnut trim. Cut strips in half lengthwise and apply by ironing the pieces onto the panel. Trim is available at home centers.

8. Decorative tiles

A few tiles leftover from another project add a touch of Florida to this door. Although it features vsmall mosaic tiles, you might try tumbled tiles or colorful glass tiles. Most tiles can be glued to doors using a construction adhesive.

9. Painted flower

Bring art into the kitchen with a painted theme that you design, or turn the painting job over to a pro. This door features a botanical painting.

Paint the cabinets

One of the least expensive tools for updating cabinets is a coat or two of paint. Here's how to obtain a professional finish that will have your property's existing cabinets looking fresh and attractive.

Step-by-step

1. Remove the doors and clean them.

Start by taking down the doors you will be painting. Remove all hardware, fasteners, and anything else that might have been applied to the door. Use a sealable plastic bag or a container with a lid to store hardware that will be reused.

Before priming or painting, clean the door surface. Start by removing the top layer of grime with a sponge and a household kitchen spray cleaner. If doors need more cleaning, use a steel wool pad. Once dry, give the door a final cleaning by wiping the surface with a solvent (Photo A). Wear safety gear when using solvents, primer, and paint.

 PHOTO A

TOOLS
- Tack cloth
- Drop cloth
- Polyester-nylon paintbrushes

MATERIALS
- Sponge and kitchen cleaner
- Steel wool or cleaning pads
- Denatured alcohol, mineral spirits, or other solvent
- Paintable wood filler
- 220-grit sandpaper
- Water-base primer
- Latex paint

■ **PHOTO B**

2. Prime.

Always apply primer to cabinet doors rather than simply applying new paint over old. Priming is the key to a long-lasting job—because it gives paint a surface it can grip.

If you are satisfied that the door is clean and there are no small cracks or holes, it's ready to prime. Should any tiny cracks show, use a paintable wood filler to close them. If you will be using new hardware, fill the old hardware holes too. Use just enough filler to do the job effectively, and lightly sand the surface smooth after the filler dries.

Choose a high-quality primer. (Ask your paint dealer for suggestions.)

Apply all finishes with a polyester-nylon paintbrush (Photo B) outside on a clean, flat surface, such as a drop cloth-covered table or a pair of sawhorses. Start with the door backs; let dry, then paint the fronts.

3. Sand the primer coat.

Run your hand over the primed surface and you'll feel a forest of bumps—raised wood grain and tiny imperfections brought to the surface by the wet primer. Smooth them out by lightly hand-sanding the surface with 220-grit sandpaper (Photo C). Take care not to rub the primer off down to the wood. After sanding, clean off the dust with a tack cloth.

■ **PHOTO C**

4. Apply paint.

When applying latex paint, put enough paint on the brush to get a nice, smooth flow that doesn't drip or flood the work (Photo D). Start by painting the backs of the center panels from top to bottom. Next paint the horizontal rails, slightly overlapping the joint with the vertical stile. Then paint the vertical stiles, starting at the top and painting down. Once the paint is dry, flip the door over and paint the front in the same order.

■ **PHOTO D**

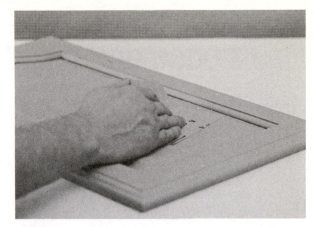

■ **PHOTO E**

5. Sand the first coat.

Just as the primer raised a few bumps, so will the water in the latex paint. Once dry, lightly sand the door with 220-grit sandpaper (Photo E), then wipe down with a tack cloth.

6. Paint the final coat.

Apply a second coat in the same manner as the first. Let the doors dry fully in a clean, dry space. Because latex hardens over time, some paint professionals let doors sit an extra day beyond the drying time specified on the manufacturer's label.

New doors?

If your kitchen cabinet doors are too damaged or even missing, you may want to order new cabinets doors. Unfinished cabinet doors in stock and custom sizes are available at most home centers. You may also find good deals through online retailers, such as cabinetdoorshop.com and newdoors.com.

Choose and install light fixtures

Change out old overhead lighting fixtures for new and you'll put your property in the best light for prospective buyers. Select styles that will best complement the house. Or create a style diversion in a post-World War II ranch or in a nondescript tract house using a light fixture to establish a new look.

Use these guidelines to help you select the best fixtures for your rooms:

Chandelier savvy

When selecting a chandelier, size matters as much as style. A fixture that's too big overpowers the room, and a too-small chandelier seems out of proportion. A good approach is to measure the width and length of the dining room in feet. Add the two numbers. The sum should be the diameter of the chandelier in inches. For example: A 12×14-foot dining room requires a chandelier approximately 26 inches in diameter. A 10×12-foot room needs a fixture about 22 inches across.

If the fixture is over a dining table, the bottom of the fixture should hang about 30 inches above the table in a room with an 8-foot ceiling. For every additional foot of ceiling height, raise the fixture an extra 1 to 3 inches.

Bulb buymanship

For best coverage, choose the longest fluorescent bulbs that fit the available space.

How high?

The bottom of a hanging fixture is typically at least 7 feet above the floor to provide adequate head clearance in traffic areas.

Lowering a fixture from the ceiling makes lighting more efficient because the light doesn't have to travel as far. Choose a pendant or another hanging fixture for use with very high ceilings. Exposed trusses and beams offer other mounting opportunities below the ceiling.

Extra-tall ceilings sometimes present special challenges. Buy additional matching chain or a longer down rod when you buy a light fixture; have a competent electrician extend the wiring.

Recessed lessons

Light from a recessed fixture spreads out in a cone-shape pattern. The farther away the light is, the bigger the area it covers and the more brightness it loses. Change from a floodlight to a spotlight bulb for more intensity, or change the route the light takes by installing a different trim ring that directs light as desired.

Most recessed fixtures are installed in a grid. You can set the fixtures as far apart as the room is high, but it's usually better if they are closer so their light overlaps. The closer they are to the wall, the brighter (and higher up) they illuminate it because the plane of the wall intersects the cone of light.

Fluorescent fixtures

Fluorescent lights are the workhorses of the lighting world, providing more light at less cost than incandescent or halogen bulbs. They come in many lengths, shapes, and even colors. When choosing tubes or compact fluorescent bulbs for your home, look for full-spectrum bulbs, which approximate sunlight, or "warm white" bulbs, which more closely resemble incandescent light.

Shown *right* are some special effects you can create by tucking fluorescent tubes behind wood structures; they are a good choice to serve as task lighting in the kitchen or workshop when mounted beneath upper cabinets.

• **Cornice lighting.** Dramatize draperies or shine a soft light downward by mounting fluorescent bulbs under a cornice. Build the cornice with 1×2 and 1×6 lumber; install the tube 6 inches from the wall and mount the cornice with large angle brackets to support the weight.

• **Valance lighting.** This light shines upward and downward to wash the wall and ceiling with light. Use 1×2 and 1×6 lumber and angle brackets. Or attach translucent plastic on the top to create a lighted display shelf.

• **Cove lighting.** Highlight a ceiling, outline a room, or accent a special feature. Build a channel from lumber and angle brackets, paint the inside surface with white paint for better reflective qualities, and mount the bulb about 1 foot below the ceiling (in most cases).

• **Undercabinet lighting.** This lighting installed directly over a work surface is particularly important in a kitchen. Install fixtures near the front, not the rear, of the cabinet where they will be hidden by the skirt. At least two-thirds of the length of the undercabinet area should be lighted.

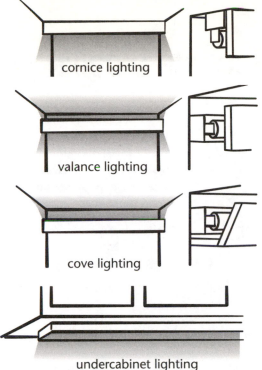

cornice lighting

valance lighting

cove lighting

undercabinet lighting

■ **Use fluorescent fixtures in a variety of creative ways as shown here.**

Consider halogen

For undercabinet task lighting, you may opt to use individual low-voltage halogen fixtures instead of using continuous fluorescent strips. If so, install the light 12 inches on center. Never use halogen bulbs in places where they could come in contact with your hands, fabric, or flammable materials; these bulbs often reach high temperatures.

Replace a ceiling fixture

Most novice do-it-yourselfers can replace a ceiling fixture with one of the same general type in about 30 minutes. Always observe safety precautions when working around electricity.

Step-by-step

1. Turn off the power.

Before beginning, turn off the power at the main control box. Use a voltage meter to make sure no power flows through the fixture.

Be style wise

Should you buy new fixtures for an older house? What if you find a chandelier you love in an antiques store? Will it look out of place in a more contemporary location?

One guideline is to choose fixtures in a style from the same time period or later than the architectural style of the house. Fixtures from an earlier time period often make the home look outdated. For example, a colonial-style house looks fine with handwrought tin fixtures or a multiarm brass and glass chandelier. But don't furnish a sleek, big-city dining room with a Western wagon-wheel fixture fitted with hobnail milk-glass shades.

TOOLS	MATERIALS
• Voltage meter	• Light fixture
• Screwdriver	• Coat hanger
• Wire stripper	• Wire nuts
• Needle-nose pliers	• Lightbulbs
• Ladder	

2. Disconnect the old fixture.

Examine how it is attached—some fixtures are secured with bolts to a metal strap (Illustration A), and others have a hickey mounted to a stud at the center of the box (Illustration B). If the new and old fixtures are different types, make sure you have all the necessary parts.

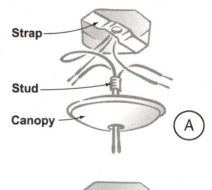

Strap
Stud
Canopy
(A)

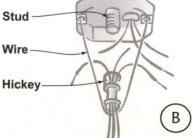

Stud
Wire
Hickey
(B)

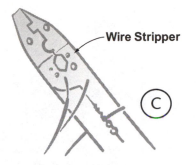

Wire Stripper

C

3. Install lightweight fixtures.

Strap mounting works best when installing a lightweight fixture. You can usually reuse the old strap. Use a wire stripper (Illustration C) to strip ¾ inch of insulation from the leads on the new fixture. If they are strand-type wires, twist the bare ends slightly.

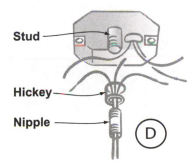

Stud

Hickey

Nipple

D

4. Support heavier fixtures.

A stud-and-hickey mounting works best for a heavier lighting fixture. To temporarily support the new fixture while you work, hang it with coat hanger wire from the ceiling mount (Illustration D). Screw a nipple into the hickey; wires exit through the side of the hickey (Illustration B).

5. Secure the fixture.

Thread the hickey on the stud, or screw the bolt into the strap.

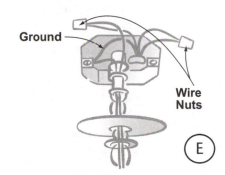

Ground

Wire Nuts

E

6. Connect the wires.

Twist the wire nuts around the ends of matching wires to connect them (Illustration E). Gently push the wires up inside the box. Turn on the power. If the fixture lights, the connect is good. Turn off the power again; raise and secure the canopy (Illustration F), then turn the power back on.

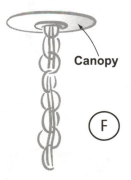

Canopy

F

Install landscape lighting

Well-designed landscape lighting not only lends drama and safety to a nighttime exterior, it also brings a sense of stylishness and value to your yard during the daylight hours.

TOOLS
- Shovel
- Phillips and flathead screwdrivers
- Wire stripper

MATERIALS
- Low-voltage landscape light fixtures and bulbs

- Transformer
- Waterproof outlet cover
- Ground stakes for light fixtures
- Wood post or stake to hold transformer (optional)

■ **Landscape lighting can be as attractive as it is functional. Lighting comes in a variety of styles.**

Leverage landscape lighting

Landscape lighting fixtures are easy to install—most anyone can put in a basic system in one afternoon. Even nonelectricians can handle the job safely because the lights are operated by a transformer that steps down standard 120-volt household wattage to a mild 12 volts.

Lights can be purchased individually or in kits. They can be completely automated by means of a timer or photocell or can be operated manually.

To design and install a lighting system, first decide on its purpose (safety, aesthetics, identification, or a combination of the three). Next, determine the optimum locations. Sketch out lighting schemes to explore your possibilities.

You then need to decide on the kinds, amount, and style of lights that will work best. Do you want low-slung fixtures that virtually

At night landscape lighting lends richness and elegance to any property.

Step-by-step

1. Install the transformer.

Find the best location for the lighting transformer—usually near the closest ground fault circuit interrupter (GFCI) outlet to your desired lighting run. Mount the transformer on a small post or stake or the outside of the house; it should be within 1 foot of the outlet and at least 1 foot above the ground. The location is especially important if the transformer contains a photocell, which shouldn't be shielded from the sun. For weather protection, make sure the outlet has a waterproof cover (available at any home improvement store). To be safe, keep the transformer turned off or unplugged (if it is operated by a photocell) while you are installing the system.

Safety first

Any household electrical current can cause a shock, so always follow safety rules for electrical projects. Shut off the power at the breaker box before beginning any wiring activities. Don't touch wires that transport currents into the box because they are always live. Use tools with insulated rubber handles, and make sure you have dry hands.

2. Attach the cable.

Determine the cable size (or gauge) needed. (It depends on the system's total nominal wattage [TNW] or the length of the run.) In a basic system, which encompasses a straight run of approximately 10 lights, a 12-gauge cable should suffice, but check the instructions. To attach the cables to the

disappear from view or taller stands that protrude over shrubbery?

How many lights do you need? Remember, less is best. You want a wonderful glow, not the glare of a miniature golf course. If your cable runs encompass too many lights, the fixtures at the end may illuminate only feebly because low-voltage power declines slightly along the length of a run.

For more illumination, you can run individual cables to separate zones but you will need to purchase a transformer that allows multiple cable connections.

Also consider what kind of material, style, and finish you prefer for your landscape lighting. Low-voltage lights run the gamut from contemporary to traditional. Match their design style to the architecture of your house.

LANDSCAPE LIGHTING

transformer, remove ⅝ inch to ¾ inch of insulation from the cable wires, then slide the stripped wires under the terminal screws on the bottom of the transformer (Photo A).

■ PHOTO A

3. Lay out the cables and arrange the light fixtures.

Referring to your sketched layout, determine the placement of fixtures and cable lines (Photo B). Keep in mind that the first fixture in the line must be a minimum of 10 feet from the transformer. For even and subtle illumination throughout the line, leave roughly 8 to 10 feet between fixtures.

■ PHOTO B

4. Bury the cables.

Dig trenches of 3 to 6 inches deep in which to bury the cables along lighting runs. (Don't bury them deeper. The lines should remain easily accessible in case you decide to change the layout later.) Lay the cables in the trenches, leaving a small amount of slack at each light juncture in order to connect the fixtures (Photo C). Smooth soil over the cables and trenches, leaving a small amount of cable protruding by each fixture location.

■ PHOTO C

5. Assemble the fixtures and attach the cables.

Assemble each fixture according to the manufacturer's directions. (To avoid corrosion, which makes it difficult to change bulbs, lubricate the screws for the lamp assembly portion.) Following the manufacturer's instructions, attach each fixture to a cable at the designated juncture. Most kit fixtures easily hook up to a cable with a two-part connector that pierces the cable and locks into place (Photo D). Turn on the transformer to make sure the connection has been successful. If the light doesn't illuminate, turn off the transformer and resnap the connector into place, making sure that it pierces the cable. You can also check the bulb and transformer to make sure they are working properly. (You should hear a slight hum if the transformer is working.)

6. Install the lights in the ground. Hide the cable.

Attach each fixture to a ground stake. Push the stake into the dirt (or dig a hole for it if necessary) until the top of the stake is flush with the ground. Examine the fixture to make sure it is upright and not tilting in any particular direction. Conduct a final check at night to see if you need to add or remove lights, then push the cable and connector under the soil about 2 inches. If installing in sod, cut the sod around the light fixture, peeling it back to sink the stake. Then press the grass down and water it.

■ PHOTO D

Select a lighting style that complements the house—contemporary to traditional.

LANDSCAPING

Lay a paver walk

You only get one chance to make a positive first impression with prospective buyers. A paver walkway—lined with flowers—can offer instant curb appeal that will set your house apart from the crowd.

TOOLS
- String
- Stakes
- Hose
- Spray paint or chalk
- Shovel or trenching tool
- Tamper (hand or electric)
- Metal spikes
- Rake
- Screed (straightedge)
- Masonry saw (optional for cutting pavers as necessary)

- Safety glasses
- Earplugs
- Dust mask
- Broom

MATERIALS
- Pavers
- Edge restraint
- Landscape fabric
- Gravel (base)
- Coarse bedding sand (optional)
- Fine-grain silicate sand (top coat)
- Top-coat sealer (optional)

Step-by-step

1. Mark the path.
To frame a straight path, use string attached to two stakes as a guide. To frame a curved path, lay a garden hose as desired. Once the outlines are established, mark the borders directly on the dirt, grass, or garden area with chalk or spray paint (Photo A). This allows for more accurate cuts along the perimeter.

■ A pathway entices visitors to enjoy the landscape and welcomes them to the property.

■ PHOTO A

2. Trench the path.

With a shovel or trenching tool, cut a level trough about 6 inches deep along the length of the path (Photo B). Slope the bottom surface of the trench slightly away from structures to facilitate drainage (approximately 1 inch every 4 to 8 feet). If the soil is porous, spread woven landscape fabric across the trench and up the sides, then a 2-inch layer of gravel, tamped. The gravel provides drainage, and the fabric keeps the gravel from working into the soil and weakening the base. (If you install a gravel base, remove soil equal to the combined thickness of the gravel, sand, and pavers.)

■ **PHOTO B**

Explore pathway options

From Old-World cobble to Southwest paver or classic brick, pathway options for remodelers have never been as abundant and as easy to install. What once required a contractor and involved the messy and time-consuming application of mortar can now be done in a weekend by an amateur without mixing any concrete at all. With sand as a base, most paver types can be secured in place using the easy steps that follow.

Paving materials of many types come in every imaginable shape, size, and color and are available at most home supply stores. Also available are interlocking varieties that fit neatly together with manufactured grooves.

Along with ease of installation, pavers set in sand offer other advantages over poured or mortared concrete alternatives. In areas where moisture may be a problem, sand-set pavers

allow water to seep between the cracks rather than divert toward the house. Sand-set pavers are so easy to replace—so save a few after installation for potential fixes.

Plan your path on paper, then use spray paint or chalk to transfer your design to the yard.

3. Add edging.

Add an edge restraint designed for pavers and purchased by the length. Install with metal spikes to both sides of the trench to stabilize the path, preventing drift from weather and foot traffic (Photo C). The edge also serves as a weed barrier.

■ **PHOTO C**

4. Partially fill the trench with sand.

Depending on the depth of the pavers, fill roughly two-thirds of the trench with coarse bedding sand and rake it smooth. (One cubic yard of sand provides a 1-inch base for 300 square feet.)

5. Level the sand with a screed.

Make a screed, or straightedge, by screwing a 2x4 to a piece of plywood 3 inches wide and as long as the trench is wide. Drive a nail into each end of the 2x4 so the distance between the nail and a plywood edge is the paver's thickness. Level the sand by guiding the screed's nails back and forth along the top of the trench (Photo D). Add sand to low spots, and remove sand that builds up. The sand should be solid but not compacted.

■ **PHOTO D**

■ PHOTO E

6. Lay the pavers.

Before placing pavers in sand, experiment with various patterns to determine the one you like best. Pavers can be set randomly or uniformly, staggered in a bricklike fashion, or even set in a herringbone arrangement. Place pavers as desired, then sink them into the base of sand (Photo E). To ensure a square ending line, stretch string lines across the walk every 10 pavers and make sure the pavers are aligned with it.

■ PHOTO F

7. Cut the pavers as necessary.

Should you need to lay pavers in a staggered fashion, or if the path is curved, consider cutting pavers to fit as necessary. A masonry saw (available for rent at most home improvement or equipment rental stores) is considered the safest way to cut pavers (Photo F). Always use safety goggles when using a masonry saw.

8. Tamp the pavers.

Once pavers are in place throughout the pathway, tamp them snugly into the sand using a hand or electric tamper. Compact the edges first, then the middle (If you are operating a power tamper, be sure to wear safety glasses, hearing protection, and a dust mask.)

■ **A paver pathway introduces attractive, rustic texture to your property's landscape.**

9. Sweep the sand into the cracks.

As a final top coat between the paver seams, pour a thin layer of fine-grain silicate sand over the pathway. Alternately sweep and compact the sand until all the cracks are full and the surface is clean (Photo G). Keep adding sand as necessary to fill the spaces between pavers.

10. Wet down the pavers.

Using a garden hose, gently wash off any remaining sand resting on top of the pavers. For a wet look, to add further protection, or to bring out the rich coloration of the stone, add a top-coat sealer to the pavers. (This step is not necessary for durability.)

11. Replant the edges.

Replace soil on the path's edges to cover the edge restraints. Plant the soil with grass or flowers.

Build a paver bench

Easy-maintenance flower gardens—even small ones—enhance a property in the eyes of most buyers. This project shows you how to quickly assemble a bench anywhere within your landscape. Constructed from tumbled pavers similar to those used for the path project on pages 208–212, this garden bench instills the same rustic appearance offered by natural stone. Best of all, you can build it in an afternoon for about $100.

TOOLS	MATERIALS
• Shovel	• Landscape pavers
• Rubber mallet	• Gravel or other base
• Tape measure	material
• 2- to 3-foot-long	• Landscape block
carpenter's level	adhesive

■ **A paver bench makes it easy for buyers to envision sitting and enjoying a garden, fountain, or other landscaping feature.**

Choose the best pavers

Dimensions, colors, textures, and prices of pavers vary, so shop around to find the style and price that suit you. Broad, flat, rectangular pieces with proportions similar to those of a standard brick produce an attractive look.

To calculate how many pavers to buy, you'll need to know the size of the pavers and have a rough idea of how large you want the bench to be. Multiply the number of pavers in each course, or layer, by the number of courses. Instead of predetermining the exact size of the bench (which might result in the need to cut pavers), let the size of the pavers dictate the dimensions.

The top course will probably look better with smaller pavers and an overhang. Often manufacturers supply different-size pavers of an otherwise similar style and material, but an entirely different kind of block can be used.

Scale is important, and pavers should be of a size appropriate for the bench; large pavers may look out of scale on a small bench. The bench shown *above* (including the top) measures 18 inches high and 45 inches long.

Step-by-step

1. Do a test run.

Before building the bench in its final location, put it together for a "dry fit" on a level surface. If you aren't happy with the size or proportions, make adjustments. You can always return unneeded pavers or buy more, if necessary. After finding the design you like, measure the base of the bench.

■ **PHOTO A**

■ **PHOTO B**

2. Choose the location.

Excavate 4 to 6 inches deep into the soil; make the hole a few inches longer and wider than the base of the bench. Fill the hole with gravel or another base material (Photo A), and level it (Photo B).

3. Lay the first course of pavers.

This is the foundation of the bench (Photo C), so make sure it's exactly where you want it and completely level. A carpenter's level at least 2 feet long will help you spot pavers that are slightly lower or higher than the rest (Photo D). If necessary, tap high pavers with a mallet or lift low pavers and fill underneath with more base material to make the first course flat.

4. Lay the second course of blocks.

Use a different pattern than for the first course. Check all sides with a level to ensure they're plumb. Tap protruding pavers, if any, into place

■ **PHOTO C**

Study the view

When deciding where to locate the bench, check out the view of the garden from each possible location. You or the future buyers are sure to spend more time viewing the garden from the bench than looking at the bench itself, so placement is important.

■ **PHOTO D**

so they're flush with the rest. Continue laying additional courses in different patterns until the desired height is achieved (Photos E and F).

5. Lay the top course of pavers.

Measure the overhang to ensure it's the same along the entire length of the ends and sides (Photo G); tap the pavers with a mallet to make minor adjustments.

■ PHOTO F

■ PHOTO E

6. Get ready to adhere the pavers.

When the top course is in place, remove the top pavers two or three at a time, brush off any dirt or other loose material, apply a bead of landscape block adhesive to the underlayer (Photo H), and replace the pavers. Proceed to the next set of pavers only after you've affixed those you previously removed—that way, you'll retain the proper positioning of the top layer. Give each block a few gentle taps with the mallet to ensure good contact with the adhesive. Let the adhesive harden for a day before sitting on the bench.

7. Wrap up the project.

Finish the bench area by planting a few ornamental grasses, colorful flowers, or green plantings next to the bench and applying mulch to conceal the gravel around the bench base.

The **best part** about building this bench may be **sitting down** and **enjoying** your handiwork.

■ **PHOTO G**

■ **PHOTO H**

PROJECT
price guide

**Maximize your
remodeling dollars
and reap the
profits by spending
your money on
what buyers want.**

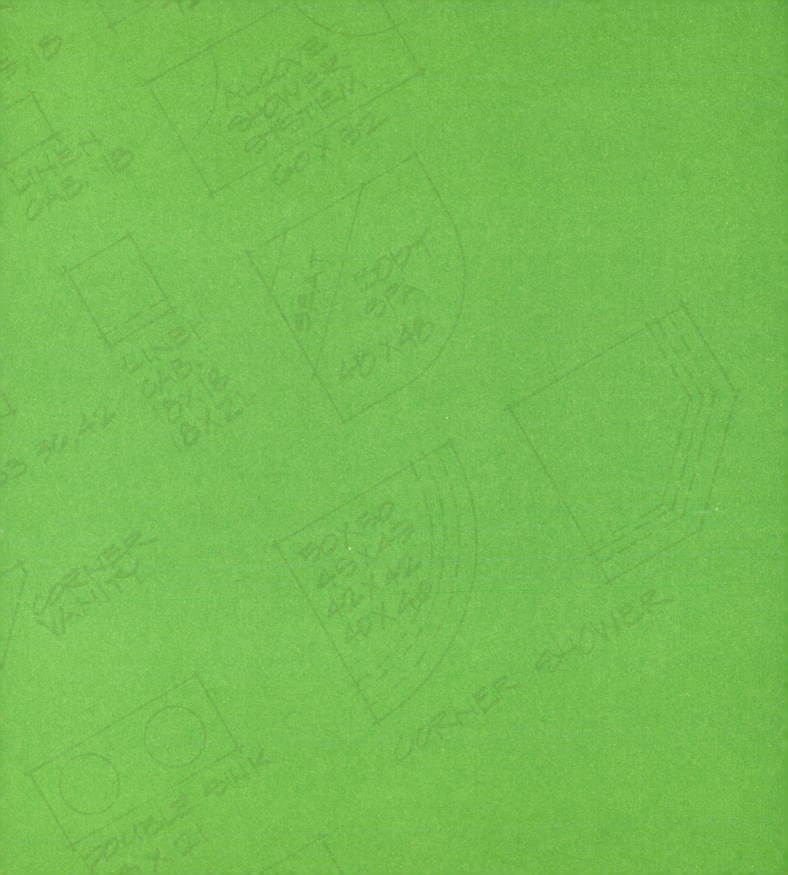

PRICE GUIDE

What's it going to cost?

The following price guides will help you determine how much you need to spend in the kitchen, bathroom, and family room to replace any damaged or dated surfaces, cabinets, or fixtures in your home.

The bottom line

Getting price quotes for all the products you want accounts for the "hard costs" of remodeling, but these numbers don't tell the complete story. These expenses may equal less than half a project's total price once you add in labor and unseen materials costs such as flooring underlayments, plumbing updates, and additional electrical lines.

Labor costs

How much of the budget goes to labor depends on the project scope and where you live. In a simple tear-out-and-replace job in the Midwest, labor may be only one-third of the total costs. On the coasts, labor expenses may double that amount. If there are structural changes—removing walls, windows, and doors—the percentage also will also be greater. Plus certain kinds of cabinets and surfaces are more difficult to install than others, which affects labor charges. Ask questions

Labor

Labor may double or triple the cost of your remodeling. Doing some of the work yourself can save thousands of dollars. For step-by-step how-to advice, see pages 146-217.

■ **On average, 60 percent of all home remodeling dollars are spent in the kitchen.**

before settling on a product: A look-alike may be more cost-effective.

Formal bids

If you request a formal bid from a prospective professional he or she will likely provide you with a list of hard costs and labor estimates. For comparison purposes, plan on asking two or three of your top contenders for formal bids. Compare these bids with your own estimate to see how accurate your hard costs are and to see if you could save money by doing some of the labor and purchasing materials yourself.

KITCHEN PRODUCT PRICE GUIDE

Range	Good	$300–$550	Painted cabinet; conventional gas or electric burners; oven window.
	Better	$550–$2,000	Large (up to 12,000 Btus) gas, glass-top electric, or induction burners; programmable convection oven; stainless-steel front panel.
	Best	$2,000–$10,000+	Dual-fuel models with burners that range from 500 to 15,000 Btus; stainless-steel cabinets; convection ovens; commercial grade; vintage look.
Range vent hood/light	Good	$80–$400	180–350 cubic feet per minute (cfm) air movement; 30–36 inches wide.
	Better	$400–$1,200	Up to 700 cfm; widths to 48 inches; larger filter area; optional stainless-steel chimney hood; halogen lamps; quiet operation.
	Best	$1,200–$5,000+	Up to 1,200 cfm; 60-inch widths; halogen lamps; dishwasher-safe, baffle-type grease traps; curved-glass canopies; custom-built.
Wall oven	Good	$400–$750	27-inch single unit; dial controls; limited finishes.
	Better	$750–$1,600	30-inch; single oven with convection or double oven without convection; digital/touchpad controls; programmable; finish choices including stainless steel.
	Best	$1,600–$5,000+	Stainless-steel or painted finishes; convection; digital controls; halogen lights; heavy-duty racks; stacked double units.
Refrigerator/freezer	Good	$500–$800	Wire shelves; icemaker option; finish choices: white, almond, biscuit, black.
	Better	$800–$3,300	Large-capacity side-by-side or bottom-freezer model; independent temperature-control zones; through-the-door ice and water dispenser.
	Best	$3,300–$7,000+	Luxury built-in (flush with cabinetry); stainless-steel housing or customized.

KITCHEN PRODUCT PRICE GUIDE

Dishwasher 	Good	$300–$525	Two-rack model; plastic interior; several wash cycles; push-button/dial controls; color choices: white, black, almond, biscuit.
	Better	$525–$900	Stainless-steel interior; touchpad controls; quiet operation; three racks or modular loading areas; more cycle options.
	Best	$900–$2,200	Heat boosters; front-panel customization; better tub; ultraquiet.
Cabinetry (per linear foot, wall and base)	Good	$60–$200	Stock/ready-to-assemble particleboard; finish choices: oak, maple, birch, white paint; three-quarter drawer-extension hardware with 75-pound rating.
	Better	$200–$600	Semicustom in more woods and finishes; dovetailed hardwood drawers with full-extension, 100-pound-rated hardware; plywood construction.
	Best	$600–$1,200+	High-grade custom cabinetry; any size, shape, or finish; exotic woods.
Countertops (per linear foot, installed)	Good	$20–$45	Ceramic tile; laminate with integral backsplash, contoured edge; many colors and patterns; prefab or made-to-order sections.
	Better	$45–$120	Solid-surfacing; maple butcher block.
	Best	$120–$300+	Stone; quartz-surfacing; stainless steel; concrete; designer tile.
Kitchen sink and faucet	Good	$110–$330	Thin-wall stainless steel or white enamel-on-steel; twin basin self-rimming; single- or two-handle faucet with polished-chrome finish.
	Better	$330–$1,000	Porcelain or cast iron; colored enamel; two or three basins; faucet in finish choice.
	Best	$1,000–$5,000+	Undermount, apron-front in heavy-gauge stainless steel, copper, stone, or engineered granite; sink accessories for food prep and cleanup; designer finishes.

BATH PRODUCT PRICE GUIDE

Sink	Good	$70–$125	White enamel or vitreous china; drop-in or wall-mount.
	Better	$125–$300	Pedestal in white; "house brands" in low-cost range, name brands at high end; some cultured-stone prefabricated vanity tops with integral sink.
	Best	$300–$3,500	Designer-series pedestal sinks; custom-fabricated solid-surfacing vanity top with integral sink; consoles; undermounts; vessel-style basins; handcrafted basins.
Faucet	Good	$40–$150	Polished-chrome or brass finish; 4-inch center-set model.
	Better	$150–$280	Solid-brass body; more single-handle models; finish choices: brushed chrome, antiqued brass; ceramic cartridges with lifetime no-leak guarantee.
	Best	$280–$1,200	Designer series; exotic finish choices: pewter, polished nickel, hammered copper, oil-rubbed bronze; widespread body style with separate handles.
Vanity cabinet	Good	$75–$150	18- to 24-inch stock cabinet in oak finish or white paint; doors, no drawer.
	Better	$150–$300	Larger-size stock or semicustom cabinet in oak, maple, or cherry; multiple drawers; choices in hardware.
	Best	$300–$3,000	Higher-grade semicustom or custom cabinet; dovetailed hardwood drawers; full-extension drawer guides; high-end hardware.
Shower enclosure	Good	$130–$250	Aluminum-track sliding door unit for tub surround.
	Better	$250–$600	One- or two-piece prefabricated units with frosted-glass door; corner placement.
	Best	$600–$4,000+	Modular enclosure with higher-quality frame and glass options; solid-surfacing wall panels; custom site-built shower with ceramic or natural-stone tiles.

PRICE GUIDE

BATH PRODUCT PRICE GUIDE

Tub	Good	$90–$175	Fiberglass or enameled steel; white finish; 60 inches.
	Better	$175–$1,400	Cast-iron or acrylic soaking tub; more color and style options.
	Best	$1,400–$7,000	Oversize soaking tub; claw-foot reproduction or other freestanding type, designer series; jetted tubs with heater and filter.
Toilet	Good	$80–$200	Two-piece; white; round bowl; gravity-action.
	Better	$200–$700	"Suite" designs to match tub and sink; one-piece models; elongated bowl; some color options; tall seat height; some with pressure-assist flush mechanism.
	Best	$700–$2,000+	Designer styles or colors; increased selection of one-piece models; metal or other decorative trim; pressure-assist flush mechanism.
Mirror/medicine cabinet	Good	$40–$100	Recessed-mount models; metal with adjustable shelves.
	Better	$100–$500	Larger-size recessed or surface-mount units; multiple mirror/door panels; mirror frame options include wood or metal trim.
	Best	$500–$1,500+	European or designer-series cabinets with multiple doors and drawers; frosted/opaque-glass doors; drawer or cubby storage; integral.
Flooring (per square foot, plus installation)	Good	$1–$3	Resilient sheet flooring or vinyl tiles; no-wax surfaces; wide variety of patterns and colors; some inexpensive ceramic tiles.
	Better	$3–$5	Laminate plank or tile flooring; better-quality ceramic tile.
	Best	$5–$30+	Natural-stone tiles such as travertine, marble, limestone, or granite; tumbled stone; glass tile.

FAMILY ROOM PRODUCT PRICE GUIDE

Hard-surface flooring (per square foot, installed)	Good	$2–$4	Resilient vinyl sheet flooring or vinyl tiles; economy-grade laminate.
	Better	$4–$7	Red oak hardwood strip, engineered wood, or bamboo; deluxe-grade laminate with glueless installation; standard ceramic tile; higher-grade resilient.
	Best	$7–$30	Maple, white oak, cherry, or exotic species hardwood; porcelain or designer-series ceramic tile; marble, granite, slate, or other natural-stone tile.
Carpet (per square foot, installed)	Good	$2–$4	Polyester or olefin with a performance (par) rating of 5 or above and a face weight of up to 30 ounces per square yard; treated for stain protection.
	Better	$4–$6	Polyester or nylon with a par rating of 10 or higher; face weight 30–50 ounces; guaranteed stain protection.
	Best	$6+	Nylon or wool; par rating of 25 or higher; face weight of 50 ounces or more.
Windows	Good	$115–$175	Extruded vinyl frame; white only; single-hung (one moving sash); insulated glass.
	Better	$175–$400	Wood-frame double-hung unit; vinyl or aluminum cladding with permanent UV reduction.
	Best	$400–$1,000+	Low-E glass for UV reduction; choice of wood for interior; tilt sash for easy care; triple-pane insulated glass; true divided lights; special glazing for hurricane codes.
Patio doors	Good	$350–$550	Vinyl-frame slider; 6-foot width; white only.
	Better	$550–$2,000	Clad-wood or aluminum-frame slider, hinged "active" door, one fixed "passive" door; snap-on muntin grids for look of divided lights; color options.
	Best	$2,000–$4,000	Wood-frame French doors with surface muntin grids or true divided lights; high-end lockset hardware; size and color options; integral shades or blinds.

PRICE GUIDE

FAMILY ROOM PRODUCT PRICE GUIDE

Molding/trim package (for a 250- to 300-square-foot room, installed)	Good	$500–$1,000	Paint-grade (finger-jointed or wood composite) material; standard profiles.
	Better	$1,000–$2,500	Stain-grade pine or oak trim; wide-profile baseboard and crown molding; rosette casing trim; wainscoting or chair-rail molding.
	Best	$2,500–$6,000	Custom-milled stock in cherry, maple, walnut, or other hardwood; wide or multilayer crown molding; raised-panel wainscoting; fireplace surround.
Lighting system (for a 250- to 300-square-foot room, installed)	Good	$2,000–$3,500	Standard recessed ceiling-canister fixtures; basic wall sconces; ceiling fan/lights.
	Better	$3,500–$6,000	Adjustable "eyelid" recessed ceiling canisters; pendent/ceiling fan fixtures; designer-series wall sconces; dimmer controls for some lights.
	Best	$6,000–$9,000	High-quality or handcrafted fixtures; low-voltage track lighting; wall sconces; halogen lighting integrated into storage units; dimmer controls.
Fireplace (installed)	Good	$375–$1,100	Freestanding electric faux fireplace or stove; prefabricated metal woodburning fireplace; modular vent-free gas fireplace.
	Better	$1,100–$4,000	Freestanding wood or pellet stove; built-in direct-vent gas fireplace; combination gas/woodburning fireplace; metal housing.
	Best	$4,000–$15,000+	Built-in masonry fireplace with gas and woodburning capability; brick facade.
Storage	Good	$250–$500	Freestanding or wall-mount shelves; stock/ready-to-assemble storage cabinets.
	Better	$500–$1,200	Semicustom cabinetry with drawers and closed-door storage; soffit shelf around perimeter of room; small wall niches.
	Best	$1,200–$10,000+	Recessed built-in storage; window seat with storage bench; custom cabinetry and shelving with integral lighting systems.

Bargains on design and project advice

Seek good advice before you undertake any project and you're more likely to avoid costly mistakes. The following are sources of free or low-cost guidance.

Specialty retailers

- **FLOORING.** When you buy flooring, find out if the store offers free installation instructions or instructional videos.
- **LIGHTING.** If you spend a certain amount, some lighting stores will provide a free lighting plan.
- **LUMBER.** Need ideas on how to stretch your buildables budget? Ask the people at the lumberyard for ideas on managing your costs, such as substituting medium-density fiberboard (MDF) for plywood.
- **KITCHEN AND BATH.** Showrooms that specialize in cabinetry or plumbing fixtures and fittings will sometimes provide free computer-generated floor plans for efficient layout. Home centers may provide a similar service.
- **APPLIANCES.** Knowledgeable appliance salespeople can provide you with all kinds of advice on which models to buy and how to install them yourself.
- **PAINT.** Buy the best paint you can afford. Talk to employees to find out what makes their paint the best or to learn which brands are popular and why.
- **FURNITURE.** Furniture salespeople can offer advice on how to choose durable furniture and fabrics. Some stores have designers who can help you plan a room arrangement for little or no cost.

Internet

- **DO-IT-YOURSELF WEBSITES, PERSONAL HOME PAGES, AND MESSAGE BOARDS.** The Internet has lots of information on decorating and remodeling projects and techniques. Read from a variety of sources, but be on the alert for misinformation. Verify advice from other resources when possible.
- **ASSOCIATIONS.** Go to association websites, such as organizations for lighting or sheet goods manufacturers, to access an abundance of quality how-to information.
- **MANUFACTURERS.** Their websites often feature tips on selecting and using products. Many manufacturer websites now include calculators to figure how much material you need. They may also feature interactive miniprograms that let you paint a room, try out new flooring, and do other virtual makeovers.
- **RETAILERS.** Retailers sometimes offer online articles with valuable remodeling and decorating ideas. Seasonal and online-only sales are available around the clock.
- **MAGAZINE- AND BOOK-RELATED WEBSITES.** Magazines, books, and other publications often promote complementary websites that are designed to augment the advice and projects offered in their printed publications.

BARGAIN ADVICE

Libraries and bookstores

- **HOW-TO BOOKS.** Look for reliable publishers and check out books on remodeling and home improvement projects.
- **MAGAZINE ARTICLES.** Find titles you trust and skim articles for ideas. Check out or purchase publications that offer specific projects or techniques you plan to incorporate.
- **LECTURES.** Watch newspapers for announcements about visiting authors. Attend their lectures to gather information and advice on how-to and decorating topics.
- **INTERNET ACCESS.** Libraries usually provide free Internet access—often on high-speed lines. If you don't have a home computer or have a slower dial-up connection, a visit to the library can kick your online research or purchasing into high gear.
- **VIDEOS/SOFTWARE.** Libraries often carry extensive how-to video, DVD, and computer software collections.

Other media

- **TELEVISION.** The tube is rife with home decorating, remodeling, and how-to shows, including Property Ladder. Tune in and take notes.
- **RADIO.** Some talk shows dish out tips and advice for would-be remodelers and decorators.
- **NEWSPAPERS, SPECIAL SECTIONS.** Watch for inserts promoting local home shows and other events. These sections are good sources of low-cost advice. Some papers feature a weekly home and garden section.

Most home centers now offer how-to advice for remodeling and decorating projects.

Home centers

- **EMPLOYEES.** Home center employees are some of the most knowledgeable folks around. Ask them where the bargains are, when the next sale is scheduled, and how to do particular tasks yourself to save money.
- **FRIENDLY CUSTOMERS.** Contractors and hard-core remodelers are wandering the aisles with you. Strike up a conversation and you may glean valuable advice and money-saving tips.
- **WORKSHOPS.** Most home centers offer free or low-cost workshops on a number of projects. Learning new skills such as laying tile, installing lighting, hanging wallpaper, or painting a faux finish may take only a few hours of your day.
- **SAMPLES/LITERATURE.** Home centers offer free printed information and samples for you to take home and try out.
- **INTERACTIVE DISPLAYS.** Larger home centers now offer high-tech displays that let you play with computer-generated room designs and palettes. Have fun mixing and matching finishes, fabrics, window treatments, and much more—all on your own for free.

Designer showrooms

- **IDEAS ON DISPLAY.** Decorators sometimes use room displays to showcase their abilities and style. These displays are often excellent free resources for gathering ideas.
- **HELPFUL EMPLOYEES.** Chat with the designer on duty and share aspects of your project. You may receive a few tips to make your plans better.
- **FREE OR LOW-COST LITERATURE.** Check racks near the door or the sales counter for free or low-cost information on decorating elements you need for your room makeover.

Continuing education

- **CLASSES.** Through community colleges and adult continuing education programs, learn how to lay tile, use power tools, and master other how-to skills, such as basic wiring and plumbing—all for very little money.
- **TEACHERS.** Chat with the instructors after class to glean additional insider's tips and ideas.
- **OTHER STUDENTS.** You may find some students who are knowledgeable about your topic of interest. Have a cup of coffee with a few good prospects and discover some fresh ideas.
- **HELPFUL TEXTS.** The books that instructors choose to augment their courses may be affordable and worthwhile additions to your do-it-yourself library.

Affordable helpers

Consider these options for finding helpers you can afford:

- **Teens and college students.** Young people need jobs; you need help. Strike a bargain and gain a helper.
- **Neighbors.** Help your neighbors paint; maybe they'll help you install tile.
- **Friends.** Have a party. Invite a group of friends to a painting party. Feed them well.
- **A pro who's willing to barter.** For example, if you don't own the tools to build shelves but have another skill, make a deal with a carpenter and trade projects.

BARGAIN ADVICE

Cyber shop!

For notable bargains on flooring, appliances, and more, switch on the computer and shop online. Here are three advantages to buying remodeling items online: 1) there is a larger selection of new, used, and vintage goods; 2) it's convenient; 3) the bargains are real. The magnitude of home improvement materials available online—everything from cabinet knobs to tools to major appliances—is staggering.

Websites associated with chain stores can outnumber in-store selections. Perhaps the greatest benefit of shopping online is the vast amount of information available. Even as recently as 10 years ago, researching products was arduous. You had to find out where a company was located, call to request a brochure, then wait.

Today you can immediately access a manufacturer's website for product information. Using a search engine such as Google (www.google.com) can turn up reviews and other information not found on a manufacturer's site.

Another advantage of shopping online is the ability to find and obtain what you need quickly. One couple, for example, enjoyed the convenience of shopping online after their contractor mistakenly ordered the wrong cabinet knobs for their kitchen remodeling. Rather than wait weeks for another special order to arrive, the couple ordered the right knobs from a website and had them shipped overnight to their home.

As for bargain pricing, the concept is this: Retail store space is expensive to maintain. Buying online direct from a factory, warehouse, or distributor often equates with lower prices. And by knowing a few tricks, you can save even more.

Smart shopping tips

Consider shipping charges. Though you may find a large item online for significantly less than the cost at a local store, be sure to factor in shipping charges. For big, bulky items shipped by truck, it can start at $50 and up. Still it's worth checking. Some online companies absorb these charges for oversize products and are still able to offer better deals than retail stores.

Look for breaks on sales tax. Sales tax, or lack thereof, can account for worthwhile savings when buying big-ticket items. Some online retailers charge sales tax only for buyers who live in the state where the company is located. Find out retailers' policies before making a purchase so you can better compare total prices.

Purchase risk-free items. Some home improvement items require exact measurements, typically done by an expert, and can be risky online purchases. A local granite fabricator, for instance, will take measurements before the granite is cut. Windows and skylights also require exact measurements, a task best left to professionals.

Where to shop

Order from reputable sellers that protect your credit-card information and privacy. Look for businesses that are certified participants in the Better Business Bureau's OnLine privacy program (www.bbbonline.org). Program participants must meet reliability standards for ethical online business practices and agree to resolve complaints using dispute resolution.

Some of the best places to find deals are at online auction sites. EBay (www.ebay.com), for example, has revolutionized the art of collecting. Items that previously couldn't be found without long shopping trips are now accessible with just a few clicks of a mouse. On auction sites, you buy from individuals or small retailers, so check out the comments left by previous buyers before making a deal.

Regional "For Sale" sites are another good bet; www.craigslist.org, for example, features community bulletin boards for many large cities all over the world. It functions much like an online newspaper classified section. It's up to you to contact a seller and determine the condition of the items for sale, but good deals are out there.

Buying **online direct** from a factory, warehouse, or distributor often equals **lower prices.**

Save big by shopping smart

Know where to shop for your remodeling and decorating needs and you'll save big.

Go to thrift stores

Goodwill, Salvation Army, and a variety of local outlets can provide a wealth of used items at greatly reduced prices. These stores offer some of the most fun and rewarding shopping experiences around. Visit often for newly stocked items, such as good used furnishings, for staging your open house.

Browse flea markets

Often vast and crowded, flea markets are worth the extra time and effort to peruse because bargains are almost always lurking there. Visit flea markets to find unusual accessories, shelves, and architectural pieces. Learn how to negotiate prices with vendors. Ask politely, "Could you do better on this price for me?" With this approach you may receive a lower price. However, also be willing to let the item go if you can't get the vendor to give you a worthwhile deal. In most cases something equally good—if not better—will turn up at another booth or flea market.

Bring packing supplies with you. Or at least bring along strong canvas or plastic shopping bags to carry all your purchases.

Plan your transportation as well. Travel to flea markets in a vehicle large enough to carry your purchases home. If you don't own a van or truck (and don't want to rent one), ask a dealer who won't budge on price if you can get free delivery or shipping.

Bargain with a buddy. Sometimes dealers will give you a better deal on an item if you and your friend purchase multiple items from their booths, especially if the two of you pay with one check or credit card.

Check out damaged freight

Some home centers, furniture stores, and appliance outlets (as well as other types of specialty stores) offer damaged freight at reduced prices.

Save gas money and time by phoning to find out which stores in your area sell damaged freight.

Be willing to sort through stacks of sinks, layers of countertops, boxes of ceramic tiles, or dozens of doors, for example, and you may find what you want with only minor damage. Even nearly invisible flaws may take 50 to 75 percent off the retail price.

Bargain with the dealer. Offer a lower price and see what happens. Most stores are eager to clear out damaged goods.

Keep in mind, however, that damaged goods are often sold "as is," meaning no warranty, no returns, and definitely no refunds.

Sleuth out other damaged goods. They aren't always labeled or placed in a designated area. Sometimes you'll find less-than-perfect items on the shelves with the good stuff. Point out the damage to a salesperson and find out if the store will offer a discount.

Visit salvage yards

Some communities accept, store, and sell used lumber, sheet goods, hardwood flooring, windows, doors, cabinetry, and other materials and supplies. Check local listings in the phone directory first and call around to find salvage yards in your area. If

Find tools for less

Many of your shopping trips will include forays to find the right tool. You need certain tools all the time—a hammer, a drill, and a screwdriver, for example. Other tools are rarely used yet crucial to particular projects, such as a rubber float for grouting. Stretch your budget with these ideas:

Borrow. After all, what are neighbors for? Why buy a reciprocating saw when you plan to remove only one stud wall in your lifetime?

Trade. If you never use your router, find someone willing to trade with you for a tool you really need, such as a drill.

Rent. Some tools are costly to buy, yet you need them to achieve professional results or to get the work done in a reasonable amount of time. If you know you'll use a tool infrequently, such as a floor sander, rent it instead of buying.

Learn a new skill. If you enjoy handiwork and you want a workshop that's well-equipped, consider learning a new skill. Hire out your newly acquired talents and tools on weekends to earn dollars for your next real estate project. Buy a high-quality diamond-tipped saw, for example; then cut marble and other rock-hard materials and install floors and countertops for extra cash. You can also hire out skills/tools that you already have and use the dollars to buy the new tools that you need.

you can't find a listing in the phone book, waste collection companies may be able to tell you who is recycling building supplies in your area.

If you'll be moving anything heavy, bring along a dolly, a wheelbarrow, or a wheeled cart to ease the chore. Also drive a vehicle that can transport what you buy. If you don't own a pickup, borrow or rent one for the job.

Try to think outside the box. You may find an architectural element that you discover can be used for something other than its original purpose. Old doors and windows, for example, make interesting decorative accents.

Consider floor models

If you don't mind that several thousand people have opened and closed that dishwasher or refrigerator door over several weeks or months, you may be able to purchase the appliance from the home center for much less than retail. The same goes for furniture floor models at department and furniture stores.

Start by asking if floor model appliances, plumbing fixtures and fittings, cabinetry, countertops, and furniture are for sale.

There may also be a clearance center in your area. Many national chains designate one retail location per region as the destination for all unsold clearance items and floor models from the stores in the area. Ask a manager at your favorite retailer if a regional clearance store exists near you.

Ask about discontinued lines

Manufacturers and retailers want to unload discontinued items to make way for new seasonal lines. Ask employees if discontinued models are available. They'll often take you to a back room or special section designated for discounted merchandise.

Keep watching for these types of bargains. Discount stores introduce, promote, reduce the price of, and discontinue new product lines quite quickly, sometimes within weeks. Shop your favorite stores frequently and pay attention to product lines you like. When the line goes on sale or clearance, buy the remaining items at a significant discount.

How much paint to buy?

Here's how to estimate how many gallons of paint you'll need for the job you have in mind.

Although many manufacturers of paint claim that 1 gallon of paint will cover 400 square feet, you're usually better off estimating 300 square feet of coverage per gallon.

Always buy slightly more paint than you need. You'll be glad you have the extra for touch-ups and in case you spill any. Also some surfaces soak up more paint than others. (For example, plaster absorbs more paint than drywall, paneling, or wallboard; unfinished wood absorbs more than finished or treated wood.)

To ensure a **perfect match,** have custom-color paint mixed in **one large batch.**

To calculate the wall area:

Refer to the illustration, *opposite,* and the instructions below.

1. Add wall lengths to find perimeter.

13 + 13 + 18 + 18 = 62 FT., IN THIS EXAMPLE

2. Multiply the perimeter by the wall height.

Most homes built in recent decades have a wall height of 8 feet, but measure your room to be sure.

62 FT. × 8 FT. = 496 SQ. FT.

3. Find the area of doors and windows.

Estimate 15 sq. ft. of area for each standard window; 21 sq. ft. for each standard door.

15 SQ. FT. × 2 + 21 = 51 SQ. FT. OF WINDOW AND DOOR AREA

4. Subtract door and window area from the total square footage.

496 SQ. FT. – 51 SQ. FT. = 445 SQ. FT.

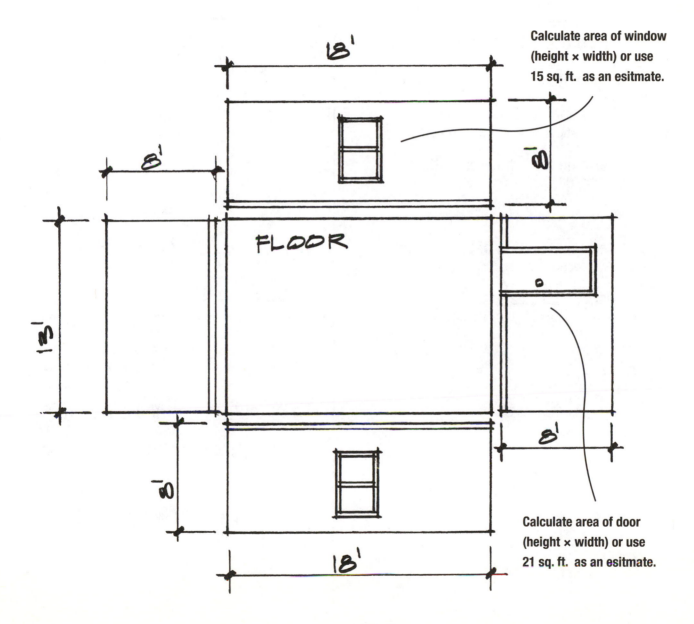

Calculate area of window
(height × width) or use
15 sq. ft. as an esitmate.

FLOOR

Calculate area of door
(height × width) or use
21 sq. ft. as an esitmate.

To calculate the stairwell area

1. Find the area of the walls around the stairs.
Divide the wall into two triangles and a rectangle, as shown in the illustration below.

2. Determine the total area of the two triangles.
Multiply the length of one triangle by its height and divide by 2. Repeat for the other triangle.

3. Determine the area of the rectangle.
Multiply the length by the height.

4. Finish the calculation.
Add the three areas to get the total square footage.

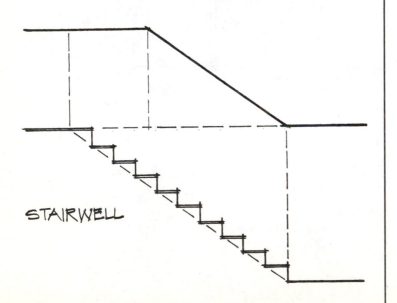

STAIRWELL

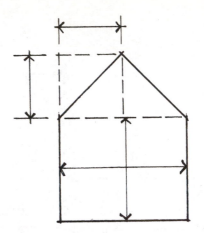

GABLED WALLS

Gabled walls
To find the area of gabled walls (walls that bump out or up to form a triangular structure), measure the wall as if it were a rectangle. Multiply the height by the width *above* to find the total area.

To calculate the ceiling area:

1. Multiply the room length by the room width.
18 FT. ×13 FT. = 234 SQ. FT.

2. Subtract areas of skylights and light fixtures, if significant.

To calculate the number of gallons you need for one coat:

1. Divide the wall area by 300, which is the average coverage in square feet for a gallon of paint.

445 SQ. FT. / 300 = 1.5 GALLONS OF PAINT

This number is for one coat of paint.

2. Multiply by the number of coats you plan to paint.

Remember that going from light colors to dark—or from dark to light—may require more than two coats of paint.

3. When in doubt, round up.

Not all walls are perfect rectangles, of course. Use the information *opposite* to calculate paint needs for stairwell walls and gabled walls.

To calculate flooring materials:

To figure how much flooring material you need for a rectangular room, multiply the length by the width, then add 10 percent. For example, a 10×15 room needs 150 square feet of flooring, plus 15 additional square feet (10 percent).

The extra flooring will ensure you have enough material for the job. Some stores will take back unused material; however, you may want to keep some extra for later repairs.

If your room has counters or protruding closets, subtract the square footage these obstructions occupy from the overall area of the room. Begin by finding the overall dimensions of the room, measuring at the widest spots.

Then measure the length and width of each obstruction. Subtract the area of each obstruction from the overall square footage, add 10 percent to the total, and then head for the store.

When **purchasing** paint, buy **a little more** than you need. That way, you'll have a **perfect color match** if you find that you do need more.

Arrange a room

This section includes a budgeting worksheet, easy-to-use templates, and a grid so you can plot the arrangement of a room in your house just like professional designers do. Use templates that fit the dimensions of existing furnishings, fixtures, appliances, and cabinetry, as well as those you plan to purchase.

How to use this kit

Measure the room you want to update, then plot the dimensions on the grid provided on pages 250–251, or use graph paper, with one square equaling 1 square foot. Use the architectural symbols *below* to designate window placement and doorways and to draw such elements as bifold doors and fireplaces.

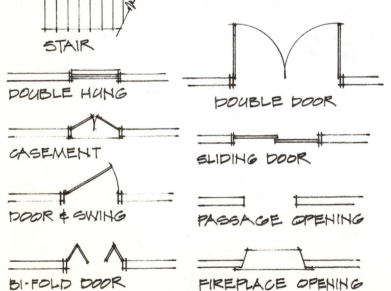

SYMBOLS:

STAIR

DOUBLE HUNG

CASEMENT

DOOR & SWING

BI-FOLD DOOR

DOUBLE DOOR

SLIDING DOOR

PASSAGE OPENING

FIREPLACE OPENING

Measure each item to be placed in the room. Trace or photocopy the corresponding templates, then cut them out with scissors or a crafts knife. Note that most templates are shown in multiple sizes, but feel free to create additional templates of special sizes for unique items.

Using the cut templates, experiment with different configurations, building around established focal points such as a fireplace or window wall, or creating new focal points with large-scale furnishings, accessories, or artwork.

Room arrangement strategies

To allow for smooth traffic flow around the room, there should be at least 3 feet of space around furniture groupings and in kitchen and bath walkways. If 2 or more people will use an aisle at once, or if the aisle provides access to an appliance, plan for 42 to 48 inches of clear space.

When placing a table in front of a sofa or chairs, keep 12 to 18 inches between them; additional space will make it difficult for people who are seated to reach items on the table.

Create one main focal point in each room. The exception: Arrange furnishings to take advantage of two focal points that can be viewed at once, such as a fireplace and a window with good views.

Balance is important. Choose furnishings and cabinetry of different heights, shapes, and sizes for interest. The balance will be interrupted if all tall or hefty pieces are placed on one side of the room. Keep the size of the room in mind when choosing and positioning furnishings: Use modest-size pieces in a small room and larger scale pieces in a grand room.

Budgeting worksheet

Cost estimates for my *Property Ladder* makeover
(See the price guide on pages 221–226 to help narrow your choices.)

Materials to purchase	Quantity	Cost per unit (Qty × Unit Cost)	Total cost	Store (source)	Purchased? Yes or no	Comments
Paint						
Flooring						
Light fixtures						
Appliances						
Kitchen and bath fixtures						
Cabinetry						
Windows						
Doors						
Staging items for the open house						
Furniture						
Artwork and accessories						

SOFA & SECTIONAL ITEMS:

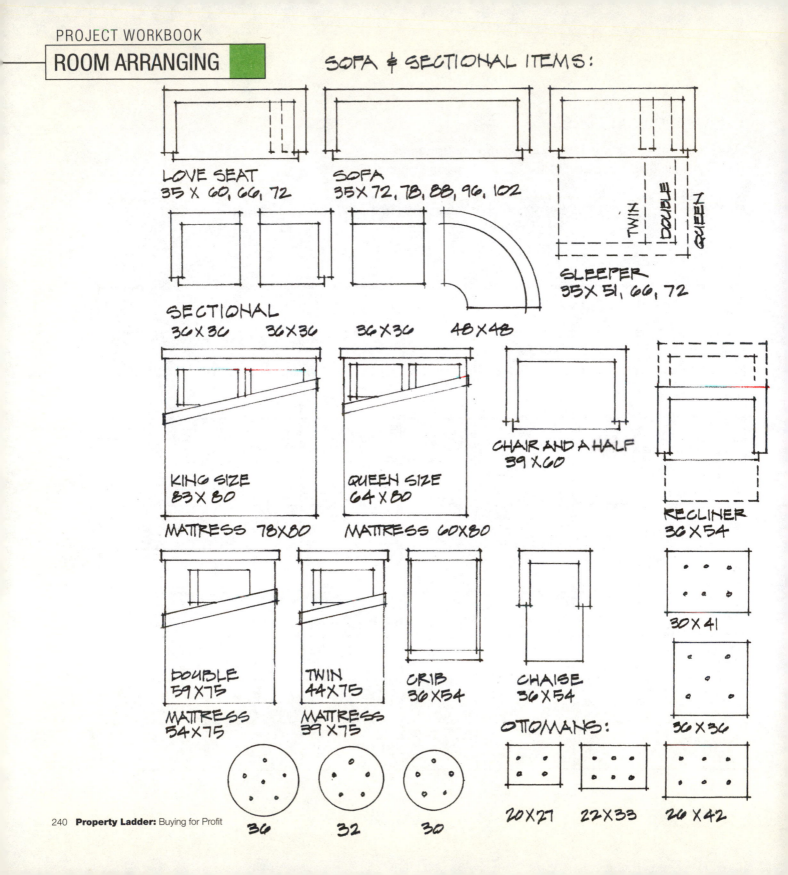

LOVE SEAT
35 X 60, 66, 72

SOFA
35 X 72, 78, 88, 96, 102

SLEEPER
35 X 51, 66, 72

TWIN DOUBLE QUEEN

SECTIONAL
36 X 36   36 X 36   36 X 36   48 X 48

CHAIR AND A HALF
39 X 60

RECLINER
36 X 54

KING SIZE
83 X 80
MATTRESS 78 X 80

QUEEN SIZE
64 X 80
MATTRESS 60 X 80

30 X 41

DOUBLE
59 X 75
MATTRESS
54 X 75

TWIN
44 X 75
MATTRESS
39 X 75

CRIB
36 X 54

CHAISE
36 X 54

OTTOMANS:

36 X 36

36   32   30

20 X 27   22 X 33   26 X 42

BASIC TABLES:

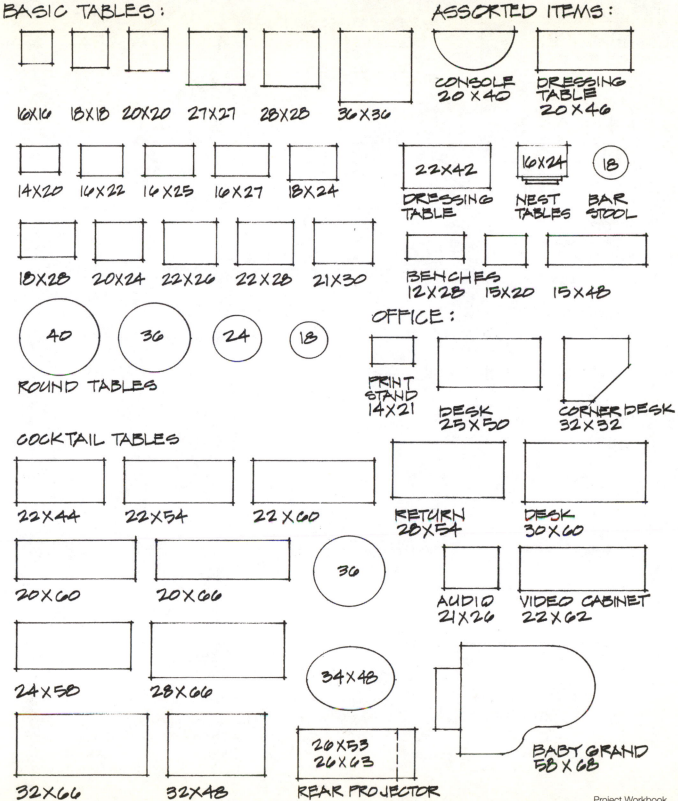

16X16 18X18 20X20 27X27 28X28 36X36

14X20 16X22 16X25 16X27 18X24

18X28 20X24 22X26 22X28 21X30

ROUND TABLES
40 36 24 18

COCKTAIL TABLES

22X44 22X54 22X60

20X60 20X66 36

24X58 28X66 34X48

32X66 32X48 26X53 26X43 REAR PROJECTOR

ASSORTED ITEMS:

CONSOLE 20 X 40 DRESSING TABLE 20 X 46

22X42 DRESSING TABLE 16X24 NEST TABLES 18 BAR STOOL

BENCHES 12X28 15X20 15X48

OFFICE:

PRINT STAND 14X21 DESK 25 X 50 CORNER DESK 32X32

RETURN 28X54 DESK 30X60

AUDIO 21X26 VIDEO CABINET 22X62

BABY GRAND 58 X 68

ROOM ARRANGING

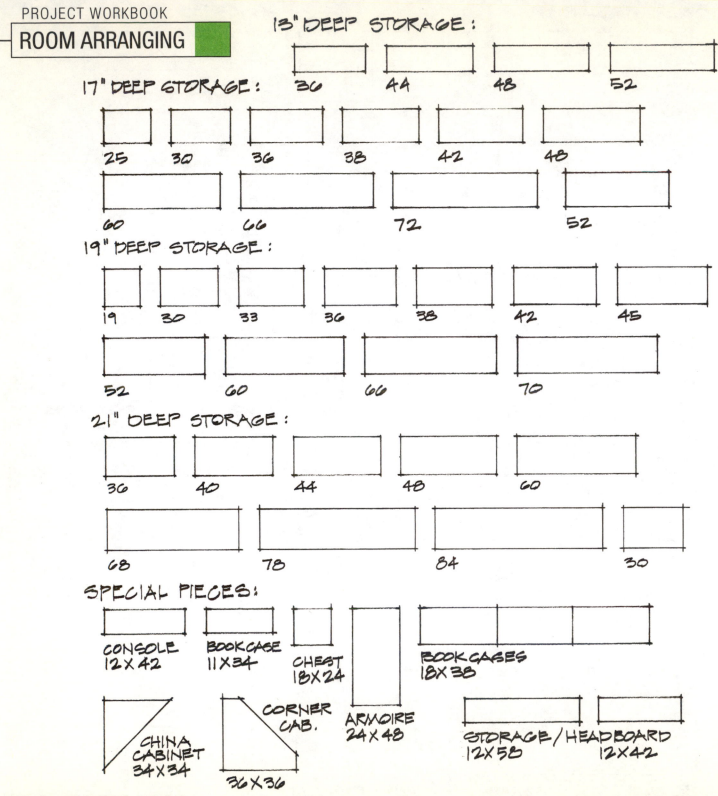

13" DEEP STORAGE:

36   44   48   52

17" DEEP STORAGE:

25   30   36   38   42   48

60   66   72   52

19" DEEP STORAGE:

19   30   33   36   38   42   45

52   60   66   70

21" DEEP STORAGE:

36   40   44   48   60

68   78   84   30

SPECIAL PIECES:

CONSOLE
12 X 42

BOOKCASE
11 X 34

CHEST
18 X 24

BOOKCASES
18 X 38

CHINA
CABINET
34 X 34

CORNER
CAB.
36 X 36

ARMOIRE
24 X 48

STORAGE / HEADBOARD
12 X 58   12 X 42

TABLES:

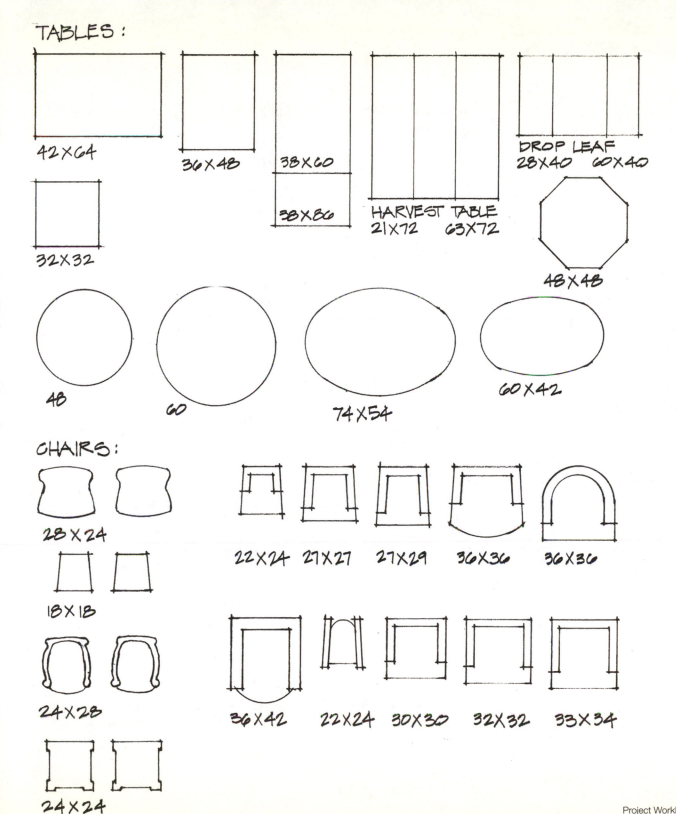

42×64

36×48

38×60

38×86

HARVEST TABLE
21×72   63×72

DROP LEAF
28×40   60×40

32×32

48×48

48

60

74×54

60×42

CHAIRS:

28×24

22×24   27×27   27×29   36×36   36×36

18×18

24×28

36×42   22×24   30×30   32×32   33×34

24×24

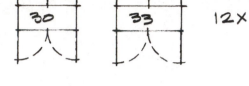

OPEN SHELF   END SHELF   CORNER SHELF

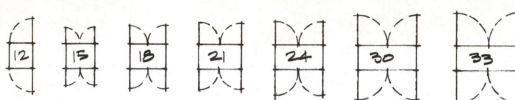

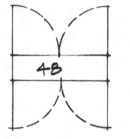
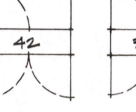
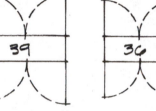

12X

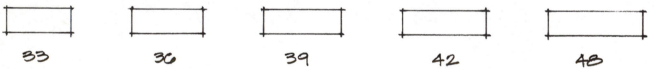

12X

WALL CABINETS: 12" DEEP

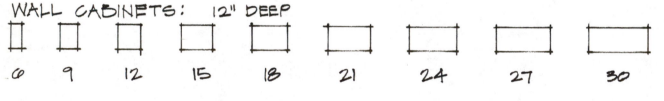

6   9   12   15   18   21   24   27   30

33   36   39   42   48

STANDARD CABINETS HGTS. 12, 15, 18, 24, 27, 30, 36, 42, & 48

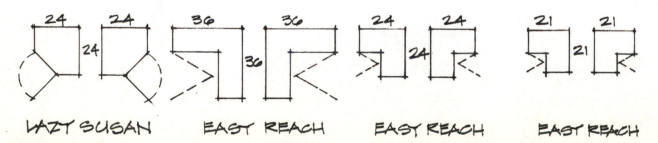

LAZY SUSAN   EASY REACH   EASY REACH   EASY REACH

WALL CABINETS:

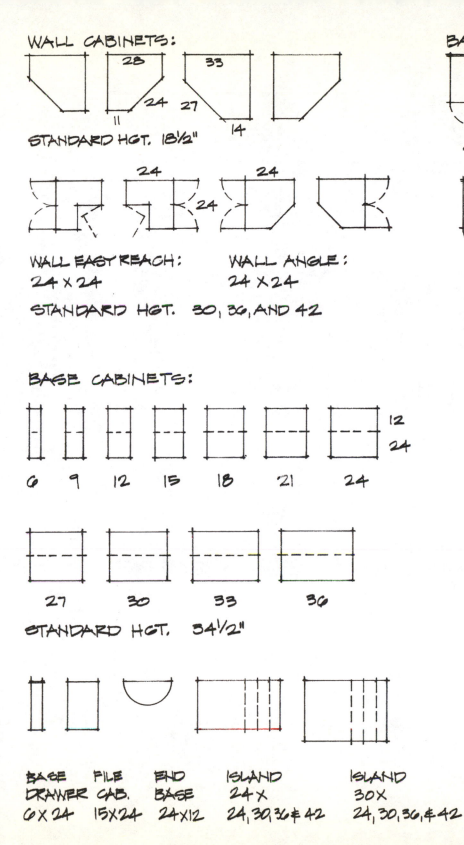

28 33 24 27 11 14

STANDARD HGT. 18½"

WALL EASY REACH:
24 X 24

WALL ANGLE:
24 X 24

STANDARD HGT. 30, 36, AND 42

BASE CABINETS:

6   9   12   15   18   21   24

12
24

STANDARD HGT. 34½"

27   30   33   36

BASE
DRAWER
6 X 24

FILE
CAB.
15 X 24

END
BASE
24 X 12

ISLAND
24 X
24, 30, 36 & 42

ISLAND
30 X
24, 30, 36, & 42

BASE CABINETS:

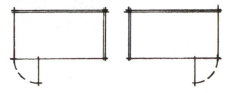

BLIND CORNER

48 X 24

45 X 24

42 X 24

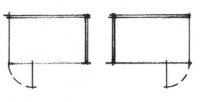

39 X 24

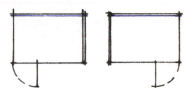

36 X 24

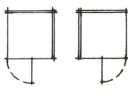

24 X 24

SINK BASES:

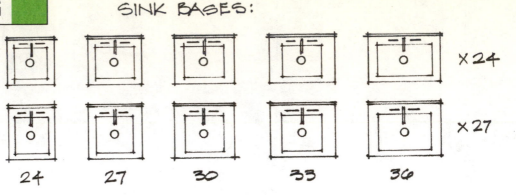

24   27   30   33   36   × 24

× 27

39   42   45   48   × 24

× 27

OPEN SHELF FOR BASE UNIT:

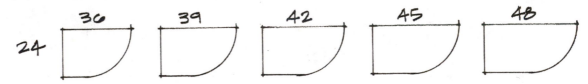

36   39   42   45   48

24

BASE CORNER CABINETS: 34½ STANDARD HGT.

CORNER SINK 36X36   LAZY SUSAN 36X36

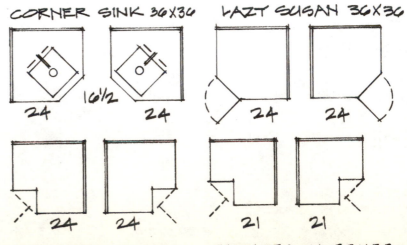

24   16½   24   24   24

24   24   21   21

EASY REACH 36X36   EASY REACH 33X33

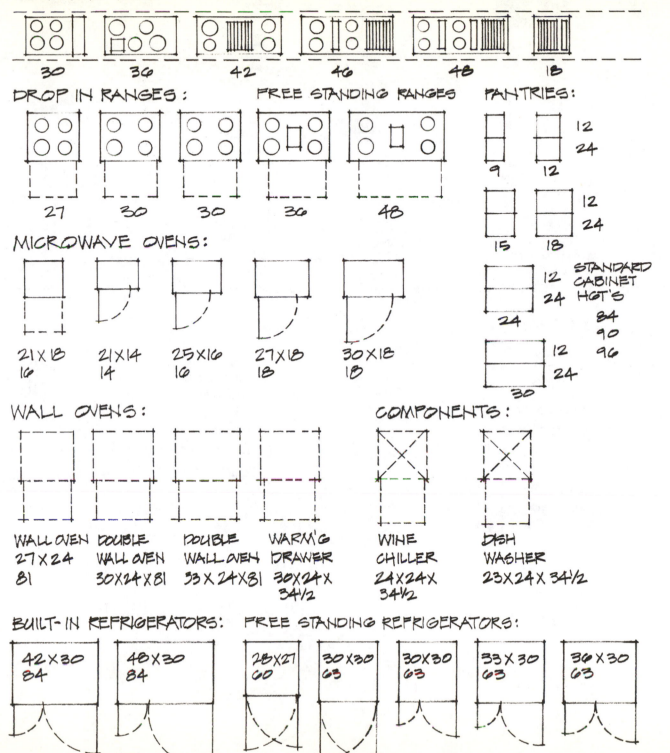

COUNTER TOPS:

30 36 42 46 48 18

DROP IN RANGES: FREE STANDING RANGES   PANTRIES:

27 30 30   36   48

9   12   12
          24

15 18   12
          24

MICROWAVE OVENS:

21X18   21X14   25X16   27X18   30X18
16   14   16   18   18

12   STANDARD
24   CABINET
     HGT'S
24   84
          90
12   96
24

30

WALL OVENS: COMPONENTS:

WALL OVEN   DOUBLE   DOUBLE   WARM'G   WINE   DISH
27X24   WALL OVEN WALL OVEN DRAWER   CHILLER   WASHER
81   30X24X81   33X24X81   30X24X   24X24X   23X24X34½
                                  34½   34½

BUILT-IN REFRIGERATORS: FREE STANDING REFRIGERATORS:

42X30   48X30   28X27   30X30   30X30   33X30   36X30
84   84   60   63   63   63   63

ROOM ARRANGING

BATH COMPONENTS:

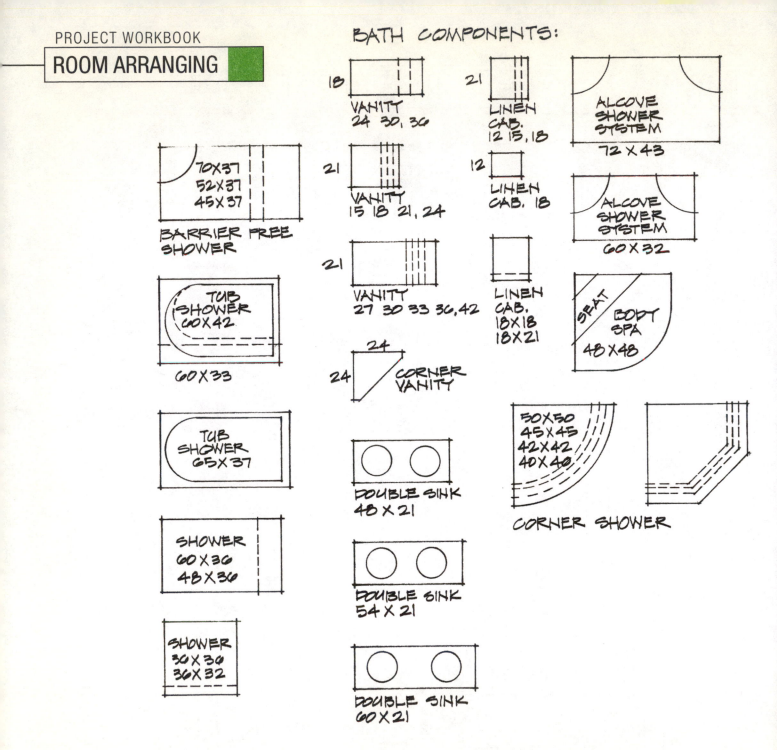

18 — VANITY 24 30, 36

21 — VANITY 15 18 21, 24

21 — VANITY 27 30 33 36, 42

24 24 CORNER VANITY

21 — LINEN CAB. 12 15, 18

12 — LINEN CAB. 18

LINEN CAB. 18×18 18×21

BARRIER FREE SHOWER — 70×37 52×37 45×37

TUB SHOWER 60×42 — 60×33

TUB SHOWER 65×37

SHOWER 60×36 48×36

SHOWER 30×30 36×32

DOUBLE SINK 48×21

DOUBLE SINK 54×21

DOUBLE SINK 60×21

ALCOVE SHOWER SYSTEM 72×43

ALCOVE SHOWER SYSTEM 60×32

SEAT BODY SPA 48×48

CORNER SHOWER — 50×50 45×45 42×42 40×40

BATH COMPONENTS:

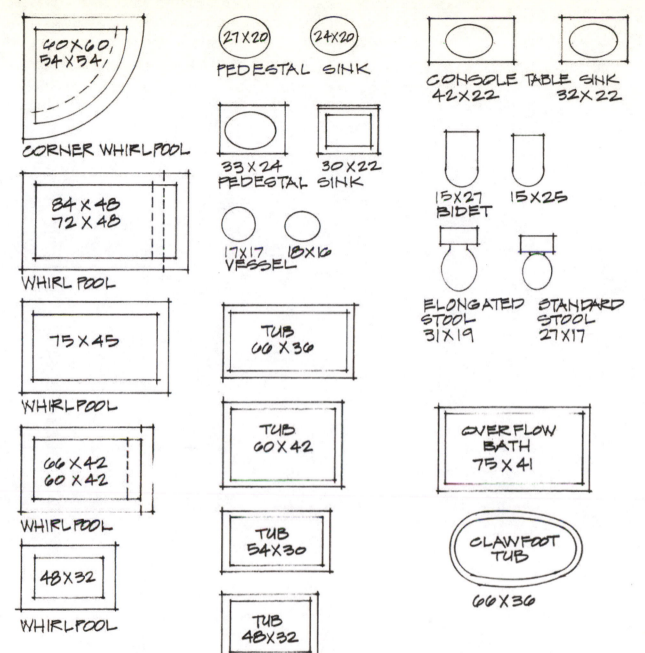

CORNER WHIRLPOOL
40X60,
54X54

27X20   24X20
PEDESTAL   SINK

CONSOLE TABLE SINK
42X22   32X22

WHIRL POOL
84 X 48
72 X 48

33 X 24   30 X 22
PEDESTAL   SINK

15X27   15X25
BIDET

WHIRLPOOL
75 X 45

17X17   18X16
VESSEL

TUB
66 X 36

ELONGATED   STANDARD
STOOL   STOOL
31X19   27X17

WHIRLPOOL
66 X 42
60 X 42

TUB
60 X 42

OVERFLOW
BATH
75 X 41

WHIRLPOOL
48X32

TUB
54X30

CLAWFOOT
TUB
66 X 36

TUB
48X32

ROOM ARRANGING

Photocopy this grid at its original size or purchase ¼-inch grid paper from an office supply store. Then photocopy and cut out the templates on pages 240–249 to begin laying out your new space. The grid is 1 square = 1 square foot.

Index